ANATOMY OF AN AFRICAN KINGDOM
A HISTORY OF BUNYORO-KITARA

To Michael
With best
Wishes
Godfrey.

Professor Godfrey N. Uzoigwe, formerly of the Department of History, Makerere University, Uganda, is now a professor of African History at the University of Michigan, Ann Arbor. He is the author of *Revolution and Revolt in Bunyoro-Kitara* (Longmans, 1970); *The Slave Trade and African Societies* (Center for Afro-American and African Studies *Monograph Series*, University of Michigan, Ann Arbor, 1971, No. 3); *Britain and the Conquest of Africa: The Age of Salisbury* (University of Michigan Press, expected Fall 1973); and has published several articles in Learned Journals. He is currently working on a biography of Kabalega, the warrior king of Bunyoro-Kitara.

Anatomy of
an African Kingdom
A HISTORY OF BUNYORO-KITARA

J. W. Nyakatura
(TRANSLATED BY TEOPISTA MUGANWA)

Edited, with Introduction and Notes, by
GODFREY N. UZOIGWE

ANCHOR BOOKS
Anchor Press/Doubleday, *Garden City, New York*
1973

The Anchor Books edition is the first publication
of *Anatomy of an African Kingdom.*

ANCHOR BOOKS EDITION: 1973

ISBN: 0-385-06966-9

LIBRARY OF CONGRESS CATALOG CARD NUMBER 72–76238

COPYRIGHT © 1973 BY GODFREY N. UZOIGWE

ALL RIGHTS RESERVED

PRINTED IN THE UNITED STATES OF AMERICA

FIRST EDITION

Contents

Part V: KITARA MONARCHY

*Part VI: KINGS OF BUGANDA, TOORO, NKORE
         AND KOOKI*

Illustrations

Author's Preface

This book has been written for the sake of young people—especially schoolchildren and students—who lack the opportunity to study the history of Kitara. In the past it was possible for young people to get to know this history. They learnt it from eminent chiefs and army leaders [who were well known in the country and within reach of almost everyone]. They also supplemented their knowledge by listening to conversations between eminent individuals when the royal drum was brought out at the new moon. This custom is no longer observed and people nowadays are more interested in their jobs than in such engagements. This has resulted in young people being ignorant of the past of their country. This book therefore has been written in an attempt to revive the study of Kitara history as something of general interest. I have written it for schoolchildren and young people in general so that each can study it on their own.

The material on which this book is based was collected from old men who knew the past history of Kitara. The book covers not only the history of Bunyoro-Kitara but also those of its neighbors. It should therefore be of general interest.

It is probable that some misguided individuals will question the validity of my sources and perhaps reject my story. I am satisfied, however, that I have done my best to try to get at the truth by collecting information from the various areas I have worked in—Bugangaizi, Tooro, Busongora, Masindi, Hoima, and Chope. I interviewed many old men who were acquainted with the past. Both my informants and I are convinced that the content of this book is the true picture of events as far as they are known. The research and the writing of this book took a very long time. A serious attempt has been made to find out the real truth by a comparison of the various sources. This is particularly so in relation to the history of kings [*Abakama*] and princes [*Abaiito*].

There is already in existence a number of history books by Europeans dealing with the kingdom of Bunyoro-Kitara. But these writers have erred especially over the names of the kings and princes. This was bound to happen, because their source materials are unreliable. Moreover, these Europeans write knowledgeably about royal tombs which they did not bother to examine for themselves. I am convinced that future historians will produce a better history of Kitara if they base their work on this book.

I am very grateful to R. A. Tito Gafabusa Winyi IV, Omukama, for his tremendous help which enabled me to locate most of my material. My thanks also go to Prince H. Karubanga, the Saza Chief Kimbugwe,[1] who supplied me with much of the information about the sazas (counties or provinces) which existed during the reign of Chwa II Kabalega. To Mr. Aramanzane Rwakiza, who gave me information about the different divisions of the Abarusura [army], I also extend grateful thanks. In the course of this work, I have profited immensely from the advice of many old people. Some in fact died before I had finished writing this book. It is not possible to mention all their names, but to all of them, however, I am very indebted.

In the course of my research I had collected a vast amount of materials. I have, however, given only a summary of them in this work in order to make it more comprehensible for the general reader. I hope to write another book about the customs of the people of Bunyoro-Kitara depending on whether the present volume is appreciated.

JOHN WILLIAM NYAKATURA,
Kimbugwe, Bunyoro

Masindi, 1947

Foreword

The main purpose of this edition of John Nyakatura's classic history of Kitara is to make the book available in English to students, undergraduates, and general readers who are interested in traditional East African history in particular, and traditional African history in general. Since its publication in Canada in 1947 this book has attracted a lot of attention but has only been accessible to a few readers outside Bunyoro who can read the Runyoro language. Hitherto, however, several scholars have been content to utilize it from secondary sources and it is not improbable that this may have resulted, in certain cases, in misinterpreting the author's mind.

That no serious attempt has been made to produce an English edition of this very important work is understandable. The Runyoro language is perhaps one of the most difficult of all Bantu languages and Nyakatura's technical expertise in it has scared off interested translators and editors. For this reason alone, we must be especially indebted to Miss Teopista Muganwa, herself a Munyoro from the Hoima area, and who holds a B.A. honors degree in history from the University of East Africa, for her courage in accepting my invitation to attempt the difficult task of translating this book into English. This is a task which several people have lacked the confidence to undertake. And as the editor's knowledge of Runyoro is very rudimentary, he would not have attempted this edition of *Abakama ba Bunyoro-Kitara* had Miss Muganwa declined the invitation. Her task was made more difficult by an instruction which requested her to "produce a literal translation of Nyakatura's *Abakama*, reflecting as far as is possible the spirit of the author." This meant, in essence, that she was not allowed to take liberties with the text. She performed her task with great diligence and competence but the final product could make sense only to the few competent in the history of Kitara. This is to be expected: a straight translation from any one language to another has always been a very difficult exercise; and a straight translation of technical Runyoro into

English more so. But this approach is justified on the ground that the editor was afraid lest some important points may be missed.

Now, the reader is entitled to know how the final product was arrived at. The editor has been carrying out some substantial research in the history of Kitara; he has published some materials on this subject; and he has also been teaching it to students for a number of years. It is hoped that this sketchy information will suffice to justify his credentials for undertaking this tremendous task. An editor's job is a difficult and thankless one: it involves a lot of hard work, a lot of responsibilities, attracts a lot of criticisms, but rarely commensurate acknowledgment. There is no reason therefore to expect that this edition of a famous book should be the exception to the general rule. But the present writer is satisfied that he has done his best to put across in acceptable English what the author has written. This was done, carefully comparing the literal translation with the original text. It was necessarily a cumbersome and time-consuming undertaking but perhaps the only way it could reasonably well be done in the circumstances. We therefore publish this work humbly acknowledging its inadequacies, but hope at least that it may make some contribution to African historiography.

Since the introduction of the teaching of the precolonial history of Uganda at Makerere, traditional histories of Uganda written in local languages—among which *Abakama* ranks very high—have acquired the status of prescribed texts. It is hoped that an English edition of this book would reduce the handicap with which our non-Runyoro-speaking students have been working. It is also particularly intended to be a handbook for lecturers and teachers as well as for those students researching into the precolonial history of East Africa.

Though a literal translation of *Abakama* would have amounted to unreadable nonsense, an effort has nevertheless been made not to deviate drastically from the original text. Liberty has also been taken to rearrange the chapter headings, and, indeed, the architecture of the book where necessary, to make it more intelligible to readers in English. The editor has, too, refused to tie himself down to certain standard spellings employed in the text. On the contrary, more attention has been paid to the present sound of words. For example, *Kabarega* is written *Kabalega* and *Toro* as *Tooro* in this edition. Another liberty taken by the editor is to translate the title of the book as *Anatomy of an African Kingdom: A History of Bunyoro-Kitara* instead of the literal *Kings of Bunyoro-Kitara*. This decision was taken because the book is much more than the activities of the kings of Kitara. Moreover, Bunyoro-Kitara is an epitome of an African Kingdom which has experienced several centuries of indigenous economic and political development before it was destroyed by the European impact. But the author's views and opinions have not in the least been interfered with. Throughout, a serious attempt has been made to reflect them. And where the editor ventures an opinion or an explanation, it is indicated either in square brackets within the text or in the footnotes. Usually long comments or explanations are indicated in the latter.

The footnotes have been supplied chiefly with a view to make the reader's task easier, to explain knotty points, to expose inaccuracies or inconsistencies where necessary, and to refer the reader to the opinions of other writers which the author has ignored or is in opposition to. Where the author has cited a published source it has been indicated in his name. At the end of the book also a select bibliography has been appended for further reading.

The introduction is designed to be a critical evaluation of the author as a traditional historian and to place *Abakama* in its proper setting in African historiography. The opportunity has also been seized to pinpoint one major problem in traditional history, namely, the lack of absolute dates; as well as to expose the major problem facing the precolonial historian of Uganda, namely, conflicting and apparently irreconcilable evidence from the sources. Finally a brief comment on the nature of historical research in Kitara rounds off the introduction.

Throughout the greater part of the text the name *Kitara* has been preferred to *Bunyoro-Kitara* or even *Bunyoro*. The decision is based on the belief that from about the fifteenth to the nineteenth century the large empire of which modern Bunyoro was a part was called Kitara. Once the empire fell apart by the first half of the nineteenth century, the small heartland became known as Bunyoro, supposedly derived from a Ganda nickname. Banyoro, however, tend to refer to their homeland as Bunyoro-Kitara. It would perhaps be more accurate to speak of Bunyoro-Kitara in the nineteenth century and of Bunyoro in the twentieth.

This book has taken more than three years to prepare, during which period I have profited immensely from the generous help of several colleagues and friends, particularly Professor J. B. Webster, History, Makerere University College; Reverend Dr. A. M. Lugira; Reverend Dr. A. Byaruhanga-Akiiki; Dr. M. S. M. Kiwanuka, who initially encouraged me to undertake this task; those numerous informants in Bunyoro and elsewhere who open-mindedly spent their valuable hours talking to an inquisitive stranger like myself; Mr. Tucker Lwanga, Librarian, Makerere University College, who contributed generously towards the typing of this manuscript; Miss Joy Mafigiri, B.A., whose skill and tireless energy as a typist made the production of this work much less laborious than it otherwise might have been, and whose understanding of the Runyoro language subjected the original manuscript to searching scrutiny; Mr. William Byaruhanga, my research assistant, whose contribution is, to say the least, invaluable; and last but most importantly, Miss Teopista Muganwa, whose courage made possible the publication of this English edition of *Abakama*.

The editor concludes this foreword with the hope that this book may help to inspire future historians to take more interest in the history of Kitara and its neighbors.

G. N. U.

Introduction

It is fitting that this first English edition of the work of a man to whom so many owe so much must carry a brief summary of his biography. The aim is merely to establish his credentials as a traditional historian.

Mr. John W. Nyakatura was born, according to his own estimation, in October 1895 in a village called Busesa, which is situated near a hill, Imirabahuma, in Buyaga County.[1] He is very reticent about his clan but is probably a Mubiito. However, in 1894 Colonel Colvile, acting independently of Downing Street, had annexed Buyaga together with the other "lost counties" of Kitara to Buganda,[2] and had used the river Kafo presumably, it would seem, as the natural but arbitrary boundary between Bunyoro-Kitara and Buganda. His action may well have been dictated by military calculations[3] but Banyoro interpreted it as a way of rewarding his Baganda collaborators at their own expense. What is clear however is that in 1896, Lord Salisbury accepted Colvile's action as a *fait accompli.* He argued that since Uganda had become a protectorate of the British Crown, these "international" boundaries had lost their significance.[4]

But he was mistaken. He had probably assumed that Africans would be reconciled to decisions by Downing Street without a murmur. Salisbury's ruling is indeed a good example of how nineteenth-century imperialists exposed their monumental ignorance of African conditions and African history. This decision is particularly important because the struggle for the return of the "lost counties" was the primary theme of Nyoro-Ganda relations for over half a century. It was a relationship marked by hatred and bad neighborliness. It also made Banyoro reconciliation to the new imperial domination particularly difficult.

Nyakatura grew up in this atmosphere of bitter ill feeling against Europeans and their Baganda collaborators. It is to his credit that this ill feeling is not reflected in his work. But it is clear that *Abakama ba Bunyoro-Kitara* was written to win sympathy for his people's struggle for the return of the "lost counties." It is a book written to encourage a down-hearted and almost fatalistic people to wake up from their slumber and work towards the regeneration of their kingdom. He exhorts them to remember the great achievements and exploits of their illustrious ancestors but warns them not to live in the past but rather to unite and work towards a glorious future. They should, he advises, be proud of whatever is left of their kingdom and build up from there. The moderation of his tone should surprise no one. This is a book written by a civil servant of the colonial government. And he had to be moderate and tactful to avoid being sent to jail and sinking into oblivion.

Is the *Abakama* therefore merely lugubrious vaticinations of a nationalist imbued with the sense of a great past that never was? It would be very unkind to hold such a view, for Nyakatura is a conscientious and objective historian who spent about thirty years gathering materials and writing this book. Moreover, he did not originate the idea that there was an empire of Kitara of which Bunyoro claimed to be the head. The *Abakama* is a detailed and authoritative account of traditional history that was well known before Nyakatura wrote. But like all traditional histories it has its own share of exaggerated claims, inconsistencies, and myths.

But let us return once more to the author's biography. In 1904 he was sent to the Church Missionary Society School at Kikangara and later went up to a high school of the same denomination at Kikoma. When he left this institution he studied for a year at Bujuni Catholic Mission School (1911). It is probable that it was during this period that he came under the influence of the White Fathers which can be detected in the pages of *Abakama*.

Having completed his formal education Nyakatura was employed (1 January 1912) as a court clerk under Kyambarango in Buyaga at an annual stipend of 120 shillings. A year later (1 January 1913) he rose to the rank of a chief clerk. His duties included that of a cashier charged with the proper maintenance of books of tax collections from the whole county. His salary also rose to 360 shillings per annum. He remained in this job until 1923, when he resigned to become Salt Inspector at Lake Kasenyi in Busongora, Tooro, at an annual stipend of 1,440 shillings. Two years later he became the Chief Salt Inspector at Katwe and Kasenyi, Tooro.

In 1928 he was transferred to Bunyoro to become the *gomborora* [sub-county] chief, Sabairu, at Kijunjubwa in Buruli County. At that time there was no fixed monthly salary for chiefs. On the contrary a chief's salary was reckoned at the rate of eighty cents per person in his area of jurisdiction who had paid his poll tax. And as there were about 400 persons in Nyakatura's *gomborora*, he earned about 320 shillings per annum, a sum by far less than what he was earning at Katwe. But not satisfied with this situation, he petitioned the District Commissioner, who privately promised to better his condition.

In 1929 he was transferred to Kinogozi to become Sabagabo in Buhaguzi County. Here there were about 700 persons who had been assessed to pay poll tax and his salary rose accordingly. The situation was still by no means satisfactory but the Colonial Administration was also becoming aware of the shortcomings of paying officials in this manner. In 1932, therefore, it was decreed that chiefly remunerations should be paid quarterly but this did not mean any increase in salary. In 1935 Nyakatura was transferred to become Sabagabo, Bugambe, in Bugahya County but remained in this post for only forty-five days.

On 15 February 1935 he was transferred once again back to Buhaguzi County, where he became the *gomborora* chief, Sabairu, at Bulindi. In this county there were some 980 taxpayers. At this time also the *gomborora* chiefs pleaded for colonial amelioration and the government consented to pay their salaries on a monthly basis.

It was not until 1 January 1940 that Nyakatura was elevated to the post of *saza* [county] chief at an annual stipend of £200. He was first appointed to the *saza* of Sekiboobo, Kibanda, where he worked for six years. He was then transferred in 1946 to Masindi to become the *saza* chief, Kimbugwe, Buruli, at an annual stipend of £280. He remained in this post for two years and was transferred in 1948 to become the *saza* chief, Kaigo, Bujenje, at Bikonzi, where he worked for three years at an annual stipend of £320. On 1 January 1951 he became the *saza* chief, Mukwenda, Bugahya, and remained there for only one year at an annual stipend of £350.

Bugahya was Nyakatura's last posting as chief. The following year, January 1952, he was appointed to the post of Chief Judge of Bunyoro. This was a newly created post and

Nyakatura was the first Munyoro to hold such a responsibility. It was an elective rather than an appointive post and he beat three other *saza* chiefs in the contest. He occupied this office for a period of one year and three months—the salary being £ 400 per annum. He retired from government service in 1953 on a pension.

But he did not retire from active service. On 1 May 1953 he joined the Ba-Kitara Transport Company as treasurer and was paid £ 300 per annum. He resigned from this post in 1956 to devote his time to fighting for the return of the "lost counties" to Bunyoro. He applied to, and was granted permission by, the then Colonial Governor, Cohen, to start the Muju-muzi Foundation. This was an organization which aimed at raising funds for the "lost counties" campaign. Nyakatura claims that this foundation proved to be a huge success.

In April 1957 he accompanied Dr. Majugo and a lawyer called Mr. Thacker, Q.C., to London to prepare for the "lost counties" negotiations. Mr. Thacker's task appears to have been to help the Banyoro delegation in contacting a lawyer to prepare their case. The lawyer they settled for was a Mr. R. W. O. Wilberforce, who prepared a document which the Omukama and his chiefs submitted to the Colonial Governor at Entebbe on 2 May 1957.

Nyakatura returned to London once more in March 1958 in the company of Katikiro (Chief Minister) Z. H. Kwebiiha, to help with the preparation of a legal document—pleading for the return of the "lost counties"—to be submitted to the court of law. Banyoro did not achieve their immediate objectives. It was not until 1964 that the Obote administration, following the recommendations of the Molson Report,[5] restored only two counties—Bugangaizi and Buyaga—to Bunyoro and neutralized Mubende. But earlier Nyakatura had paid two more visits to London—in October 1961 and in April 1962—"to witness the preparation for the granting of independence to Uganda."

This brief summary of the career of Nyakatura, as has already been noted, is intended primarily to emphasize the experiences which made it possible for him to produce a history of his country. It can of course be pointed out that only two of his contemporaries—Bikunya[6] and Karubanga[7]—who had similar experiences in chiefly administration attempted to record the traditions of their country. But none of these works can stand any comparison with Nyakatura's

Abakama. We cannot all, of course, be historians even if we all have such an ambition. Nyakatura has all the makings of a traditional historian—background, patriotism, pride in the culture and tradition of his people, dedication to a cause, inquisitiveness, and above all, a long memory.

His interest in history started from the days of his father, who served in both the palaces of Omukama Kamurasi and Omukama Kabalega. He recollects that at home his father used to narrate the history of Kitara to his friends and John, as a young boy, used to sit nearby and listen. This impudent intrusion was highly resented by his father. But the young boy ignored his father's reprimands and preferred to risk his wrath rather than give up his interest in history. "Actually, on one occasion," the author told the present writer,

> I sustained serious injuries on my leg as a result of the punishment he inflected on me for defying his orders to attend to the goats and for having chosen to listen to his stories instead. I still bear a big scar on this leg—a lasting testimonial to my profound interest in history. Fortunately, whatever I heard from him became deeply rooted in my head as traditional tales. In 1912 I started jotting down some of these things in pamphlet form which I later showed to the Assistant District Commissioner at Mubende in 1922. He wrote me a letter congratulating me for my good work and urged me to write more. My interest was stimulated further and I carried out intensive research into the history of Kitara up to 1938, when I completed the first draft of *Abakama ba Bunyoro-Kitara.*

It was not until 1946, however, that Nyakatura secured the help of a Roman Catholic priest who was a friend of his to arrange for the publication of this manuscript. And in 1947 the *Abakama* was published in Canada by St. Justin, Province of Quebec. Ever since then the book has been acknowledged by students of Kitara history and culture as a classic. It also soon became a textbook for schools in Bunyoro. But its circulation was necessarily limited because it was not only written in a vernacular language not widely spoken nowadays but contained too many technical phrases and expressions that even good Runyoro speakers find difficult to comprehend.

Now that the study of African history has become fashionable in many parts of the world it is hoped that this first

English edition of the *Abakama* will prove to be a useful contribution to African historiography. It is also hoped that not only scholars but also the general reader will find it useful.

Although the first manuscript of the *Abakama* was completed in 1938, the author continued to collect further information, some of which was used to update the 1938 manuscript before its publication in 1947. And for the purposes of this edition he has also written a further chapter, bringing the story up to the present time. He also admits that he has a lot of materials which he is finding difficult to turn into a book.[8] It is hoped that one day this additional information will be made available to scholars. Perhaps a lot of these materials have already found their way into Nyakatura's new book,[9] to be published by the East African Literature Bureau.

Mr. J. W. Nyakatura now lives in retirement in Kiganda village, about a mile from Hoima on the Butiaba Road.

II

With the exception of Apolo Kaggwa's *Basekabaka be Buganda*, Nyakatura's *Abakama* is perhaps the only other historical masterpiece of its kind in the lacustrine region of East Africa and compares favorably with traditional histories written in vernacular languages in other parts of Africa. And this book together with those of Kaggwa,[10] Katate and Kamugungunu,[11] Winyi,[12] Bikunya,[13] among others, has made Uganda one of the richest countries in traditional history throughout the African continent. Indeed, it has been pointed out that "Uganda has some of the most detailed and reliable traditions in Africa, particularly in the west where some twenty generations of hereditary rulers can be traced."[14] The *Abakama* is one of the most detailed and reliable of this *corpus* of traditions. Its fundamental importance in the study of the history of the lacustrine region in particular, and of African history generally, has for long been noted by students of African history.

Sir Apolo Kaggwa has rightly been described as "the father of historical writing in Uganda".[15] And it is probable that his works may have influenced John Nyakatura, who holds him in the highest regard,[16] even if the traces of this influence are rather faint in the pages of *Abakama*. It is of course well known that traditional historians, unlike modern scholars, rarely acknowledge their indebtedness to their predecessors.

The *Abakama*, for example, makes no mention of the writings of either Sir Tito Winyi or P. Bikunya and yet these two authors wrote before Nyakatura and on a similar topic. The degree therefore of Kaggwa's influence on Nyakatura must be left to conjecture.

A critical study of Kaggwa's writings—especially *Basekabaka*—has already been made by Kiwanuka.[17] And his conclusion that Kaggwa was objective in his judgments and rigorous in his techniques is basically correct. However, as Rowe has pointed out, "Kaggwa's 'fault' could easily be claimed as the very reverse, that his narrative is too sterile, factual and colourless."[18] Perhaps this is not a fault; perhaps Kaggwa has kept impeccably within the bounds of the traditional historian. If this is so, then Rowe's statement could hardly be a sound criticism against him. This point is worth stressing because oral tradition is far from being history so-called. And Kaggwa's writings as well as those of Nyakatura must be regarded as source materials for history and should therefore be treated as such.

In a certain sense Nyakatura may be regarded as a better historian than Kaggwa in the accepted sense of the word. He is clearer than Kaggwa in his exposition, more penetrating whenever he attempts an analysis, more colorful in his expressions, and generally more controversial. Indeed Nyakatura is not afraid to place his own value judgments on events and is ready to "take on" those who had written before him where he disagrees with them. And his judgments and criticisms are usually based, not on assumptions, but on the facts at his disposal. But he is still basically a storyteller who is not particularly concerned with the ramifications and implications of his facts. For example, Nyakatura tells us that Kabalega created the *Abarusura* (national standing army) and goes to great pains to name their *ebitongole* (battalions) and their locations.

But it did not occur to him to investigate why Kabalega considered it absolutely necessary to create this army and how this revolutionary idea affected the politics of Kitara. These are the questions an historian is likely to ask. Nevertheless our original point that Nyakatura is perhaps a better historian in this particular sense is not invalidated by this example. The point is that he attempts more analysis than Kaggwa. There is of course no suggestion that *Basekabaka* is a less reliable source of traditional history than *Abakama*. On the contrary, Nyakatura, by being less cautious than Kaggwa, has exposed himself to more searching criticisms.

This is particularly so when, unlike Kaggwa, he fails to make available to us the names of his informants[19] and how he went about collecting his information. On this point he is content to say only: "The material on which this book is based was collected from old men who knew the past history of Kitara." He goes on to mention the names of Sir Tito Winyi, Prince H. Karubanga, and Prince Aramanzane Rwakiza. But his readers would still like to know who the other old men were—their status in society, their functions, their closeness to, or distance from, the monarchy, their clans, their geographical locations, and even their approximate ages. By these omissions he has naturally strengthened the hands of those critics who may doubt the veracity of his story. Indeed Nyakatura was not unaware of the possibility of this happening, for he wrote: "It is probable that some misguided individuals will question the validity of my sources and perhaps reject my story. I am satisfied, however, that I have done my best to try to get at the truth by collecting information from the various areas I have worked in—Bugangaizi, Tooro, Busongora, Masindi, Hoima, and Chope. I interviewed many old men who were acquainted with the past. Both my informants and I are convinced that the content of this book is the true picture of events as far as they are known. The research and the writing of this book took a very long time. A serious attempt has been made to find out the real truth by a comparison of the various sources. This is particularly so in relation to the history of kings (*Abakama*) and princes (*Ababiito*)."

But Nyakatura must be forgiven, for, unlike Kaggwa, he does not seem to have been surrounded by the literary circle which may have given Kaggwa much needed criticism. This point is worth stressing when it is remembered that the first edition of *Basekabaka* did not carry the names of informants.

When all this is said, a careful reading of *Abakama* will portray Nyakatura as a basically honest storyteller and essentially objective in his judgments. His "fault" lies not in the handling of his materials but perhaps in his research techniques. Admirers of this book may argue—and perhaps rightly so—that we are making a mountain out of a molehill. They may point out that his qualities and credentials as a traditional historian outweigh his "faults." They could argue that he had held responsible positions throughout the counties of Bunyoro and even beyond and had collected his information during this period supplementing it with what he had learnt from his father. Moreover, he has shown considerable acquaintance with the traditions of Kitara's neighbors. And more importantly, *Abakama*, unlike Nennius' *History of the Britons*, does not make the Bakitara win every battle which they had obviously lost. On the contrary Nyakatura gives credit where it is due. This is indeed a remarkable achievement because he was working among, and writing about, a people who were very bitter at the way British *fin-de-siècle* imperialism had treated them and had caused the emphatic collapse of their once famous kingdom. It is only on rare occasions that his nationalism and patriotism intrude into his story. But even then he is sober, polished, and restrained. There is no hatred, no acrimony, no recriminations, no crying over spilled milk. Throughout he is proud, dignified, and deals fairly with all the *dramatis personae*.

All this is fair enough, but so is our suggestion that he would have performed an invaluable service had he treated exhaustively his research techniques and had he made available to us the names of his informants. Had this been done we would have been in a better position to assess his work. It is probable and indeed very likely that he may have, for one reason or another, left out some would-be excellent informants.

This point is particularly relevant because the publication of *Abakama* has at once enhanced and hindered researches into the traditional history and culture of Kitara. It is, for example, difficult nowadays to assess whether informants are reciting by rote what they have read from *Abakama* or telling their stories independent of it. On many occasions potential informants have referred the present writer to Nyakatura as the sole embodiment of their traditions and would only talk after some persuasion and, at times, tactful pressure. For them he is the official, national historian; and whatever he has written is bound to be correct. A few, in fact, during the course of an interview, read out aloud page after page of *Abakama* and, oblivious of the fact, taxed the writer's patience to the limit. And there are yet others who would not dare challenge Nyakatura in public but are prepared to do so in private. This is why in the course of my researches I have relied more on individual rather than on group interviews. In private interviews, given the kind of society we are studying, individuals are more likely to express their opinions freely.

The other point worth mentioning about *Abakama* is in fact true of all oral histories—namely, the lack of absolute dates. The result is the irritating telescoping of events which may have taken place over the span of a century or more as if they happened within a matter of months. We are, for example, still at a loss to know the time lag between the "disappearance" of the Bachwezi and the arrival of the Babiito. Were it possible to know this we may perhaps be in a better position to attempt the solution of the thorny problem as to whether or not the supposed Babiito hegemony in the lacustrine region was the result of military conquest or peaceful penetration.

Nyakatura, however, like other historians of centralized kingdoms, has supplied a chronology upon which one can attempt to set up a time scale. And his chronology has been based on the royal genealogy. It must be warned, however, that however reliable a genealogy might be, it would be futile to expect absolute dates from it. This is because for any genealogy to be meaningful it has to be based on generations and the best we can hope for is to establish through these generations only relative dates. Moreover, chronologies dealing with kingdoms must depend to a large degree on the system of succession. Oliver has argued that generation tends to be long where the succession law is not based on primogeniture, and has accepted twenty-seven years as a reasonable average.[20]

It may perhaps be useful at this stage to explain what we mean by a generation and to see how it can provide a time scale upon which to set up a chronology. A generation may be defined as the average date between the birth of a father and the birth of his first child. In Britain such an average is reckoned at one third of a century, or more generally, at thirty years as a time measure. Succession in Britain, it must be pointed out, is based on primogeniture, and must, according to the Oliver thesis, tend to be short. If this is so, one wonders how Oliver considers an average of twenty-seven years as long in the lacustrine region, where the law of succession is not based on primogeniture and where, *ipso facto*, generation must tend to be long. He must indeed have considered his calculation as near absolute when he writes: "Figures calculated on this basis should be regarded as liable to a margin of error of two years plus or minus for every generation back from the present."[21] But working on this assumption and basing a relative chronology of the Baganda kings on either nineteen or twenty generations, Kiwanuka has exposed margins of error ranging between twenty-two years (in the reign of Muteesa II up to 1960) and sixty years (in the reign of Kato Kimera).[22]

The conclusion then would seem to be that the issue of relative chronology in the lacustrine region has to be looked into afresh. Indeed Kiwanuka has already demonstrated "that the Banyoro genealogy is an unsatisfactory basis for calculating the chronology of the Kiganda dynasty."[23] Conversely, it would be even more futile to use Baganda genealogy to attempt any meaningful computation of the Kitara dynasty. Simply put, the root of the matter is that historians are yet to agree on the nature of the relationships between the dynasties of Bunyoro-Kitara, Buganda, Nkore, Karagwe, and Kiziba. But perhaps unanimous agreement is impossible. What, however, has emerged is that the traditions of Bunyoro-Kitara, Nkore, and Kiziba are to a large extent fundamentally in agreement. Who copied from whom or who was influenced by whom is difficult to determine. Nor should the possibility of independent development be ruled out. What is clear is that there is a discernible "lacustrine culture" all the way from Karagwe, Bukoba, Kiziba, Kitara (to the west of Kiziba),[24] through Nkore to a greater part of Buganda, the principalities of Busoga, Tooro, and Bunyoro. This is certainly not an historical accident. Most of what we call Buganda today was conquered and annexed to the nuclear kingdom from about the eighteenth century upwards. Strictly speaking only the counties of Busiro, Busuju, Kyadondo, and part of Kyagwe could be said to comprise this nuclear kingdom. "Its extent," writes Oliver, "would have been easily comprised within a twenty-five mile radius drawn from Kampala."[25] The tantalizing question then is: how could this small enclave have remained an island unto itself and maintained its independence either of the Bachwezi or the Babiito? According to Kitara tradition this region was an integral part of the Kitara empire until the rebellion of Kimera; according to Kiganda tradition it was not; and according to Luo tradition, the nuclear Buganda kingdom was a subdynasty of the main Biito line.[26] And if it is accepted that the Biito were Luo, then Kitara and Luo traditions are agreed at least on this point. Indeed the *Abakama* deals primarily with the Banyoro account of the history of the empire of Kitara. This account must be read with the reservation that there exist different traditions of the same story.

The precolonial history of Uganda is an exciting and challenging one and must pivot around the axis of the Kitara Kingdom. Anyone who attempts a study of any part of this history without reference to the rest must do so at his own peril. What this statement amounts to is that an "acceptable" and comprehensive precolonial history of Uganda can only be written when the histories of the various groupings that make up the present Republic of Uganda, parts of the Republics of Kenya, Tanzania, and the two Congos, and even that of the Southern Sudan have been written or even raw materials relating to these histories have been collected. This is not to suggest that any harm would be done if a tentative rather than definitive history of Uganda, based on the present state of our knowledge, is attempted, frankly acknowledging its obvious inadequacies. In fact it is by attempting such a task now that we will be in a better position to weigh the magnitude of our problems.

In so far as Uganda is concerned, the Uganda History Project under the direction of Professor J. B. Webster is a modest step towards this goal. And Nyakatura's *Abakama* is an invaluable contribution to this project. Whether or not Nyakatura's history is authentic should not be the overriding consideration. What should be borne in mind is that it should be studied, considered, and rejected or accepted only in relation to the traditions of Kitara's neighbors. Nyakatura was perhaps not unaware of this fact when, following Kaggwa, it would seem, he appended short histories of the other kingdoms of Uganda at the back of his book. But again, like Kaggwa, these are skeleton histories not based to any tangible extent on researches carried out in the areas concerned.

A further point must need clarification: is *Abakama* merely a source for the royal history of Kitara as the title would lead us to expect? With certain qualifications this is true to a large extent. But the book contains in addition commentaries on the geography, religion, military organization, myths and fables of Kitara, and so forth. The larger part of it, however, deals with the political and administrative setup of each monarch's reign. The information supplied varied from one monarch to another; some are given fairly detailed treatment while others are simply mentioned in passing. The hero and warrior kings receive a lot of attention mainly because wars and rebellions tend to stand out clearly in oral tradition. This is true of those nineteenth-century Abakama—Nyamutukura, Kamurasi, and Kabalega—whose reigns are treated fairly exhaustively. Indeed the author devotes an entire part of his book to the reign of Kabalega alone and the information heaped on this one reign is almost equal in volume to the information supplied for the preceding twenty-two reigns. The reason is obvious. Kabalega was a warrior and hero king of Kitara, the events of whose reign are within living memory. Moreover, there exist written accounts of Kabalega's conflict with the Europeans, which the author has utilized presumably with the help of his missionary friends since he could not read or write English. It is likely that these missionaries supplied the dates attached to the reigns of the kings of Kitara starting with Omukama Olimi III Isansa at the beginning of the eighteenth century.

There has of course been a tendency to criticize historians of monarchical states for writing purely royal history. This criticism is not always justified. It could indeed be argued that since the influence of monarchies tends to pervade all aspects of the lives of their subjects, it would be naïve to draw a sharp distinction between court traditions and the traditions of the people, especially as the people tend to see their own traditions in terms of "dynastic time." Indeed the present writer's own researches in Bunyoro and Tooro have revealed that these people tended to migrate to places where royal influence was strongest primarily in search of protection and security. One of the reasons why the people of Tooro and Busongora supported Kaboyo's rebellion was the lack of effective control exercised over them by the central government. They felt ignored, unprotected, and defenseless. In Kaboyo they found a king they could at least call their own. This feeling seems to confirm the medieval European belief that in a monarchy the private and public interests are reconciled. Even among the so-called segmentary peoples such as the Langi the position of the *rwot* "was sufficiently formalised for the concept of *Ker* (royalty) to be associated with it."[27]

Nevertheless, Nyakatura can be justifiably criticized for ignoring clan, local, and family histories. These histories invariably supply useful information which helps to fill out the

history of a particular reign. So also do biographies of outstanding individuals as well as the customs of the people.[28]

III

Finally, some comments on the nature of historical research
in Kitara. Until fairly recently this history has been neglected.
This is indeed surprising, for the source materials are fairly
copious. Besides the occasional references to Kitara history
by the nineteenth-century travelers—Speke,[29] Grant,[30] Baker,[31] Stanley,[32] Emin Pasha,[33] Casati,[34] and Johnston,[35]
especially—the first detailed collections of the traditional history of Kitara were made by Fisher,[36] Gorju,[37] and Roscoe.[38] Later on Bikunya,[39] K.W.,[40] Nyakatura, Karubanga,[41] and Rukidi[42] greatly added to our knowledge of
this history. Other important sources include works on the traditional histories of Buganda, Kooki, Nkore, Kiziba, Buhaya,
Karagwe, Rwanda, Alur, and the Luo, as well as the scattered
references to Bunyoro-Kitara in *Munno, Bunyoro Church
Magazine, Mengo Notes, Matalisi, Ebifa Mu Buganda,* etc.
All these are primary source materials for Kitara history,
among which Nyakatura's *Abakama* is the most outstanding.
   The first scholarly attempt at the study of Bunyoro-Kitara
was made by Beattie,[43] who spent twenty-two months (between 1951 and 1955) doing original fieldwork in Bunyoro.
True, he was merely concerned with the cultural anthropology
of this kingdom but his researches have proved immensely
helpful to historians. It is regretted that some historians still
do not seem to realize the great debt they owe to social an-
thropologists, who, in a sense, could be said to be the first
"historians" of Africa.
   The first modern attempt, however, to write a history of
Kitara was made by Dunbar,[44] who worked in Bunyoro between January 1954 and March 1955, and again from February 1961 to August 1962. His history is based on part-time
researches carried out during these short periods. But far from
being a history of Kitara, his work is primarily a catalogue
of European activities. Indeed, as the present writer has
pointed out in a recent review of this book,[45] the history
of Kitara is yet to be written. But Dunbar's book is still useful
not only as a pioneering attempt at an almost impossible subject but also because of its bibliographical information. And
successive researches must remain indebted to him.

Recently the History Department of Makerere University College has been paying a lot of attention to the history of Kitara and its neighbors. The present writer, with a team of students and research assistants, has been collecting oral tradition relating to various aspects of this history with the aim in view of updating the existing information. Already some monographs and articles have been produced but there is still a lot to be done.[46]

This English edition of Nyakatura's *Abakama* is in fact a direct consequence of this new interest in a neglected subject.

APPENDIXES

TABLE I

LISTS OF BATEMBUZI KINGS VARIOUSLY COMPILED[47]

Fisher and Bikunya	Gorju	Roscoe	K.W. and Nyakatura
Ruhanga	Ruhanga (Hangi)	Ruhanga	
	Rugaba	Enkyaya	
		Enkya	
Nkya		Enkya	
Kantu			Kintu
Kairu			
Kakuma			Kakama
Kakama		Twale	Itwale
Twale			
		Hangi	Ihangi
		Nyamenge	
	Ira (Iya Hangi)	Ira	Ira lya Hangi
		Kabangera	
	Kazoba (Nyamuhanga)		Kazoba ka Hangi
			Nyamuhanga
	Nkya		Nkya I
			Nkya II
Baba	Baba	Baba	Baba
			Kamuli
			Nseka
			Kudidi
			Ntonzi
			Nyakahongerwa
Mukonko	Mukonko	Mukonko	Mukonko
Ngonzaki	Ngonzaki	Ngonzaki	Ngonzaki
Isaza	Isaza	Isaza	Isaza Mukama
			Isaza Nyakikoto
			Bukuku

TABLE II

BACHWEZI GENEALOGY[48]

Isimbwa (not counted as a Muchwezi because he was born in the underworld)

Karubumbi (Ndahura)	Mugenyi	Mulindwa	Mugasa	Kyomya

Wamara	Ibona	Kiro		Kagoro

TABLE III

LISTS OF BACHWEZI KINGS VARIOUSLY COMPILED

Fisher and Gorju	Roscoe, Bikunya	K.W. and Nyakatura
	Ndahura	Ndahura
		Mulindwa
	Wamara	Wamara

TABLE IV

DATING THE BACHWEZI DYNASTY[49]

K.W.	A.D. 1300–1400
Sir John Gray	pre 1462 or pre 1492
Cox	pre A.D. 1399
Lanning	pre A.D. 1350–1550
Crazzolara	A.D. 1600–1650
Ingham	A.D. 1550
Haddon	pre A.D. 1575 or pre 1478

TABLE V

RELATIONSHIP BETWEEN THE BATEMBUZI, BACHWEZI AND BABIITO[50]

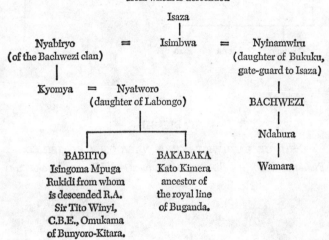

BATEMBUZI
from whom is descended

Isaza
|
Nyabiryo = Isimbwa = Nyinamwiru
(of the Bachwezi clan)   (daughter of Bukuku,
| gate-guard to Isaza)
Kyomya = Nyatworo |
(daughter of Labongo)   BACHWEZI
| |
                                   Ndahura
                                       |
BABIITO   BAKABAKA   Wamara
Isingoma Mpuga   Kato Kimera
Rukidi from whom ancestor of
is descended R.A. the royal line
Sir Tito Winyi,   of Buganda.
C.B.E., Omukama
of Bunyoro-Kitara.

TABLE VI

GENEALOGY OF THE BABIITO KINGS[51]

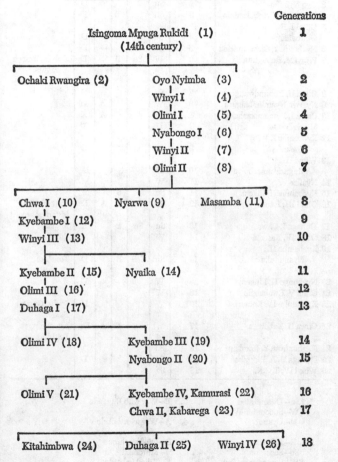

	Generations
Isingoma Mpuga Rukidi (1) (14th century)	1
Ochaki Rwangira (2) Oyo Nyimba (3)	2
Winyi I (4)	3
Olimi I (5)	4
Nyabongo I (6)	5
Winyi II (7)	6
Olimi II (8)	7
Chwa I (10) Nyarwa (9) Masamba (11)	8
Kyebambe I (12)	9
Winyi III (13)	10
Kyebambe II (15) Nyaika (14)	11
Olimi III (16)	12
Duhaga I (17)	13
Olimi IV (18) Kyebambe III (19)	14
Nyabongo II (20)	15
Olimi V (21) Kyebambe IV, Kamurasi (22)	16
Chwa II, Kabarega (23)	17
Kitahimbwa (24) Duhaga II (25) Winyi IV (26)	18

TABLE VII

ANALYSIS OF BABIITO DYNASTY[52]

MUKAMA	GENERATION	1	2	3	4	5	NOTES
1 Isingoma Mpuga Rukidi	1		SeB			D	Buganda lost
2 Ochaki Rwangira	2	Su				D	
3 Oyo Nyimba	2	Su				D	
4 Winyi I, Rubembekantara	3	Su		B		D	
5 Olimi I, Rukidi Rwitamahanga	4	Su	R	B		D	
6 Nyabongo I, Chwa Rulema	5	Su	R			D	
7 Winyi II, Rubagirasega	6	W	Se	B		D	Ankole, Busoga Karagwe. Rwanda lost
8 Olimi II, Ruhundwangeye	7	Su				D	
9 Nyarwa Nyamlirahaiguru	8	W			A	M	
10 Chwa I, Rumomamahanga	8	Su			A	K	
11 Masamba Omubitokati)	8	U				M	
12 Kyebambe I, Winyi Omuzikya	9	Su				D	
13 Winyi III, Rugurukamacholya	10	Su				D	
14 Nyaika	11	W				M	
15 Kyebambe II, Bikaju	11	Su		B		M	
16 Olimi III, Isansa	12	Su		B	A	D	Start of historical record
17 Duhaga I, Chwa Mujuiga	13	Su	Se	B		K	Koki lost
18 Olimi IV, Kasoma	14	W				M	
19 Kyebambe III, Nyamutukura	14	Su	SeS R	B		D	Toro lost
20 Nyabongo II, Mugenyi	15	W				D	
21 Olimi V, Rwakabale	16	W				M	
22 Kyebambe IV, Kamurasi	16	W				D	Speke, Grant, Baker
23 Chwa II, Kabarega	17	W		B	A	Dp	Egyptians, British
24 Kitahimbwa, Y. Karukara	18	Su				Dp	
25 Duhaga II, A. Bisereko	18	Su				D	
26 Winyi IV, T.G.K.	18	Su					

Key:
1. Su—Uncontested
   W—Succession War
   U—Upstart

2. R—Rebellion
   Se—Secession
   SeS—Secession by Son
   SeB—Secession by Brother

3. B—War with Buganda

4. A—War with Ankole

5. D—Died on throne
   M—Murdered
   K—Killed in battle
   Dp—Deposed

Each reign is judged on five counts.

TABLE VIII

LISTS OF BABIITO KINGS VARIOUSLY COMPILED[53]

FISHER	GORJU	TERELLI	ROSCOE	BIKUNYA	K.W. AND NYAKATURA
I.M.R.	I.M.R.	I.M.R.	I.M.R.	I.M.R.	Isingoma Mpuga Rukidi
Ocaki	Ocaki				Ochaki Rwangira
Oyo	Oyo		Oyo	Oyo	Oyo Nyimba
			Nyimba		
		Olimi			Winyi I, Rubembekantara
		Nyabongo			Olimi I, Rukidi Rwitamahanga
		Winyi I	Winyi	Winyi I	Nyabongo I, Chwa Rulemu
			Olimi		Winyi II, Rubagiramasega
					Olimi II, Ruhundwangeye
Cwa	Cwa	Chwamali I	Chwa I	Nyarwa	Nyarwa Nyamuhukahaiguru
Dunego	Dunego			Cwa I	Chwa I, Rumomamahanga
					Masamba Omubitokati
		Kyebambe I			Kyebambe I, Winyi Omuzikya
Winyi	Winyi	Winyi II		Winyi II	Winyi III, Rugurukamacholya
		Nyaika	Bikaju	Rukidi II	Nyaika
		Kyebambe II	Isaza	Winyi III	Kyebambe II, Bikaju
		Olimi II		Olimi II	Olimi III, Isansa
Olimi	Olimi				
Isansa	Isansa				
Duhaga	Duhaga	Duhaga	Duhaga I	Duhaga I	Duhaga I, Chwa Mujuiga
	Kasoma	Kasoma			Olimi IV, Kasoma
Dubongeza	Dubongeza	Kyebambe III	Kyebambe II	Kyebambe II	Kyebambe III, Nyamutukura
Mugenyi	Mugenyi	Nyabongo II	Nyabongo II	Nyabongo	Nyabongo II, Mugenyi
					Olimi V, Rwakabale
Kamurasi	Kamurasi	Kamurasi	Kamurasi	Kyebambe III	Kyebambe IV, Kamurasi
		Kabagungu			
Kabarega	Kabarega	Kabarega	Kabarega	Chwa II	Chwa II, Kabarega
Kitahimbwa	Kitahimbwa	Kitahimbwa	Kitahimbwa	Kitahimbwa	Kitahimbwa, Y. Karukara
Duhaga	Duhaga	Duhaga	Duhaga	Duhaga II	Duhaga II, A. Bisereko
				Winyi IV	Winyi IV, T.G.K.

G. N. UZOIGWE

Kampala, November 1969

ANATOMY OF AN AFRICAN KINGDOM
A HISTORY OF BUNYORO-KITARA

Part I
PREHISTORY

CHAPTER 1

The Foundation of the Kingdom of Kitara

The Kingdom of Kitara is now called Bunyoro, its language being Runyoro. The name Bunyoro is a new invention. Originally the kingdom was known as Kitara, and its people referred to as Abakitara. It must be stressed that Kitara was a very extensive, prestigious, and famous kingdom at the height of its power. It extended as far as Madi and Bukidi in the north, Kavirondo in the east, Kiziba, Karagwe, Rwanda, and Kigezi in the south; to the westward, it encompassed the Ituri forest and the lands of Bulega, all of which now belong to the Congo. Isingo [Ssingo] and Bwera [Buddu] also formed part of the kingdom. But slowly, the kingdom declined as parts of it were captured by some warlike ethnic groups. Some parts too became independent kingdoms under some rebellious princes. Buzimba, Kooki, and Tooro kingdoms were established in this way during the reign of Omukama[1] Nyamutukura [1786–1835]. The height of this decline coincided with the coming of the Europeans. It was these Europeans who annexed Bugangaizi, Rugonjo, Buruli, Bugerere, and other parts of Bunyoro-Kitara to other kingdoms.

The People of Kitara

The people of all the different regions mentioned above were called Abakitara. All Banyamwenge, Bagangaizi, Banyabwiru, Bagahya, Bachope, Batuku, etc. belonged to the kingdom of Kitara. In fact, people in those days were proud to be called Abakitara, and out of this grew the proverb: "*Mbere, Mwenda gwa Kitara njuna* [Please do help me my countrymen of Kitara]." The county of Mwenge [now in

Tooro] was inhabited mainly by the Abahuma,[2] the *Ababiito* [princes], and the *Ababiitokati* [princesses]. All princes and princesses were born in Mwenge. The county of Bugangaizi was reserved for royal tombs and the people of this area specialized in iron working and pottery. The county of Rugonjo was [agricultural and pastoral]. The counties of Mboga [now in the Congo], Bukidi [Lango], Ganyi [Acholi], and Bulega provided soldiers for the King's army.

The Language of the People

In spite of its large size, Kitara had one major language, now known as Orunyoro. This language is still spoken and is used more widely than Luganda. For example, a Runyoro speaker can be understood in such areas as Chope, Busoga, Bugangaizi, Buhekura [Buwekula], Nkore [Ankole], Kiziba, Karagwe, Bukerewe [now in Tanzania], Rwanda, Kigezi, Makora, Busongora, and Mboga, without the necessity of using an interpreter. There are of course, local variations in dialects.

It would be a very healthy development if we all endeavored to preserve this one language so as to be able to listen to the same news, as the British do. It is important to note that despite their different languages and various dialects, the British have one common language—English—to unite them. Brethren, be proud of your now small kingdom which still remains and also of your language! Both are great symbols of the glory of the past history of a country. Do not be dismayed by the present small size of our kingdom. Empires have risen and fallen in the past. Such stories abound in history books. Every citizen of Kitara should therefore do his best to revive the country's glory and should praise his country. Let us love our country, Kitara, because of the glory that was Kitara and let us not emigrate from our country. Let us also cherish our language and speak it everywhere we go. For as the proverb says: "One can exile the body, but not the language."

THE PEOPLING OF BUNYORO-KITARA

In the beginning the world was void. It consisted of waste land uninhabited by people. On it, however, there lived animals ruled by Kalisa—the lord of wild animals. This gave rise to the saying "Kalisa, look after your herds and do not come near." It is not known whether Kalisa was an animal or a reptile.

Then there came people on earth. These people originated either from the Sudan or Abyssinia. They were ruled by a king called Kintu. His wife's name was Kati. They brought their cattle with them. Kintu and Kati had three sons. The first son was called Kairu, the second Kahuma, and the third Kakama.

Kakama Becomes King

When Kintu had reached old age, he began to worry about the successor to the throne. He decided to set his sons a test to discover the ablest of them. He tried them in many ways. But one day he called them together and spoke thus: "Children, death is near; but I would like you to do something for me and the one who does it best will be my successor. He will sit on my royal throne and will rule over his brothers." In the evening Kintu milked the cows and filled three bowls with milk. He summoned his sons and handed them the bowls of milk, saying: "If by morning all your bowls of milk are still full, I will divide my kingdom between the three of you. But if only one of you passes this test, he will be my successor and will rule over you." Having said this, he retired to sleep. The sons remained in the sitting room, each with his bowl of milk on his lap. After a short time, Kakama, the youngest son, was overcome by sleep and spilled some of his milk. He wept. He begged his brothers to give him some of their milk with which to refill his bowl. His brothers took pity on him and granted his request. They did so because he was their youngest brother and they loved him dearly. Now all the three brothers had the same amount of milk in their bowls. At cockcrow, Kairu, the eldest son, was also overcome by sleep and spilled nearly all his milk. Kairu nevertheless retained his courage and, instead of grieving over his misfortune, shared the little milk he was left with between his brothers. After some time, Kahuma, the second son, fell asleep and spilled a lot of his milk. In the morning their father came into the sitting room and greeted them. Kairu was the first to report his failure. His father was not angry with him but teased him about his physical strength. Kahuma tried to explain to him his unsuccessful effort to save his own milk.

Again his father was not angry with him but teased him about his bodily weakness. Then Kakama said to his father triumphantly: "Here is my milk, father." His father was surprised and said: "The ruler is always born last." But his elder brothers protested, saying that Kakama had been the first to spill his own milk and that they had been kind enough to give him some of theirs to fill his bowl. But their father only replied: "Since you have consented to give him some of your milk, you should also consent to be ruled by him." On hearing this, the two brothers decided to recognize their young brother as their future king, partly because they were jealous of each other.

Then Kintu admonished his sons thus: "You, my child Kairu, never desert your young brother. Serve him well." To Kahuma: "And you, my child, never desert your young brother also. Help him to look after the cattle and obey him." And to Kakama [the successor]: "You have now become the eldest of your brothers. Love them and treat them well. Give them whatever they ask of you. Now that you are king, rule the kingdom well." Sometime after this incident Kintu vanished. People searched for him everywhere but in vain. It was therefore presumed that he must have disappeared into the underworld.[3]

Our neighbors, the Baganda, regard Kintu as their king, arguing that "He is Kato, the brother of Rukidi." But this is not true. Admittedly one cannot with all confidence dismiss their claim outright, because the events in question took place a very long time ago and were witnessed by no living person. Moreover, there are no written records to substantiate their authenticity. However, both Banyoro and Baganda are agreed on one fact, namely, that Kintu was the first man to come to this world and that he preceded the Bachwezi. The Babiito came later on, as we shall see in Part 3. The name of the king of Buganda was Prince Kato Kimera, the younger brother of Rukidi. Their mother's name was Nyatworo. The disintegration of Kitara into the three kingdoms of Nkore, Bunyoro, and Buganda occurred during the period of the Babiito dynasty following the disappearance of the Bachwezi. Since no written records existed during this period, it is very probable that not all the names of the kings of Kitara are extant. European writers, however, believe that the history of Bunyoro [meaning Kitara] goes as far back as between 2,000 and 3,000 years ago.

THE KINGS OF KITARA

Abatembuzi

The Abatembuzi dynasty was the first to rule Kitara. In other words, they preceded both the Bachwezi and Babiito. The names of the kings of this dynasty are as follows:

1. Kintu
2. Kakama
3. Twale
4. Hangi
5. Ira s/o Hangi
6. Kazoba s/o Hangi
7. Nyamuhanga
8. Nkya I
9. Nkya II
10. Baba
11. Kamuli
12. Nseka
13. Kudidi
14. Ntonzi
15. Nyakahongerwa
16. Mukonko
17. Ngonzaki Rutahinduka
18. Isaza Waraga Rugambanabato
19. Bukuku

Abachwezi

1. Ndahura of Mubende
2. Mulindwa, regent during the period of Ndahura's disappearance
3. Wamara of Bwera

Ababiito

These are the names of the Babiito Kings of Kitara—excluding those of Buganda and Nkore. [You will find their names later on in this book.]

1. Rukidi I Mpuga Kyeramaino s/o Nyatworo
2. Ocaki I Rwangirra
3. Oyo I Nyimba Kabambaiguru
4. Winyi I Rubembeka—Ntara, Kiburara
5. Olimi I Rwitamahanga, Kalimbi
6. Nyabongo I Rulemu, Kyambukyankaito, Muyenje
7. Winyi II Rubagiramasega, Lapenje
8. Olimi II Ruhundwangeye, Burongo
9. Nyarwa I Omuzarra Kyaro, Kyaka
10. Chwa I ayacwire ente Nkole, Rwanda
11. Mashamba I yali mubiitokati Rwembuba

12. Kyebambe I Omuzikya, Kijaguzo
13. Winyi III Ruguruka—Macolya, Miduma
14. Nyaika Omuragwa—Macolya, Kihwera
15. Kyebambe II Bikaju, Nyamiryango
16. Olimi III Isansa Gabigogo Omukwata-galemire,
    Kiguhyo
17. Duhaga I Chwa Mujwiga, Ngundu, Kisiha, Irangara
18. Olimi IV Kasoma, Ruhunga
19. Kyebambe III Nyamutukura Lubongoya Lwabunyana,
    Kibedi
20. Nyabongo II Mugenyi Biranga s/o Mwenge, Bukonda
21. Olimi V Rwakabale, Kitonya
22. Kyebambe IV Kamurasi Mirundi Rukanama, Kanembe,
    Busibika
23. Ohwa II Kabalega Yokana, Mparo
24. Kitahimbwa I Karukara Yosia William
25. Duhaga II Bisereko Andrea, M.B.E., Kinogozi
26. Winyi IV Tito Gafabusa, C.B.E.[4]

CHAPTER 2

Abatembuzi

Kintu, as we saw, was not born in Kitara. He came from
a distant land and found no one living in that area. He therefore ruled over the few people he brought with him. He is
very much remembered as the great forefather of Bunyoro.
The manner of his death is still a mystery. He is said to
be the father of Kakama, who was the father of Twale. Hangi,
the son of Twale, had sons Ira and Kazoba who later became
kings. Kazoba, the younger of the two brothers, succeeded
his elder brother, Ira, who died without an heir. The population increased considerably during the reign of Kazoba.
Kazoba was loved by his subjects and was deified after his
death. He is still well remembered in our time. He was the
father of Nyamuhanga, known by the Banyankore as Rugaba
and by the Baganda as Muwanga. People made a cult of
him as well.

Omukama Nyamuhanga also ruled over many people, because during his reign there was further increase in population. He was greatly loved by his people. A long time elapsed before he could have a child. This happened after he had consulted a witch doctor, who advised him to marry a certain girl called Nyabagabe, the daughter of one of his servants called Igoro. Nyabagabe bore him a son, whom he named Nkya [meaning "Lucky"]. People were delighted at Nyabagabe's good luck. They were glad that the daughter of a mere servant had married a king. Even today when something lucky happened to someone, people would comment: "That one must have been born at about the time Nyabagabe was in labor." King Nyamuhanga is still remembered today by many people.

Nkya I ruled over many people and was also loved by them. Like his father, he was barren for a long time. Like his father, too, he had to consult a witch doctor, as a result of which he begot a son, whom he declined to name. When questioned about his decision he replied that he saw no reason to give his son a different name from his, because both of them were born under similar circumstances. When Nkya, Junior, therefore succeeded his father he assumed the title of Nkya II. Nkya II was succeeded by Baba, and Nseka by Kudidi. Kudidi reigned for a very long time and died a very old man. He was succeeded by Ntonzi, who came to be known as "Ntonzi who ruled by the sword" because he put down rebellions in the country. Ntonzi was succeeded by Nyakahongerwa and Nyakahongerwa by Mukonko, his son. Mukonko's reign lasted for a very long time and those who lived under him were also to experience Bachwezi rule. Rutahinduka ["the one who never turns to look behind"], son of Mukonko, came to the throne already an old man [on account of his father's long span of life]. He was nicknamed "Ngonzaki Rutahinduka" because he used to say to people who teased him about his father's long life: "*Ngonzaki* [What do I need!]." He was a very rich man and did not feel that becoming king was particularly important to him. This was how he came to be called "Ngonzaki Rutahinduka."

He had a son called Isaza Waraga Rugambanabato, who ascended the throne while still very young. Consequently, the young monarch continued to play around with his fellow young friends and hated old men. He did his best to harass them and even went as far as putting some of them to death.

The frightened old men feared him and avoided him. The young monarch was therefore nicknamed "Rugambanabato [he who talks only with young people]." This nickname was to become his official title. Waraga Rugambanabato enjoyed hunting. One day it transpired that when he had gone out to hunt with his young friends, he expressed a wish to put on the skin of the young ejazelle they had killed. His friends skinned the dead animal, made the skin into the form of a sack, and helped him to put it on. The king was extremely delighted. But, unfortunately, the skin dried on him and became too tight. It pressed against him to the point of squeezing him to death. His friends tried unsuccessfully to extricate him from his misery. And when he exclaimed to them in anguish: "Friends, I am at the point of death," they answered mockingly at him: "You may die, since you have enjoyed the throne." When, however, they saw that the situation was getting out of hand, some of them rushed off to the king's aunt called Kogere and his sister called Nyangoma and narrated to them the tragic story. On hearing the bad news, these ladies summoned some old men from among their servants and sent them off to the rescue of Waraga. When they arrived at the scene they ordered Waraga's friends to convey him to the river and dip him in water. When emersed in water, the animal skin softened, and with the aid of a knife, the old men were able to cut the skin open and extricated the king. They had thereby saved his life! To his aged saviors, the king was very grateful. He rewarded them by making them his court favorites and ordered them not to depart from his presence. From then onwards, Waraga cut off his associations with the young. But he refrained from killing or even punishing them. But his love was now transferred from them to the old, for whom he threw a banquet to celebrate the occasion, as it were. In the course of the banquet he thanked them once more and declared: "My fathers, you saved my life. My young friends could only advise me on how to put on the animal skin but not on how to take it off. If it was not for these ladies [his relatives] I would not be among you here." Turning to the youths, he said: "I was nearly dying in your presence. Always give reverence to the old people."

In order to demonstrate further his gratitude and respect to these old men, the king gave each a county to rule. He warned them, however, to regard him as their overlord and unifier. They were commanded to come to him whenever he summoned them and to obey him always. The word *Amasaza* [counties or provinces] was coined from the name of the king, Isaza. King Isaza Waraga therefore was the first monarch to divide Kitara into large areas called sazas and to appoint a *saza* chief to rule over each area. These old men, his saviors, were to become the first *saza* chiefs of Kitara. From this period Isaza Waraga came to be called "Isaza Nyakikoto [the greatest of all the *saza* chiefs and the lord of all]." To the following people he gave the various sazas: Kitara[1] was given to Nyamenge, Buganda to Ntege and Koya, Nkore to Macumulinda, Busoga to Ntembe, Bugangaizi to Kabara, Mwenge to Nyakirembeka, Busongora to his aunt Kogere, Buruli to Nyangoma, his elder sister, Bugahya to Nyamurwana, Bugoma to Nsinga, Bugungu to Kwamango, Chope to Kaparo, Bulega to Kalega, Bwera to Mukwiri, and Busindi [Masindi] to Nyakadogi. These were the original sazas of Kitara before disintegration set in. However, these sazas existed during the rule of the Bachwezi.

Brief notes on some of these sazas may be necessary at this stage. Buganda was given to an old man called Koya, but due to his old age he delegated the job to his son, Ntege. That is why Buganda County was referred to as "Buganda of Ntege and Koya." Two counties were given to women— Kogere, Isaza's aunt, and Nyangoma, his elder sister, as a token of his gratitude to them for having helped to save his life. Omukama Isaza Nyakikoto himself lived in Kitara County, but would visit the other counties to inspect his cattle.

Omukama Isaza's Friendship with Nyamiyonga

Omukama Isaza lived to a ripe old age and his fame spread all over the country. One day a certain ruler of a foreign land in the underworld sent a messenger to Isaza making six requests. This foreign ruler did not say exactly what he wanted. He merely supplied Isaza with six clues and wished him to deduce his requests from these. The clues were as follows:

1. The measure of time.
2. The rope that arrests water.
3. What makes Isaza [the king] turn to look behind.
4. One who knows no duty or responsibility.

5. One who knows no suffering or cares and becomes drunk
   without alcohol.
6. The door that shuts out poverty.

The king, lost over these riddles, decided to call an assembly of elders for counsel. But this assembly could solve nothing. The *saza* chiefs were sent for, but they, too, failed to
solve the conundrum. It transpired, however, that Kogere, the
Saza Chief of Busongora and the king's aunt, had a maid who
offered to be taken to the king to unravel the clues. She also
offered to give up her life in the event of failure. Accordingly,
Kogere brought the maid to her nephew, the king, and said
to him: "Here is my maid who says she can solve your mystery." The king then addressed the maid genially: "Adyeri
[for that was her pet name], are you sure that you know the
answer?" The maid replied that she did. The king dismissed
those present except the *saza* chiefs. The maid then began
to unravel the meanings of the foreign king's puzzle. For the
first problem, she requested a cock to be brought before her.
When this was done, she said to the king: "This is the measure
of time." For the second problem she asked for water, which
she heated in a cooking pot, mixed millet flour in it, and made
it into a dough. Turning to the king she said: "This is the
rope that arrests water." As for the third problem, she asked
for a calf to be brought. As this animal was being brought it
uttered a cry and Isaza turned involuntarily to find out what
was happening to the calf. The maid then said to him: "Sir,
that is what makes Isaza turn and look behind." As for the
fourth problem, she asked for a dog to be brought in and be
given a smoking pipe. The dog just stared at the pipe dis-
interestedly. Then the maid said: "Here is one who has no
sense of duty." For the fifth problem she asked for a baby to
be brought forward. When this was done she requested the
king to place it on his lap. The baby started scratching the
king's face and then wetted his clothes. Whereupon the maid
said to the king: "Here is one who knows no sorrow and be-
haves like a drunkard though without alcohol." Finally, she
requested the foreign messengers to come forward and then
asked them: "Did your king, Nyamiyonga,[2] give you anything
to bring to this king?" The messengers opened their baskets
and produced a small vase containing two coffee seeds, the
one smeared with Nyamiyonga's blood and the other untainted by blood. There were also some pieces of *ejubwa*

[name of a kind of grass], four *omutoma* leaves stuck on a stick, and a shearing knife. Then the maid said to the king: "Sir, that is the door that shuts out poverty, which Nyamiyonga asked you about. If you are ready to comply with his requests, cut up some part of your stomach with that shearing knife. You should cut the area near your navel and smear the untainted coffee seed with your blood. You should then swallow the seed tainted with Nyamiyonga's blood. I have done my duty and now leave you to do yours." With these words the maid left the king's presence. The king thanked her for her efforts and the help she had rendered.

Isaza sought the advice of his *saza* chiefs as to whether or not to swallow the coffee seed sent to him by Nyamiyonga.[3] A certain old man called Kyarunda advised the king against the idea of becoming a blood brother with someone he did not know, someone, indeed, he had neither met nor seen. "If that king really loves you," asked Kyarunda, "why doesn't he come and see you and talk to you? Then after that you can become friends." Isaza accepted this advice. But since custom demands that one should not deny another an offer of friendship, Isaza delegated this ceremony (of making a bond of friendship) to his servant Bukuku, and said to him: "Bukuku, I have delegated this task to you, make this bond in my name." Bukuku swallowed Nyamiyonga's coffee seed, then cut open part of his stomach, smeared the other coffee seed with the blood, and put it in the vase in which it was brought. He then put back the vase into the basket, which he handed to the messengers. The messengers took leave of Isaza and went back to report to Nyamiyonga.

The Birth of Isimbwa

When the messengers reached home they narrated to their king what had transpired in Isaza's palace. On hearing their story, Nyamiyonga became very angry. He inquired from the messengers the main interests of Isaza. They told him that the king loved two things—cattle and women—above all else. Burning with revenge, Nyamiyonga decided to play a trick on Isaza. He summoned his daughters and chose one of them —Nyamata [literally, of milk]—and dispatched her to Isaza's palace with strict instructions neither to disclose her true identity nor to reveal who sent her there. Nyamata, accompanied by her escorts, left by night for Isaza's kingdom. Just before they reached Isaza's palace, Nyamata's escorts left her on her own and returned home. Alone, she proceeded to the palace and entered the visitors' house, known as *Mucwa*. There she met Bukuku, the guard of that house. Bukuku was astounded by her beauty. Nyamata expressed a wish to be announced to the king. Bukuku, blinded by the girl's beauty, lost his head, and breaking convention, marched straight to Isaza without ascertaining the young lady's identity, her mission, and where she came from. Bukuku said to the king: "My lord, there is a lady in front of your palace, and though I have no intention of insulting my ladies, there is no one as beautiful as she in your entire household." On hearing this news, Isaza sent off his young sister, Runyunyuzi [star] Nyanzigombi, to inspect this beauty. Like Bukuku, Runyunyuzi, taken aback by the visitor's extraordinary good looks, rushed back to her brother and exclaimed: "My lord, I must not be jealous of her because I am not as beautiful, but must declare that she is very beautiful. You, too, have never set your eyes on such a beautiful creature. There is no one as beautiful as she in this kingdom." Isaza ordered the young lady to be brought before him at once. On seeing her, he fell in love with her at first sight and decided to take her to wife. At night, Isaza inquired from Nyamata: "Where do you come from?" She laughingly replied: "I am a daughter of Bahuma parents who live in your kingdom. There are so many of them that it is not possible for you to know my parents even if I told you their names. However, I ran away secretly from them because I respect and love you and wish you to marry me. You do not have to wait for long before my people come looking for me. Then you will have the opportunity to see them." Isaza, consumed by love for her, was in no mood to ask further questions.

After they had been married for a long time, Nyamata wished to test her husband's love for her. She said to him: "Who do you love more, me or your cow Bihogo bya Gaju?" The king replied: "Surely, my dear, I love you as much as I love my cow Bihogo bya Gaju." After this incident, Nyamata was in no doubt as to where Isaza's first love lay. One day, as Isaza and Nyamata were seated together and conversing playfully, the king's cows happened to stray towards their direction. All of a sudden, Isaza got up and went to find out what was happening. Nyamata was furious, and the king, realizing what he had done, came back to her and spoke coaxingly: "My dear, do not be angry with me, because I lose all sense of proportion whenever I see cows." Nyamata simply kept quiet and only ruminated over her mission to Isaza.

In her sixth month of pregnancy, Nyamata decided to go home. "I am going back home to tell my people about you and your kingdom," she told her husband. "I do not want my child to have no maternal relatives. You know that it is a long while since I left them and they may rightly believe that I am dead." Isaza was impressed by these words and bade her farewell and gave her an escort. When Nyamata and her escort reached the border of Nyamiyonga's kingdom, she stole away from them. They searched for her in vain. Disappointed and terrified, the escort headed for home to report to Isaza his wife's disappearance. "My lord," said their leader, "your wife vanished from us at the border." Isaza said nothing and showed little emotion.

Nyamata reached her father's palace unaccompanied. After three months she had her baby. It was a boy and was named Isimbwa. On the day of her arrival, her father had asked her many questions concerning Isaza—how he was, the things he loved best, his wealth and his subjects. Nyamata explained everything to him, emphasizing Isaza's love for cattle. "There is nothing he loves more than cows," she told her father.

Isaza Visits Nyamiyonga

Having found out a great deal about Isaza, Nyamiyonga summoned all his herdsmen [who were usually Bahuma] and ordered them to herd his flock together. From this collection he chose two of his best animals—Ruhogo the bull, and Kahogo the cow. He instructed two of his herdsmen to lead these animals to Isaza's palace but warned them to travel secretly by night. Nyamiyonga's herdsmen accomplished their mission splendidly. When Isaza's herdsmen saw the two animals standing in the palace, they put them among those of their master. Not unnaturally Isaza's animals resented the intruders and fighting was started. When Isaza saw the new arrivals the following morning, he loved them very much. He even took the trouble to prevent the new bull from attacking his own. And when he saw the new bull attempting to make love to his beloved Bihogo bya Gaju, he was delighted and decided to make the new animals his own. It transpired, however, that the new animals eloped with his beloved Bihogo bya Gaju. They headed back to Nyamiyonga's palace, fol-

lowing the route they had come by. Isaza and some of his
herdsmen ran after them in an attempt to stop them. Isaza
sent a message to Bukuku, the guardian of the visitors' house,
ordering him to "Go and look after my household. I am going
after Bihogo and Kahogo wherever they go."

Isaza kept his word and with his herdsmen wandered about
until eventually they reached some foreign land they had
never heard of before. Then they saw a palace, whereupon
Isaza asked some passersby: "Whose palace is this?" "It belongs to Nyamiyonga," the people replied. The name rang a
bell in Isaza's ears. "Couldn't this be the king who requested
my friendship?" But the people interjected: "Who are you?"
and Isaza answered: "I am Isaza Nyakikoto, the king of
Kitara." "True," the people replied, "this is the palace of your
friend. We have often heard him talk about you." Whereupon Isaza ordered them to announce his arrival to the king.
When the two monarchs met, Nyamiyonga asked Isaza:
"Who showed you the way up here?" And Isaza answered:
"Are you not my friend? And is it not natural that I should
know the way to your house?" On hearing this, Nyamiyonga
ordered a house to be prepared for Isaza. He prepared a feast
in his honor, sent him some cows to kill, and others for
milking.

The next morning Nyamiyonga ordered two royal chairs to
be got ready—one for him and the other for Isaza. He asked
that Isaza be shown in. He greeted his guest cheerfully.
After some conversation between the two monarchs, Nyamiyonga decided to send away the other people present so that
he and his guest would be left alone. Then he said to Isaza:
"You have done me wrong. Why did you decline to perform
the bond of friendship I asked of you but instead delegated
the ceremony to Bukuku, a mere servant?" To this Isaza replied: "I did so through the influence of bad advice. I personally do not hate you." Nyamiyonga accepted this
explanation and added: "It is true indeed that you acted under the influence of bad advice. I am sure you yourself do not
hate me."

At this juncture Nyamiyonga decided to introduce his queen
and princesses to Isaza. When they assembled and took their
seats, Isaza immediately recognized his wife, Nyamata, and
was very delighted to see her. "Who is that one?" Nyamiyonga asked Isaza. "This is my wife, who has been lost for
some time now," he replied. Again Nyamiyonga inquired:
"Who is that child she is holding?" "It could be my child be-

cause Nyamata left my house in her sixth month of pregnancy," he answered. "True, that child belongs to you, and his uncle, Rwogamata [one who bathes in milk] before you here, is the one who performed all the rituals and gave him the name of Isimbwa," said Nyamiyonga. Isaza was childless and therefore was very delighted to hear all this. But then Nyamiyonga posed the inevitable question: "Were you following your wife or did you come merely to see me?" Isaza truthfully told him that he was following the three animals—Bihogo bya Gaju, Kahogo, and Ruhogo. Then Nyamiyonga said to him: "Would you know your cows from mine?" Isaza said he would, and the cows were ordered to be assembled. On hearing the cows moo, Isaza turned instantly to look at them. This time Nyamata did not get annoyed but rather pretended not to have noticed her husband's reaction. She only nodded to her father, thereby drawing his attention to Isaza's love for cows. "Look at him," she whispered to her father. "My friend," said Nyamiyonga to Isaza, "how you love cows! Cows seem to mean more to you than your wife and son!" "It is not true," Isaza replied, "because I love them too. I love cows especially now because they have given me a son" [meaning that were it not for cows he would not have discovered his wife and son].

Whereupon Nyamiyonga rose from his royal seat and went with Isaza to the cows' quarters so that Isaza could pick out his own animals from the flock. Isaza had no difficulty in picking out his own animals and Nyamiyonga gave him some two hundred more. He also permitted him to be reunited with his wife and son and bade them farewell. But Isaza could not find his way back to Kitara and so remained in Nyamiyonga's kingdom for the rest of his life.[4]

In the meantime, Bukuku, the guardian of Muchwa [visitors' house] and who belonged to the Baranzi clan, had proclaimed himself King of Kitara, having acted as regent for too long. He therefore became Isaza's successor.

Bukuku of the Baranzi Clan

King Bukuku of the Baranzi clan, a relative of Kairu, son of Kintu, former chief guard of the visitors' house and in charge of Isaza's household, having waited for a long time for the return of Isaza, proclaimed himself king. But having sat on Isaza's royal stool, he soon discovered that he was acceptable to only a few people. Some of the *saza* chiefs appointed by Isaza refused to accept his overlordship. They declared: "We cannot worship a *muiru*[5] [common man or peasant]." Some *saza* chiefs therefore declared their independence of Kitara, thereby becoming kinglets in their various sazas. Nevertheless, very few *saza* chiefs accepted Bukuku as the sovereign mainly because Isaza had left no heir to the throne. Some of the people, however, still hoped for Isaza's return. "Isaza will come back one day," they used to say. And this worried Bukuku very much.

Bukuku himself had no son. But he had a daughter called Nyinamwiru [a name which indicated her peasant origin]. This Nyinamwiru was a very beautiful girl. The witch doctors therefore advised Bukuku to kill her. They argued that her beauty was such that she was destined to bring misfortune to her father's house. "Kill that daughter of yours. If you refuse to take our advice, do not blame us for the terrible consequences of your refusal." Bukuku was not prepared to take away the life of his only child. When, however, Nyinamwiru grew older Bukuku decided to incapacitate her by cutting off one of her breasts and gouging out one of her eyes. By so doing he was convinced that she would not attract the attention of men. He then built her a separate palace without any entrance to it. One could only get to Nyinamwiru's palace through Bukuku's own house. He gave her a maid called Mugizi to serve her and look after her needs.

Part II
ABACHWEZI

Introduction

During the reign of Isaza Nyakikoto Rugambanabato, there appeared a race of white people known to us as the Abachwezi. The Babiito clan, now ruling over Bunyoro, Buganda, Tooro, and other parts, the Bahinda clan ruling in Nkore, Karagwe [part of modern Tanzania], and Rwanda, are descendants of these Bachwezi.

These people had very white skins and it is thought today that they may have been Portuguese. The word Abachwezi, it is argued, may have originated from the word Portuguese. It is also thought by some that the Bachwezi may have come from some other European countries whose names we do not know. But we are sure that they had white skins. What is in doubt is their country of origin. It is probable that they were not Europeans but may have been either Arabians, Abyssinians, or Egyptians [Abamisri] since they migrated into Kitara from the northern direction. They have left many traces of their presence and because of this they will be remembered by all generations.

European writers have attempted to compare things found in this country and those found in Egypt. Certainly there are many things which bear similarities in the two countries such as painting, engraving, pottery, and so forth. These Egyptians also were familiar with the geography of Central Africa and particularly with the pygmies in this region. It is thought that they came as traders in the areas south of the Nile [Kihira], and west of the Sudan. It would have been surprising if the countries of Egypt and Nubia, which were established trading states, did not attempt to extend their tentacles to their neighbors in Central Africa. Egyptian boats sailed from Khartoum along the Nile down to Bunyoro and Buganda. The Sudanese people were powerless against these traders and could not put a stop to their expansion through the Sudan towards Bunyoro and Buganda.

Boats and musical instruments—drums, guitars [*endingidi*], etc.—found in both Bunyoro and Buganda also testify to the Egyptian presence since similar items are found in Egypt as well. Egyptian geographers, too, were familiar with our Lakes Albert [Mwitanzige] and Victoria. In A.D. 150 Ptolemy had described the kingdom of the moon where the mountains of the moon stand, while Herodotus, writing some 2,000 years ago, described the country lying north of these mountains— the land of the pygmies.

It is possible that the people in the west of Buganda, Bunyoro, Tooro, and Nkore are descendants of peoples who came to this kingdom very long ago. Because of their relatively sophisticated way of life, they regarded themselves as the ruling class, and extended their influence southwards to Bukidi [Lango] and slowly southwards to Bunyoro, Tooro, and Nkore.

CHAPTER 1

The Coming of the Abachwezi

Isimbwa Comes to Bukuku's Palace

When Isimbwa, son of Isaza Nyakikoto [who had failed to find his way back to his kingdom] and Nyamata, grew into a mature man, his father found him a wife called Nyabiryo. Isimbwa and Nyabiryo had a son and named him Kyomya. Isaza used to tell his son, Isimbwa, stories about his lost kingdom of Kitara. Isimbwa was filled with the desire to see this kingdom. Fearing that he might be killed by his father's former subjects if he disclosed his identity, he decided to find his way to Kitara disguised as a hunter. He was accompanied by many white people like himself who were also disguised as hunters. When they reached Madi, Isimbwa left his wife and some of his luggage there. They passed through Bukidi [Lango] and Buruli to Nyakatema and Mpongo and then headed eastwards through Buganda and then on to Buhemba, Rwembuba, and Kikwenuzi. Finally Isimbwa reached Bukuku's palace and that of his daughter, Nyinamwiru, which were at Kisengwe [in Bugangaizi].

Isimbwa paid Bukuku a visit and gave him gifts; beads and many other things. But Isimbwa and his followers happened to be seen by Mugizi, Nyinamwiru's maid. She immediately rushed to her mistress and told her of the good looks and tremendous riches of these people. Nyinamwiru, determined to see these newcomers, instructed Mugizi to ask their leader to pay her a visit. Isimbwa accepted her request in a return message but asked her to be patient until the opportunity was ripe. He also sent her some small gifts.

Then Isimbwa and his followers, pretending to be continuing their hunting expedition eastwards, begged King Bukuku to excuse their departure. Bukuku granted them permission to proceed with their plan. They passed through Mubende and having reached Kisozi, Isimbwa decided to leave his men and their luggage there. Taking only two men with him, he stole his way back to Nyinamwiru's palace. With the aid of a ladder he climbed into Nyinamwiru's apartment. The lady was very glad to see him and hid him in her house. Isimbwa stayed with her for three months, at the end of which he decided to rejoin his companions. He gave her many presents and bade her farewell and comforted her thus: "Do not worry, I will come back one day." Clearly, Isimbwa's intention was to recover his father's throne. But he was well aware that the moment was not opportune. Moreover, being white, he looked different from the rest of the population. In the meantime, Isimbwa and his followers retired to Bukidi.[1]

The Birth of Ndahura

Six months after the departure of Isimbwa, Nyinamwiru gave birth to a baby boy. The baby was white like his father. Bukuku was very surprised when he heard the news and wondered from whom she got the child. "Women are a terrible lot," he exclaimed. "How on earth did she get the child?" It was from Bukuku's words that the child came to be called "Ndahura." Bukuku wanted to kill the child but his witch doctors advised him against adopting such a drastic course of action, arguing that the child's milk teeth were not yet visible from the gum.[2] When the child grew older and the teeth appeared he was brought before Bukuku, who ordered him to be thrown into a river. It is believed that Ndahura was

thrown into either the river Nguse or the river Muzizi because
these were the two nearest rivers to Bukuku's palace. But the
child wore charms around his neck which got stuck to a tree.
Consequently, he did not drown but hung to the tree howling.

There happened, however, to be nearby a man (a potter)
who had been collecting clay from the river. When he heard
the child crying he decided to find out what was going on.
On seeing the child he guessed to whom it belonged and decided to rescue it. He carried the child to his house and went
secretly to Nyinamwiru to tell her of his discovery. She advised him to look after the child well and warned him not to
disclose his identity. As a curious gesture Nyinamwiru asked
the potter to prepare dishes for the king and announce them
as a present coming from her. She also sent to the king, her
father, two cows—one for milking, and the other in gestation
as a token of her thanks and also for feeding the baby.[3] The
child now became known as Ndahura Kyarubimba after the
potter who had saved his life and was bringing him up. On
his part, Bukuku was convinced that the child was dead.

Ndahura Kills Bukuku, His Grandfather

When Ndahura Kyarubimba grew up, he developed interest in cattle and became a shepherd. He also became unusually very determined and feared nothing. He was indeed
such a naughty young man that he used to neglect his flock
and watched them as they grazed in the gardens thereby
demolishing the flowers. When Bukuku's herdsmen led their
cows to drink the king's salty water, Ndahura would also lead
his to drink the same water. As a consequence, he got into
incessant quarrels with the king's herdsmen. Finally, they decided to report him to the king. "That potter's child," they
told the king, "is a nuisance. He usually brings his cows to
drink the salty water before your cows have had their fill."
"I will give him a beating," retorted Bukuku. One day,
Bukuku was called to witness the little boy's impudence.
Ndahura had brought out his cows as usual and the herdsmen
said to the king: "Sir, now you have seen the potter's little
boy!" Whereupon Bukuku, infuriated, got hold of a spear,
moved near Ndahura and hurled it at him, but missed his target. Ndahura bolted for the spear, seized hold of it, aimed,
and speared Bukuku to death. Then he seized the throne. The
frightened herdsmen ran to Nyinamwiru, exclaiming: "Our

lady, bad things have happened. Rubumbi [their version of Kyarubimba], has killed the king." Whereupon Nyinamwiru said: "The ears cannot refuse to hear. Today, I have heard bad news and good news. My father, Bukuku, is dead; but my son, Ndahura, has succeeded his grandfather on the throne. What are you waiting for? Go and put Ndahura on his grandfather's throne." Few people disputed the fact that Ndahura was Nyinamwiru's son. Then Nyinamwiru gave the following instruction: "Go and pull down my palace and remake it. This time, make sure you put in a door. In the meantime, I will wear the royal robes" [of the king's mother]. All these things were done and Bukuku was buried at Kisengwe in Bugangaizi.

Nyinamwiru is very much remembered in Bunyoro-Kitara and people refer to her as: "Adyeri Nyinamwiru, the one-breasted, the breast which fed a fighter and a conqueror."

CHAPTER 2

Abachwezi Rule

There were only two Bachwezi kings. And between these two intervened the regency of Mulindwa, the custodian of the drums, when Ndahura got lost. Their names are as follows:

1. Ndahura Kyarubimba, Rwesakara Myambi, Rusoma Mahanga.
2. Mulindwa—the regent.
3. Wamara Bwigunda, Njojo eyona Rwabwera.

1. OMUKAMA NDAHURA OMUCHWEZI[1]

Ndahura ascended the throne in succession to his maternal grandfather, Bukuku. He moved his capital from Kisengwe to a hill in Mubende so as to have a clear view of his kingdom.

His First Wars

After establishing himself on the throne, he proceeded to bring back to obedience those rebel chieftains who had refused to accept Bukuku as king. He first moved against Nsinga, Saza Chief of Bugoma, and captured him. Ndahura accused the chief of attempting to bewitch him: "I hear you have been bewitching me," he said to Nsinga. On reaching Kabale,[2] Ndahura dethroned him, then made him a mock king with a crown made out of leaves before executing him. He gave the saza of Bugoma to his son, Kanyabugoma, whose title was *"Omugamba Ikwenu* [one who speaks without reflecting on his words]."

With the same determination and equal ruthlessness, Ndahura moved against the other rebellious chieftains, as well as the rulers of foreign kingdoms, and executed them all. It is said that during his reign, Kitara was afflicted by various kinds of diseases. These diseases were contacted by Ndahura's armies while fighting in foreign lands. They were infected with sores when they fought against Omukama Nyamuhangara [the name of whose kingdom is not mentioned in the text], and other skin diseases when they fought against Kwaku Nkodo of Itaka [literally, Earth]. The most serious disease of all which Ndahura and his soldiers brought back to Kitara was smallpox, which they contracted while fighting against King Fumura. This is why the disease is called *Ndahura* [after the king's name]. And when they launched an attack on Omukama Tongoka they contracted another skin disease, called *ebisonde*.[3] Contrary to some other views, it was not until the reign of Omukama Cwa II Kabalega (1870–99) that jiggers became known in Bunyoro-Kitara.

Isimbwa Returns to Kitara

Having heard news of his son's activities, Isimbwa decided to return to Kitara. He passed through Bukidi, Isaka, Kafo, Buruli, and reached Miduna through Bujogora. He crossed over to Kirahoiga and passed through Kikonda, Kiewabugingo, and having crossed over to Mpongo and Bukonda, he proceeded to Kitahinduka through Kicunda, Bujagule, and Kikwenuzi.

Finally he arrived at Nyinamwiru's palace and immediately

sent for Rubumbi [the potter who had brought up Ndahura].
When Rubumbi arrived Isimbwa asked him to relate to him
all that had happened during his absence. Having heard all
the news, he dispatched Rubumbi to Nyinamwiru to announce
his name. When the visitor met her he resolutely refused to
give his name but requested instead that the maid, Mugizi,
be summoned. Immediately, Nyinamwiru guessed who he
was and complied with his request. After her discussion with
Isimbwa, Mugizi returned to her mistress and with a broad
smile confirmed her suspicion. Isimbwa was warmly welcomed
back and a big feast was prepared in his honor. Many cows
were slaughtered to celebrate the reunion. People ate, drank
beer, and made merry.

Two months elapsed before Isimbwa expressed a wish to
see his son, Ndahura. He was accompanied by Nyinamwiru
to the king's palace. They set out from Kisengwe [where
Nyinamwiru still lived] and traveled by the Kyankuba route.
They crossed the Nguse River and proceeded through Busesa,
Rwanjali, and Bugogo. They halted at Bugogo and sent word
to Ndahura to announce their arrival. Then moving through
Kamwema they crossed the Muzizi River and finally reached
Mubende. Here they were welcomed by a large cheering
crowd who had lined the routes to welcome them. Here, too,
they discovered that the royal Bachwezi drum, *Rusama*, had
been commanded to be sounded all night to announce their
arrival. Ndahura was overcome with joy and emotion when
he first set eyes on his father. He was now convinced beyond
doubt that Isimbwa was his father. In the past, some people
had doubted the authenticity of his story, believing tena-
ciously that he was the son of the potter. But when they saw
father and son together they were struck by the resemblance
between them and thus ended their doubt. As a result of this,
Ndahura's prestige among his subjects was greatly increased.
Ndahura threw a big party in honor of the distinguished visitors. People ate to their satisfaction, drank, danced, and made
merry all night.

Isimbwa decided to settle in Kitara and Ndahura made him
the ruler of Kisozi [the area to which Isimbwa had originally
retired] and of Karokarungi [Nkore]. He made his mother
the ruler of Nkoni and Rwamwanja, which were good grazing
areas.

The Abachwezi Multiply

Then Isimbwa went back to Bukidi to fetch his family and belongings. He found his son Kyomya with four children who had been begotten to him by Nyatworo, the daughter of a Mukidi [a Lango man] called Rabongo [Labongo] who belonged to the Mukwonga clan. The names of Kyomya's children are as follows:

1. Nyarwa [the first-born].
2. Isingoma Mpuga Rukidi } twin brothers.
3. Kato Kimera
4. Kiiza, who came after the twins.

When Isimbwa reached his old home, he said to his son Kyomya: "Let us all pack bag and baggage and go to Kitara and live with your younger brother, who is now king. He is the lord of all the country." But Labongo, the father of Kyomya's wife, refused to allow his daughter to undertake the journey because Kiiza, the youngest child, was still a very young baby. Isimbwa advised Kyomya to leave his wife behind on the strict understanding that he would be coming back to fetch her later on. They set out on their journey, following the route Isimbwa had taken during his first journey, and reached Mubende, Ndahura's capital. Ndahura was delighted to welcome back his father and was particularly pleased to see Kyomya, his half brother. After this touching family reunion, Isimbwa retired to his saza of Kisozi.

Ndahura, too, had the following children:

1. Wamara [from a woman called Nyante].
2. Kiro Muhimba [from a woman called Katutu].
3. Kazoba.
4. Nyabiryo [a daughter].

When Kyomya was well settled in Kitara country he begot more children. Kagoro was born to him by his maid, Kacubya. But the child was taken away from the maid and handed over to Nyakweyogya, Omusaigikati. Isimbwa also begot more children and these are their names:

1. Mugarra was born to him by a woman called Kogere of the Bachwezi clan.

2. Mulindwa was born to him by Nyakwahya of the Basaigi clan.
3. Obona was begot by a woman called Waraga, a Muchwezi.
4. Kange
5. Byangambwe } begot by Rugomya of the Basamba clan.
6. Mugenyi was begot by Nyangoma of the Basingo clan.

In this way, the Bachwezi population increased and they reigned in peace and prosperity.[4]

The Expeditions of Ndahura and His Brothers

Ndahura's first expedition was launched against Buganda. Ntege, the ruler of Buganda, had assumed the role of the overmighty subject. Ndahura and Kyomya, his brother, attacked Ntege and killed him. The *saza* of Buganda was given to Kyomya to rule, and Ndahura went back to his capital, Mubende.

Then, with the concurrence of his brothers, Ndahura embarked on the ambitious policy of conquering other countries so that they would be the virtual rulers of the whole interlacustrine region of East Africa and even beyond. They took Bukidi and Bulega [now in the Congo] by storm and then moved against Buruli, Nyangoma's county, and annexed it. He also conquered and annexed Bunyara, Busoga [Ntembe's county], Sukuma, and Budora. Then he passed through Karagwe, Rwanda, Karokarungi [Nkore], and having crossed the Kazinga, went back to Bulega.

His son, Kiro Muhimba, moved against Madi, and having subdued it, annexed it to Kitara. He also captured, as part of his booty, a stool with eight legs, a special animal skin, and a maidservant called Nyankwengere. He was at the point of killing this old maid but she prayed him to spare her life and promised to dress him every day. Whereupon he took pity on her and spared her life. He also captured many cattle as part of his booty. Kiro crossed to Buligi and from thence to Bugungu, from where he took a boat across Lake Albert and arrived at Butuku. He conquered and annexed Butuku. Moving northwards through Nsorro, he crossed the Mpanga River and reached Tooro, which he conquered and annexed. Then he moved against Busongora, which he also conquered and annexed. He moved on to Bugemeke of Nkwerre, then to

Bwamba, and reached the Busenya River. Here, he suddenly heard the sound of a familiar drum and, greatly puzzled, said: "That drum sounds like that of my father." To prove his point, he started beating his own drums, and when Ndahura heard their sound, he said: "Those drums sound like those of my son, Kiro Muhimba!" By that time Kiro had a lot of booty including many prisoners of war. He ordered his men to clear the forest and made his way to his father. The forest cleared by Kiro is called Kakiromba. Ndahura also had a lot of booty, which included many cows. When father and son met they proceeded to Butebwaigombe. Here, Kiro presented his father with the eight-legged stool, the calf called Kahogo, and the old maid, Nyankwengere. Ndahura sat on the stool and, all of a sudden, stood up and praised his son and declared that he would rather have one son of Kiro's caliber than be saddled with a whole lot of seven or eight sons. Thereupon Kiro replied: "Indeed, you have seen my worth." When Ndahura saw Kiro wearing the special animal skin he had captured in Madi, he requested to have it too. But Kiro refused to hand it over because he had already decided to make a present of it to his aunt [his father's sister], Nyakaranda. The party then decided to return home. And following the route Ndahura had taken, they passed through Nkoni [near Nyinamwiru's former residence], Kikankana, Kigimba, Nyakabimba, and finally reached Mubende.

The Distribution of Sazas during Ndahura's Reign

Now that Ndahura had subdued all the rebels who had defied the authority of Bukuku during the absence of Isaza, he decided to redistribute the sazas of Kitara. He gave:

1. Bwera [Buddu] and Nkore to his son Wamara.
2. Buruli to Rubanga.
3. Mwenge to Mugenyi.
4. Kitara [Kyaka] to Ibona.
5. Bunyara to Mugarra.
6. Bulega to Mulindwa.
7. Muhwahwa [Buganda] to Kyomya and later on to Rusirri.
8. Sese to Mugasa Ibebe.
9. Bugoma to Kanyabugoma of Nsinga.

10. Tooro and Busongora to Kahuka.
11. Bugahya, Bugungu, and Chope to Kiro, his warrior son.

Far away in this extensive empire of Kitara, Ndahura also distributed sazas among other eminent people.

The Introduction of Crops during Ndahura's Reign

In periods of famine, the people of Kitara used to import coffee seeds from foreign countries. Ndahura's interest in coffee developed in this way. He therefore decided to make coffee an important cash crop of Kitara and ordered that it be grown throughout the empire. Coffee was first grown in this manner in Bugoma, Kijura, Kyabaranga, Mwenge, and then coffee farming spread to many other areas. People now began to roast coffee for commercial purposes. Gradually coffee became a symbol of the kingship of Kitara. It played an important part in royal ceremonies. It was also used for entering into blood brother relationships. Coffee planting was introduced to Kyagwe in Muhwahwa [Buganda] by Kyomya, Ndahura's half brother; and to Bwera [Buddu] by Wamara [Ndahura's son]. It also spread to Kiziba, which is now part of Tanganyika territory [now modern Tanzania].

Cotton [ewaro] was introduced to Kitara from Egypt in the north. Ndahura was also responsible for the popularization of cotton growing in Kitara. The people of Ganyi [Acholi], Madi, and Bukidi[5] wove it into cloth for covering their bodies. Cotton also played an important part on royal occasions. It was used for covering the crowns, royal beads, and other items of regalia. Even the common people used it for covering their ancestral implements. The chiefs, too, used it to cover their crowns, and other precious belongings. It will be seen therefore that cotton was very popular in Kitara and people used to plant it in their compounds. It was also used for covering coffee seeds when being sent as presents to friends. For those suffering from skin diseases, especially sores, the introduction of cotton proved very useful. After putting some medicine on the affected part, they bandaged it with cotton wool to keep out flies and bacteria. When someone was speared or shot, cotton wool dipped in some sort of ointment was pushed inside the wound to act as a catalyst and produce pus quickly.

Ndahura Loses His Throne: An Heir Is Chosen

We saw how success crowned Ndahura's initial expeditions. After some time, he became restless for action and decided to move against Kyaihangiro [in Tanganyika], where Bwirebutakya was ruler. A bitter battle was fought, in the course of which Bwirebutakya caused darkness to fall on Ndahura's army. In the ensuing confusion Ndahura himself was captured by the enemy. And people, ignorant of what had happened spread the rumor that Ndahura was swallowed by the earth. With his capture panic spread among his soldiers and many of them were slaughtered. Only a few managed to reach Kitara in safety. When the Bachwezi heard the news of the disaster, they were filled with rage. Some of them wanted to choose a ruler at once so as to keep the machinery of government running smoothly but Kyomya, Ndahura's elder brother, was against the idea and refused the throne which was offered him. On the contrary, he decided to proceed to Tanganyika as a spy to satisfy himself that Ndahura was really dead. Meanwhile, Mulindwa, his half brother, was installed as regent. Kyomya set out on his expedition accompanied by a few hand-picked people. They took with them tobacco and coffee, which they hoped to sell on the way.

When they reached Kyaihangiro, they made various inquiries about the fate of Ndahura, and were told by some people: "Ndahura is not dead but was captured by Bwirebutakya, who is still holding him." Kyomya then decided to find out where he was being held. After many secret investigations he at last found Ndahura with his servant Nyamutale. Kyomya stole them away and brought them back to Kitara. They decided to enter Mubende, the capital, during darkness because Ndahura was ashamed as a result of his disgrace and had no wish to face his subjects. He decided to forsake the throne as the honorable course open to him. His subjects, however, were very pleased to see him back and welcomed him warmly.

But Ndahura refused to rescind his decision, and declared before the Bachwezi: "Choose from among my children the one you consider fit to be king. I can no longer rule over you after my disgrace, and having been made to work like a peasant." The Bachwezi saw his point of view and concurred with it. Some decided in favor of Mulindwa, the regent,

as suitable for the throne, but others disapproved of him.
After much wrangling and politicking the Bachwezi settled
for Wamara, his eldest son, as king of Kitara. Nyangoma,
mother of Mugenyi [one of Isimbwa's sons], was very disappointed that her son was not considered for the succession
and blamed Mulindwa [her husband's son] for it. From that
day onwards she hated Mulindwa and vowed secretly to have
him murdered even if that was the last thing she would do.
Nyangoma was a very pretty lady and Mulindwa had a weakness for pretty women and had been planning to make love
to her. Mulindwa played into her hands when he expressed
a desire to pay a visit to her, apparently with the aim in
view of satisfying his desires. But the lady had other ideas
and carefully planned her plot. She made a deep hole in
the sitting room and prepared boiling water ready for action.
When she saw Mulindwa striding towards her house, she
quickly emptied the boiling water into the hole and covered
it with an animal skin. She then placed a chair on top of
the skin. In came Mulindwa, and, suspecting no mischief,
sat on the chair. And almost immediately he fell into the
hole with a bang. He screamed for help and his servant, who
heard the scream, rushed to report the incident to the other
Bachwezi.

Kagoro [son of Kyomya] came immediately to the scene
and without asking questions started killing everyone he found
on the spot. When he threatened to kill Gwinekyakyo, Nyangoma's maid, she prayed him not to kill innocent people and
revealed that Nyangoma [his own stepmother] was the cul-
prit. Thereupon Kagoro rushed into the house and rescued
Mulindwa. He was very scalded and was on the point of
death. Kagoro, blinded with rage, killed Nyangoma as well
as her two sisters, Nyangoro and Nyanteza. He swore to put
an end to the Basingo clan, to which Nyangoma belonged.
But his father [Kyomya] said to him: "Do not kill them for
they gave birth to Mugenyi." This advice prevailed.[6]

The Disappearance of Ndahura

After Ndahura had renounced the throne, he retired to
Kibale in Buyaga. After some time he moved to Rubazi and
spent two years there. But before his departure he planted
a tree [omutoma tree] near a well and instructed his servant
Ntwara to look after it. He then moved to Kitagweta and

having passed through Kijuma reached Butara. Here, he and
his dogs halted for a rest. In the meantime, he built himself
a makeshift hut in which to spend the night. The marks he
left still exist and the place has come to be called "*Oburaro
bwenaku* [a sleeping place for the poor]." From here he
moved to Muhumba and, having reached Tooro, established
himself at Bulembo, where he dug wells for his cows. These
wells still exist and are known as *Bijongo*. Ndahura spent
four years at Bulembo before moving on to Butanuka, where
he spent only a year. He then moved to Rwagimba, from
where he proceeded to Rwisamba. He settled on the plain
near Lake Busongora and dug a big well to serve as a drinking place for his cows. This well still exists and is known
as *Kikorongo*. He channeled the water from Lake Bunyampaka into this well.

It would appear that his mother, Nyinamwiru, had also decided to leave Kitara and follow after her son. Tradition
indeed states that she settled at Irangara on the island of
Rwakasese [Rwisamba and Rwakasese are adjacent to each
other]. It was in these places that they spent the rest of
their lives before vanishing from the face of the earth.

It was during the reign of Ndahura that the empire of
Kitara reached the summit of its expansion. He ruled an empire which extended as far as Kavirondo, Abyssinia, Congo,
and parts of modern Tanzania. Those who may wish to dispute this fact must first of all explain why the Kitara language
is spoken all over the areas mentioned.

2. OMUKAMA WAMARA OMUCHWEZI

Wamara became king while his father was still alive. After
his coronation, he moved his capital from Mubende[7] to
Bwera.[8] Ndahura, as we saw, had also left the capital after
his abdication. Mubende was therefore left to be ruled by
Ndahura's eldest wife, Nyakahuma. This position was to become hereditary until 1907, when the British authorities abolished it and expelled the last Nyakahuma. Mubende thereafter became government headquarters. There are very huge
trees in this area and it is believed that they were planted
by Ndahura.[9]

The Government of the Empire

When Wamara had established himself on the throne, he divided the Kitara empire among his brothers and close relations. Kagoro, son of Kyomya was given the county of Kahanga, Mugarra, son of Isimbwa, got Kisozi [Mubende], an area still remembered as Kisozi of Mugarra.[10] Katukura ruled Karokarungi, Mulindwa, his uncle, Buyaga, and Mugenyi, Bwongero and Mahogora. It was Mugenyi who built that cow-shade which still exists and is associated with his name as "the cow-shade of Mugenyi." Ibona was given Bugusuru, Swera, and Rwanda. Of all Wamara's brothers, Ibona was reputed as the best hunter. Bugungu was cut off from Kiro's county and given to Kahuka. Mugasa Ibebe retained the island of Sese, whither he had been exiled by Ndahura. Rubanga retained Buruli, which he had been ruling since the time of Ndahura. Kyomya gave up Muhwahwa [Buganda] and was transferred to Bugahya [Hoima]. Buganda was then given to Kaganda Rusirri, the father of Ssebwana. All of these chiefs belonged to the Bachwezi clan. No changes were made in the government of the other counties, which were hereditary.

The Origin of Rainmaking in Kitara

After Wamara had ruled Kitara for a long time, he left Bwera and went to hunt in Bugahya. On his way back to his capital, he passed through Pacwa and Kasimbi, having crossed the rivers Nguse and Ruzaire. He then proceeded to Kicunda, where a man called Munuma lived. Munuma had a son called Birenge, and Birenge a son called Kapimpina. Munuma was a very old man and was probably born during Isaza Nyakikoto's reign. This family had built their houses on the slopes of a hill called Misozi. Wamara decided to camp at this place. He called at Munuma's house and asked for water to quench his thirst but got none because it was dry season and water was scarce. The king, disappointed, said to Munuma: "Go to your room and there you will find water." The old man went to his room and discovered to his surprise that the water pots had been filled to the brim. He gave Wamara a glass of water and hardly knew what to say. When the king had quenched his thirst, he presented Munuma with omulinga [a sort of bangles worn round the arm] and commanded him thus: "Henceforth, whenever there is no rain, stir the well with this *omulinga* and you will have rain." This *omulinga* is still among the treasures of the Kinyoro monarchy.

After this incident Wamara retired to a rocky place called Nyabaigara for a rest. This place was for some time used for a game which is similar to chess. The holes for that game still exist and some people even claim that Wamara's footsteps are still visible on that spot.

When Wamara visited Birenge's and Kapimpina's fire-places, he discovered that water had appeared beneath them and had developed into wells. These wells still exist and these are their names:

1. *Kaisabusa*, Munuma's well.
2. *Muhangisima*, Birenge's well.
3. *Nyabisodo*, Kapimpina's well.

From now onwards these three men possessed powers to make rain. During dry seasons people flocked to their homes with gifts and implored them to cause rain to fall. Munuma was the chief rainmaker. When he died, Birenge succeeded him, and when Birenge died, he was succeeded by Kapimpina. In this way the position became hereditary, and remained so until it was abolished by the British in this century. Indeed, during the reign of Cwa II Kabalega, these rainmakers were hunted down and killed. The chief rain-maker, however, escaped death because he usually caused rain to fall whenever the king's men were searching for him. By this century the rainmakers of Bunyoro-Kitara had lost their prestige primarily due to the impact of the new religions. Worse still, they had been chased out of their dwellings on the hill slopes by the Roman Catholic missionaries to whom this area had been granted as *mailo* [freehold] land. The hereditary chief rainmaker at the time of writing this book is Zakaria Rwangirra.[11] Munuma is still praised by traditional dancers as *"akatemba iguru atakwatirire* [he who went to heaven without any support]."

King Wamara and his fellow Bachwezi were endowed with supernatural powers. They used these powers especially when they lived in Mubende. They also left many traces of their presence mostly around Bugangaizi and Buyaga. This may account for the reason why the Babiito had chosen this region for the royal tombs and for the coronation of their kings.

Every king was crowned in either Buyaga or Bugangaizi and built his first palace there.

Tradition also claims that Wamara was responsible for the digging of Lake Wamara, which is now located in the Ssingo County of Buganda. Before his disappearance, he left the royal drums, *Nyalebe* and *Kajumba*, with a man called Mubimba of the Abasita clan.[12] The royal spears, crowns, and other regalia were left with a man called Mugungu. They were commanded to hand them over to the Babiito when they took over the government of Kitara. When the Babiito clan, which we shall deal with presently, took over Kitara, they found the aforementioned counties intact. Aware that the Babiito were ignorant of the customs of Kitara, as well as of the institution of kingship, Omukama Wamara left behind two queens—Iremera of the Banyagi clan, and Bunono of the Mwitira clan, to instruct them in these matters.

Kantu: Friend of Wamara

During his reign, Wamara had cultivated the friendship of an old man called Kantu, who was probably born in the reign of Mukonko. They became blood brothers and from him Wamara learnt the history of Kitara. One day Kantu paid a visit to his friend Wamara, but found him all prepared to go out hunting. Wamara ordered one of the servants to show Kantu to the house and to request his wives to look after him properly until his return. But the king's wives despised the little old man. They merely laughed at him and ignored Wamara's orders. They even refused to allow him to stay inside the house. Instead, they ordered the servant to deposit him in one of the outer huts, where food and drink could be brought to him. Having carried out his instructions, the servant rejoined the king's hunting expedition. Meanwhile, the king's wives went about their business and forgot all about Kantu. Neither the food nor the drink was therefore offered him. When he became very hungry, he staggered out of the hut to see by which way the hunters might be returning. As he came out he saw a bull and a cow making love. When the bull noticed Kantu it charged at him and kicked him to death.

On his return Wamara inquired about his friend. Nobody seemed to know what had happened to him. The king was very angry and put the blame on his wives. At last Kantu's dead body was discovered lying outside the outer huts. The king was furious when this news was broken to him. But nobody foresaw what would happen next.

The following morning the herdsmen went to milk the cows and then discovered to their horror that the milk had changed color, turning into *mutara* [red milk]. Whereupon they consulted the witch doctors, who solved the mystery by declaring: "Wamara's blood brother relationship with Kantu has caused the milk to change into *omutara*." It was therefore decided that this blood brotherhood [bond of friendship] must be loosened in the traditional fashion. This was done and after four days the cows began producing normal milk once more. From now onwards, the Bachwezi decided to avoid the *obusito* [milk that is from a cow that is with a calf] totem. When a cow was expecting a baby they refrained from drinking its milk until four days had elapsed. The Babiito also later adopted this totem, although we are not quite sure that they necessarily copied it from the Bachwezi. Perhaps this question will be gone into in greater detail in the author's projected work on the clans of Bunyoro-Kitara.

The Abachwezi Lose Respect: Evil Forebodings

During this period the Bachwezi had a lot of things to worry about. Moreover, they began to be despised by their subjects and lost respect among them. While eating or drinking they would hear strange noises. But they neither saw who made these noises nor precisely where they came from. Perhaps on account of these curious developments, the royal pages and other servants ceased to respect the royal family. The magic of the Bachwezi appeared to have gone. Now, instead of looking at them with awe mixed with admiration, their subjects assumed an arrogant posture when dealing with them.

Gradually, it became the practice that when a Muchwezi volunteered a remark, a woman or even a mere servant would retort: "What can you say, but rubbish!" Sometimes they said mockingly to the Bachwezi: "What kind of people are you after all? How on earth did you come into this world?" Even their personal servants obeyed orders grudgingly and unwillingly.

This was not the end of their troubles. Whenever their cows went to the streams to drink water, they were driven off by some evil creatures. These creatures were two in number and black in color. One day, one Muchwezi, Kagoro, son of Kyomya, decided to put an end to all this nonsense. So he took his cows to the Muzizi River for a drink. As soon as the animals settled down to drink, they were attacked by the evil creatures. And, all of a sudden, Kagoro sent his spear flying in their direction and speared the male creature to death. The female one, which was nearing the last stages of pregnancy, escaped, but having gained a safe distance between her and her assailant, stopped and shouted at Kagoro: "Do not delude yourself by believing that you have destroyed us creatures by killing Kyenserikora. I am pregnant and there are many more of us." Having delivered this message it vanished into the swamps. When the story of this incident was related to the Bachwezi they got very worried and fear spread among them.

At that time there lived a Muhuma called Ntuma. He had been given many cows by Mugenyi and very soon became a very rich man who possessed, in addition to his many cows, countless kraals. He was the son of a man called Munyonyi. Ntuma had a special bull called Rutale [which was reputed as an animal of great powers]. One day, Ntuma decided to sacrifice the bull to the gods and tied it to an iron post.[13] Tradition also states that the reason for Ntuma's great wealth was primarily due to a certain custom which he and his household had observed. According to this custom, none in his house would say plainly that "the moon has appeared," but would instead use a more subtle expression like "the biggest star is up in the heavens." It is claimed that the gods looked kindly on him because of this custom and heaped riches on him. But during this period of disrespect for the Bachwezi which we have already seen, Ntuma's wife blundered one day and uttered the forbidden expression. Suddenly, Ntuma's entire flock rushed out of the kraals and disappeared. The distracted Ntuma followed in hot pursuit of them and never came back. His entire family also disappeared. And so it is that when one's family goes astray, people will remark: "His family has been swallowed up like that of Ntuma, son of Munyonyi."

But it is said that Ntuma went straight to another rich man, called Ntuma Kinywananabaingi [literally, Ntuma who makes friends with many people], but neither disclosed his name to this man nor related to him his past history. On

the contrary, he disguised himself as one of the itinerant
Bahuma and was accepted as one of his namesake's herdsmen.
After some time, Ntuma Munyonyi's servants, who had gone
astray with him, showed up in his new residence and burst
out crying when they saw him in the unusual role as one
of the many servants to a rich man. But because Ntuma was
still determined to hide his identity, he slipped away from
them. One of the landlord's servants introduced the newcomers to his lord's Bahumakati [female Bahuma], who wished
to buy the coffee seeds they had brought with them. "These
are the brothers of the other Muhuma living with us" [refer-
ring of course to Ntuma Munyonyi], he told the ladies. But
when Munyonyi saw them he once more made fast his escape.
Whereupon the Bahumakati asked the newcomers: "Do you
know where this man comes from?" And unaware that Ntuma
had been living under another identity, they let the cat out
of the bag. "This man you see here," they replied, "used to
be very rich in the past." Then the Bahumakati wished to
know his name since he had resolutely refused to disclose
his true identity to anyone. "He has no other name," said
the servants, "but only one, and that is Ntuma Munyonyi.
He used to be very rich and we were his servants. To find
him employed as a servant sweeping the kraal, carrying dung,
and looking after cattle, made us cry." The Bahumakati were
very surprised at this disclosure. But then it dawned on them
that they used to hear of another Ntuma reputed for his great
wealth. Now, when their husband came back from work, they
broke the news to him thus: "That Muhuma who lives with
us is none other than Ntuma, son of Munyonyi, of whom
you undoubtedly have heard. Seated here are his servants."
Ntuma Kinywananabaingi, the landlord and husband of the
Bahumakati, was at once surprised and glad to hear this news
for he was well acquainted with the reputation of Ntuma
Munyonyi as a very wealthy man. Whereupon he summoned
this unusual servant and asked him: "Are you Ntuma, the
son of Munyonyi, the rich man who never visits his friends,
of whom I have heard so much before?" Embarrassed and
confused, he replied: "Yes, I am." Then Kinywananabaingi
asked him: "But why did you not tell me so in the beginning?
Why did you not tell me what had happened so that I might
be of some assistance to you?" He replied: "True, I am to
blame for not being frank with you. But I was afraid that
you might also lose your wealth as I lost mine. I shall tell

you the whole story of my misfortune when we take the cows to drink tomorrow." The next day, the two Ntumas went to the lake, whereupon Munyonyi stood on the banks of the lake and, calling on those present, said: "Come, for I want to tell you how I lost my property." Kinywananabaingi, shocked at the unfortunate story that followed, said frankly: "I am not prepared to experience what you went through." Thereupon, he got hold of his companion and both men threw themselves into the lake. Their bodies were never discovered. Nor were they heard of again.

Misinga Raids the Cows of the Bachwezi and Is Later Killed by Kagoro

During these difficult times for the Bachwezi, there came from the direction of Burundi, a man called Misinga. This man, accompanied by a very large army, captured the kraals of Mugenyi, Kagoro, as well as those of Mugasa Ibebe, who had left Sese Island. Mugasa, however, counterattacked, defeated Misinga, and managed to recover his own cows.

During one of the raids, a man called Nyamutale was standing on top of a hill shouting himself hoarse. Kagoro Omuchwezi was also at that time playing a game with his sisters-in-law. On hearing this shouting, he said: "That sounds like the voice of Rukungarwitabyaro." "No," replied his sisters-in-law, "it is just noise made by birds." To which Kagoro retorted: "Do not bamboozle me. You ladies never hear anything. You are only interested in detecting the smell of perfumes." He angrily bolted away from them and ran towards Nyamutale's direction. On seeing him, he inquired what the shouting was all about, to which Nyamutale replied: "All the kraals of the Bachwezi have been captured and Mugenyi has been hurt. Bitale and Mugasa, however, have managed to recover their cattle. But, unfortunately, Mugasa has exterminated his own cattle in an attempt to recover them."

Thereupon Kagoro decided to engage Misinga in a duel. He found him near a well and challenged him: "Use your spear. I want to see how well you can fight." Then the duel commenced and Misinga seemed to have the upper hand. He speared Kagoro twice but each time failed to kill him. Then Kagoro's aunt said to Misinga: "You do not know how to fight. A man cannot spear another twice without killing him." The fighting, however, continued and with one good

aim, Kagoro speared Misinga and killed him. He immediately
moved against Misinga's army, which he routed, and recovered all that they had captured from the Bachwezi.[14]

But the misfortunes of the Bachwezi seemed never to end.
Mugenyi had two cows he loved very much—Bihogo and
Rusasa—and swore that he would kill anyone who destroyed
them and would kill himself if they died a natural death.
One day he gave them salty water as usual, but unaccount-
ably, the animals dropped dead as a result. Whereupon, he
decided to kill himself in obedience to his vow. But his brothers frustrated his plan and gave him many cows. Moreover,
they always watched his movements and made it impossible
for him to execute his planned suicide.

CHAPTER 3

The Disappearance of the Abachwezi from Kitara

This series of misfortunes perturbed Wamara and his brothers very much. Wamara therefore decided to seek the help
of his witch doctors and asked them to explain the meaning
of this disastrous series of events. But these doctors were unable to be of much use to him. It transpired, however, that
at about this time there happened to appear two men from
Bukidi. These men were the brothers of Nyakoka and
Karongo. They belonged to the Basuli clan and practiced
abafumu [divination].[1] They had found themselves in
Wamara's palace while in pursuit of an eagle which had
snatched away their cock which they used in the practice
of their profession. On arriving in Kitara they announced
themselves as diviners. Wamara was happy to hear this
news and promptly offered them lodging in the residence of
his own diviners at Kasoira. When the king's doctors
went to attend to the king and display their craft, they took
the two strangers with them with the intention of discover-
ing how much in fact they knew. As a test, they killed
a calf and when they opened the stomach found it quite
empty. The two Bakidi doctors were called upon to solve

the mystery. They studied closely the dead animal and requested their examiners to cut open its skull. There they found
the intestines! Then they requested that the legs be also cut
open. There again, to everyone's surprise, the other contents
of the stomach were found! When asked to explain what all
this meant, the two Bakidi doctors, knowing that what they
had to say would be unpleasant, attempted to evade the question. It would seem that their compulsive pursuit of the eagle
was in obedience to a force beyond their control. They had
come to prepare the way for the coming of the Babiito! Such
news would certainly be unwelcome for the Bachwezi.

Wamara was unsatisfied with their vague answers to his
simple questions but refrained from pushing them too far.
On the contrary, because of the mysterious event he had witnessed, he was convinced that the two Bakidi were powerful
diviners endowed with great powers. He ordered their
separation from his own doctors and gave them a separate
house inside his palace. The following morning he summoned
them secretly to appear before him and his fellow Bachwezi,
who had gathered together as a result of the mysterious event
that had happened. Omukama Wamara gave them another
calf to use for their craft. When they killed this calf, everyone
found to their amazement that its blood was spouting in many
directions like a fountain! This was not all, for, like the first
calf, they found nothing in its stomach when it was cut open
but discovered the contents of the stomach inside its skull
and feet. Then while they were examining the entrails, a black
smoke oozed out of the calf and settled on them and could
not be removed either by washing or scraping with a knife.
Then Nyakoka asked Wamara and the other Bachwezi thus:
"Have there been any discontents among your subjects? Has
there also been a lack of respect among your wives and
servants? And have your cows been producing milk as red
as blood for four days?" To these questions they answered,
"Yes." Then Nyakoka inquired whether there ever was a
friend of Wamara's who paid him a visit but was neglected
by his queens and was in the end killed by a cow. The king
answered that that was correct. This was the reason why the
cows produced bad milk for four days, Nyakoka explained.
The intestines found in a tangle in the head of the calf, he
went on, meant that the time had come for the Bachwezi
to pack their luggage and put them on their heads. The intestines found in the legs were a sign for them to start on their

journey back to their country of origin. The blood which came in many spurts was meant to show them the way. And the black stain which could not be washed off the intestines meant that the throne of Kitara would be taken over by black men who did not resemble the Bachwezi. Wamara and his fellow Bachwezi were astounded by these explanations and their perturbation increased.

Some of them suggested that the two Bakidi doctors be killed. So too did the king's doctors, who had become jealous of them and feared that they might be superseded by them. They argued that the two men might have been undesirable characters who were run out of their country. They accused them of being the cause of all the misfortunes of the Bachwezi. They then persuaded Wamara to set the foreigners another test to establish without doubt their authenticity and the veracity of their claims. The test which the king's doctors prescribed was rather an unusual one. They said to Wamara: "We shall put a bead inside a cow without the knowledge of these Bakidi doctors and if they can tell that there is a bead inside the cow, then their lives will be spared. But if they fail and kill the cow as they are told, then there is no doubt that they are the ones responsible for your misfortunes." It happened, however, that these men had made friends with a servant of the king's doctors who used to carry their medical bag. When, therefore, this servant heard of this plan, he went straight to his friends and revealed it. The two Bakidi doctors were therefore prepared for the occasion. When they appeared before the king, he said to them: "Kill that cow so that you can foretell what is going to happen." Thereupon Nyakoka replied: "My Lord, this cow has something inside it." He asked his young brother, Kagoro, to put his hand inside the cow and bring out the king's property. Kagoro did as he was told and brought out the bead, which was handed back to the king by Nyakoka. The king and his fellow Bachwezi were greatly surprised. The Bakidi doctors were asked to repeat what they had done the previous day and see if their forecast could be different. They repeated the process but got the same results, thus confirming their original explanations. This made the king's doctors more jealous than ever. In their envy they plotted to set on fire the house in which the foreigners slept and thus burn them to death. But one of their servants, who was a friend of the Bakidi doctors, happened to have overheard this plot and ran quickly to warn his friends of the impending danger. "You must leave this place today," he said to them, "because there is a plan to burn down your house when you are asleep." They took this warning seriously and left the palace during the night, unnoticed, and returned to Bukidi. Wamara made several unsuccessful attempts to discover the whereabouts of these Bakidi. The worries and anxieties of the Bachwezi further increased and they decided to leave Kitara for good as soon as possible, because they had found their position very intolerable. Whereupon Kyomya asked the important question: "Who will rule this country if we go away? Let us send a message to Bukidi for my sons, asking them to come over and rule in our place. If they fail to hold the country, the fault will be theirs." Kyomya's suggestion was unanimously accepted and Kanyabugoma [Saza Chief of Bugoma] was delegated to go to Bukidi with instructions to seek out Kyomya's sons and summon them to become the successors of the Bachwezi in Kitara. It was also expected that the first Omukama of this line would be Isingoma Mpuga Rukidi. Kanyabugoma set out on his journey but it soon became clear that Kyomya's sons had been preparing to come over to join their father. Apparently, the two Bakidi doctors, Nyakoka and Karongo, had explained to them the intolerable position of the Bachwezi. They were already grooming themselves as their successors.

The Journey Begins

Soon after the Bachwezi had sent off Kanyabugoma to Bukidi, they started on their journey to an unknown destination. They passed through Kisozi and proceeded from there to Kahanga. Here, Wamara remembered the *Akasale* [Drum] of Love, also called the *Kaijuire* [It Is Full],[2] which they had left behind. He immediately sent a servant to go back and bring it to him. But when the servant had fetched it and was running hurriedly to catch up with his companions, he shook the drum and the butter in it melted and was considerably decreased. When Wamara learnt of what had happened, he declared: "This is the end of any feeling of love between human beings. When one loves another one is repaid with hatred."[3]

From Kahanga the Abachwezi headed towards Buyaga. When they arrived at Buyaga, they decided to leave their

brother, Mulindwa, behind. Mulindwa, however, refused to
be left behind. His brother, Kisinde, therefore tied together
his luggage and servants were hired to carry him and these
belongings.[4] Having traveled some distance, it was discovered that Mulindwa's *kyebungya* [milk vessel] and his charm
had not been packed among his luggage. They had been left
behind.

Mulindwa had made a blood brotherhood with a very old
man called Mihingo, who belonged to the Bayaga clan.
Mihingo had a son whose name was Kyanku. And these two
men had accompanied their friend Mulindwa on his journey.
When they had got near to the Bugoma forest, Mulindwa
became so ill that it was feared that he had not got much
longer to live. The Bachwezi decided to leave him in the
charge of Mihingo, who was instructed to bury him if he
died and, if he got better, to look after him; and when he
had fully recovered his strength he would rejoin them.
Mihingo was also asked to explain this development to the
new rulers of Kitara. Mihingo then brought Mulindwa back
to his house in Buyaga. The charm which Mulindwa had
left behind him had now grown into a shoot, but the milk
vessel was still resting on the ground where he had left it.
This vessel has been preserved to this day. In days gone by,
when superstition was more current than now, people used
to spread the rumor that when this vessel was removed, or
transferred to another place, it would mysteriously return to
its owner. There is, however, no truth in this superstitious
rumor.

The charm which grew into a shoot eventually grew into
a tree which came to be called *omutoma*. This species still
exists. Omuchwezi Mulindwa died in Buyaga, which, from
then onwards, became a place of great importance. The
Babiito kings, heirs to the Bachwezi, would neither climb the
hill near Mulindwa's residence nor indeed venture near the
place. And whenever Baganda soldiers raided that area, they
never ventured to seize anything from Mulindwa's section of
Buyaga but would, on the contrary, offer sacrifices to him
and thus propitiate his wrath.

On Mulindwa's death, this section of Buyaga became the
property of Mihingo and consequently became hereditary.
When Mihingo died, Kyanku succeeded him. And from then
to this day the ownership of this section of Buyaga had been

held either by a Mihingo or a Kyanku. They had their own royal drum called *Kyabakumbwire*.

In the past [pre-Christian era], the Mihingos and Kyankus were forbidden to see a Mubiito king not only because they buried a Muchwezi, but also, like the Babiito, they too had inherited some of the things belonging to Abachwezi, including two beautiful bangles [*ebikomo*] made of gold. These bangles were attached together. In the old days it used to be said that if the lord of this place died without choosing an heir, these golden bangles would proceed to choose one. When the lord died they would extricate themselves from his arm and would float to the arm of his successor. The people, this story goes on, never questioned the authority of a successor chosen in that way. But the coming of foreign religions shattered such beliefs to the extent that it became clear to many people that such incidents never took place. They were merely dreams. At this time [1947] the present heir is Zakayo Banura Kyanku.[5]

Kagoro Leaves Some Other Royal Drums Behind

As the Bachwezi progressed on their journey after they had left Mulindwa behind, they reflected on the wisdom of taking with them all the royal insignia. They therefore decided to leave some of these behind for the sake of the Babiito and in the belief that these would prove of great help to them in the art of government. After all, Omuchwezi Kagoro was aware that it was his half brothers who were coming to rule Kitara and saw no point in making the task any more difficult for them. Among the things they left behind were a throne, two spears, a shield, and so forth. These royal emblems were left with a man called Mugungu, who belonged to the Mubwijwa clan, and was a friend of Kagoro's. These things still exist and some of them are in the possession of the King of Bunyoro-Kitara.

When the Bachwezi reached Bugoma, they met their brother called Mubyasi, whose wife was pregnant. As this lady was in the last stages of pregnancy, Mubyasi prayed them to wait for him until the child was born but they ignored his prayer. They left them behind with the pregnant woman holding on to a piece of grass [*ekinyansi*] and the couple thus became the founder of the Babyasi clan. The other members of this clan included Oyo of Bugoma, Mbihwa of Bulega, and others. This clan had a royal drum called *Kananura*.

It is also worth mentioning that there was a certain man called Kisegu, son of Mpaka, who elected to vanish with the Bachwezi because he refused to be ruled by another clan.

The Abachwezi Vanish

Curiously enough, after the Bachwezi had vanished from Kitara, their former subjects started once more to respect them very much. Moreover, their disappearance began to cause a great deal of worry and uncertainty. Many speculations about their fate became current. It was believed by some that they had gone to Bugoma from Rubindi and had drowned themselves in Lake Mwitanzige[6] [Lake Albert]. But the more intelligent and less gullible people refused to believe this story. They argued that the Bachwezi had not drowned themselves but had gone to other countries to the southward, passing through Mboga (now in the Congo) and Busongora, and from here had headed further south towards Ankole, Rwanda, Usinga [Businga], Urundi [Burundi], and thence to some unknown countries still further south.

The names of Ndahura and Wamara are foremost among the names of the Bachwezi. But people were uncertain as to what had befallen them precisely because they had traveled far away from Kitara. When the Europeans first came to the lacustrine region, people mistook them for the Bachwezi and used to exclaim: "Behold, the Bachwezi have come back to recover their lost throne!" Because of their white skins, people were convinced that these Europeans were the "red sons of Mugasa"[7] who had lived on the Sese Islands and had refused to marry black women. Indeed it was believed strongly by some people that these Europeans had emerged from the Sese Islands and were white-skinned because they lived underwater like fish. It is from this belief that they concluded that the Bachwezi may have disappeared underwater and had settled there. Such fanciful beliefs are not entirely without significance. After all, Europe is surrounded by great rivers and seas!

Summary

The place from where the Bachwezi are supposed to have disappeared is still called "Bugoma ha Rubindi." It was from here that they were supposed to have drowned themselves in the lake. But there is yet another school of thought which believes that they crossed the lake (in other words, did not drown in it) and went over to Egypt following the route they had taken when they first established their authority over Kitara, and were mistaken for Nyamiyonga's men.[8] And because Abakitara showed a lot of reverence to Nyamiyonga's men, who were supposed to have originated from the underworld, it was therefore believed by this school of thought that the Bachwezi, having crossed over to Egypt, disappeared into the underworld. This is why the Bachwezi cult is important and why people in difficulties ask them for anything they want.

Names of Some Famous Bachwezi

The Bachwezi were many and it is not possible to write down all their names. Below, therefore, are only the names of those of them who were well known:

THE MEN

1. Isimbwa Ruhiga
2. Ndahura Kyarubimba
3. Wamara Bwigunda Njojo
4. Nulindwa Nyabweliza Ngango
5. Kyoma Ruganda
6. Kagoro Byarankanduro Nkubaitera Matambara Gatosa
7. Ibona
8. Irungu Bwekale Omusambwa Nyama
9. Mugasa Ibebe Kirimani
10. Kahuka Muzinga Nyabagabe Igoro
11. Rubanga Binonkondo Mujumbajumba Hongo
12. Ruboha Kabombo

THE WOMEN

1. Kaikara Ihiga
2. Nyabuzana Rubumbuguza Mugizi
3. Rwose Banyiginya [who wears skins with *enambo*]
4. Rukohe Nyakalika Irikangabu [who wields shields like men]

THE OTHERS

1. Kange	22. Kabagyo
2. Mugenyi	23. Bwihura
3. Mugarra	24. Bwogi
4. Byanyabwe	25. Mukulebya
5. Kiro Muhimba	26. Kasabiko
6. Kazoba	27. Nyamumara
7. Waraga	28. Isorro
8. Kacope	29. Nyamisale
9. Muruli	30. Ngusuru
10. Rwandana	31. Rwakwata
11. Kihimba	32. Nyamutale
12. Muhazi	33. Nyakaranda
13. Nkuna	34. Nyambaka
14. Samaga	35. Nyabiryo
15. Waraga	36. Nyabibungo
16. Kalega	37. Rukwanzi
17. Nyakingo	38. Nyakalembe
18. Nyanja	39. Mugizi
19. Buhukuma	40. Kagole
20. Nyaihengere	41. Kinyabwiru
21. Mukawamara	42. Aguda or Kitule

and many others.

The Abachwezi and Abatembuzi Cult

As has been pointed out earlier, when the Abachwezi and Abatembuzi had disappeared the people of Kitara still reposed a great deal of confidence in them and worshiped them as gods. They believed that their former rulers would grant them whatever they wanted—strength, long life, wealth. Some people still worship the "dark" Bachwezi, that is, those begot by the black women of Kitara. These "dark" Bachwezi had therefore a color between red and black. It is interesting that people still worship them while refusing to worship the one, true, and only God and Creator. And yet Abakitara also know that the Bachwezi were in fact not gods but human beings who had ruled their country and then disappeared. Be it as it may, the Bachwezi are still remembered as the rulers of Kitara. Those most remembered are Kazoba, son of Hangi, Nkya I, son of Nyamuhanga, and Nkya II.

Some people also regard the Abatembuzi as gods and wor-

ship them as such. They utter their names whenever they are
in difficulties and request their help. True, at this time, God
had not yet revealed himself to the people of Kitara and had
not yet sent them his messengers, but he not only forgave
them for their ignorance but also, in his mercy, sometimes
granted them whatever they asked for. O God, help open
our eyes to your greatness so that we may follow and obey
you, so that the whole country may leave its pagan ways and
follow the Christian Way through our Savior Jesus Christ,
who died for our sins.

ABAHUMA

There was a certain ethnic group known as Bahuma who
lived in Kitara. They were not Bachwezi but were rather the
descendants of Kahuma, the son of Mutembuzi Kintu [the
Batembuzi dynasty is discussed in the first part]. It is said
that during the reign of Ndahura there appeared in Kitara a
group of people who had a different type of cattle which were
bigger and taller than the normal breed in the country and
had very long horns.[9] These people were given the name of
Bahuma—meaning the people of Huma, their king. The names
of their clan heads were: Muhumayera [Umayera], Nyarwaki
[Nyarwa], Burumata, Kapupa, Kyera, Kacoco, and many
others. Omukama Ndahura gave them land in Bwera,
Rwamwanja, and Karokarungi to settle in. These people came
from Misri [Egypt]. It is generally believed that the Bachwezi
and the Bahuma are different peoples. The Bachwezi did not
bring cattle with them but were very good hunters. They also
brought with them things which were different from those
found in the country. The Bahuma, on the other hand,
brought many cows with them. They may have come from
Egypt or Ethiopia [Abyssinia] but were certainly not the same
breed of people as the Bachwezi. There are of course some
historians who contend that the Bahuma may have been the
descendants of the grandchildren of Sem [Shem] and Cham
[Kham] and may have originated from the lands surrounding
the Red Sea and the river Nile, where these descendants of
Shem and Kham lived.

After settling for some time in Kitara, the Bahuma completely lost their mother tongue and acquired the language
of the indigenous population though they speak it with a different accent. They belong to the same racial group as the

Bahinda and the Tutsi of Rwanda and Burundi. These people refused to intermarry with the indigenous Bairu population because they were proud of their superior culture and good physique. But this was not true of the Bachwezi and their descendants, the Babiito. But since the Babiito were the ruling clan they could marry also among the Bahuma. This, however, did not prevent the Bahuma from looking down on the Babiito. In fact they despised them and dismissed them as also belonging to the Bairu group.

Part III
ABABIITO

Introduction

Let us explain the situation in the three kingdoms of Bunyoro, Buganda, and Nkore before we go into the subject of the Babiito and the manner of their coming into Kitara. Since the coming of Kintu and his people [the Abatembuzi] and before the arrival of the Bachwezi, these three kingdoms formed parts of the Kitara Empire. During the reign of the Bachwezi, however, Karokarungi [Nkore] broke away from Kitara and established itself as a separate kingdom. The leader of this rebellion and subsequent ruler of Nkore was a Muhuma called Ruhinda. He refused to be ruled by any other clan and so made himself master of Nkore by force. This incident in fact happened during the reign of Wamara [the period when the Bachwezi had lost respect of their subjects]. Ruhinda grew to be feared and respected by the Bachwezi, who honored him with the title of "Ruhinda, son of Muchwa," when they mentioned his name. After the Bachwezi had vanished from Kitara, Ruhinda seized the opportunity to confiscate the cattle in their kraals which still remained in his kingdom and took them to Buzinja. He now declared himself the first *Mugabe* [king] of Nkore. He built his capital on a hill called Mweruka. From then onwards, Nkore became a separate and sovereign kingdom. But Bunyoro and Buganda still remained part of the Kitara Empire.

CHAPTER 1

The Coming of the Ababiito

As we saw in Part II, Chapter 2, Omuchwezi Kyomya had married a woman, the Lady Nyatworo, daughter of Labongo, a Lango man [*Omukidi*]. We also saw that when Kyomya had decided to join his younger brother Ndahura [now ruler of Kitara] in Mubende, Labongo had refused to allow his wife and children to accompany him. The children were therefore brought up by their maternal uncles and aunts. Let us once more repeat their names:

1. Nyarwa, the eldest son, became the head of the Babiito clan (*Okwiri*).
2. Isingoma Mpuga Rukidi ⎫
3. Kato Kimera   ⎬ twin boys.
4. Kiiza, the youngest son, became the ruler of Busoga and adopted the name of Nyaika.

It has also been said that Kiiza became *Okwiri* after the death of Nyarwa. Rukidi, the second son, was called Rukidi because he was born in Bukidi; and was called Mpuga because he was partly fair and partly dark, thus indicating both his Bachwezi and Bukidi descent respectively. The younger twin, Kato, became the ruler of Buganda, but took on also the name of Kimera after he had broken away from Kitara and had declared Buganda an independent and separate kingdom. The name Kimera was added to emphasize the fact that Kato had shaken off his allegiance to his overlord, the King of Kitara, and had become his own master, just as the branch of a *mutoma* tree breaks away from its parent body and grows into a separate *mutoma* tree.

Now, to go back to our story. These boys grew up into strong young men and, like their fathers, the Bachwezi, became good hunters. They were greatly loved by the people of Bukidi. It will be recollected that these boys were those who had been prepared for the succession to the throne of Kitara by the two Bakidi doctors, Nyakoka and Karongo, who had assured them: "You will become the kings of Kitara." They were also the ones Kanyabugoma was ordered by

Wamara to ask to come over to Kitara and be the rulers. It was to them, too, that Kagoro and Kyomya had left the royal drums and other insignia of office and had kept them in the charge of a man called Mugungu, who was instructed to hand them over to these young men when they became rulers of Kitara.

Now, let us see how the Babiito came to Kitara and what they found in Wamara's palace. Let us also examine how they ruled the country up to now. We are not here concerned with the traditions of the other kingdoms in the lacustrine region, but mainly with Kinyoro tradition. In Buganda, we regard Kato Kimera as the first Kabaka, leaving out Kintu and Chwa Nabaka, who were not Babiito. In Nkore, we count from Ruhinda, but leave out Ruhanga Rugaba, Nyamate, Simbwa, Ndahura, Wamara, all of whom we regard as Bachwezi who lived before Nkore became a separate kingdom. Let us now examine the Babiito dynasty.

Why They Were Called Babiito

When Nyatworo became pregnant by Omuchwezi Kyomya, her father, Labongo, built her a hut inside his own compound under a *biito* tree. When the children were born the Bakidi people nicknamed them "the children of the *biito* tree" and, when inquiring about them, would say, "How are the children of the biito tree?" From this time onwards they got stuck with that name and it eventually became the name of their clan. It must be pointed out that they had not at first assumed the clan of their father because he had deserted them. In addition, however, they also assumed the clan of their mother, the Mukwonga clan. The totem of this clan is the bushbuck, which consequently became the totem of all Babiito. In Buganda, the Babiito kings had perpetuated this custom by adopting the clan of their mothers. But the Babiito of Bunyoro, however, consequently adopted also the clan of their forefathers—the Bachwezi—and thus observe the *obusito* totem.

When these young men had met Kanyabugoma, the messenger of the Bachwezi, and had had everything regarding the situation in Kitara explained to them, they were delighted at this formal invitation to rule a great empire. Then Nyakoka and Karongo inquired from them thus: "What will you reward us with for our pains?" "We shall love you like our own brothers," replied the young men. Mugungu of the Mubwijwa clan also arrived post haste in Bukidi and advised them to go straight to Kitara. "Did you not see the messenger sent to you?" he inquired. "Are you going to dillydally here until the people of Kitara turn against you?" He went on to explain to them further as to how the Bachwezi had vanished and had left some royal regalia behind under his charge. The rulers-elect thanked him for his pains but Mugungu also wanted to know how he would be repaid for his pains. They assured him that he would be a very great man, almost as great as the king himself, and would also be recognized as their elder. At this point Nyakoka advised them to make themselves a drum which would be used for summoning the people. This drum, too, could be used to let the Babiito know of one another's whereabouts.

This advice was welcomed and accepted. A big tree was felled, out of which they made their drums. Rukidi took the lowest part of the tree, with which he made a big drum [*empango*] and named it *Tibamulinde*. He also used the branch of the same tree to make a smaller drum to be used for the journey to Kitara and named it *Nyakangubi*. Kato [Kimera] took the trunk, out of which he made his drum, and called it *Musambwa* [or *Mujaguzo*]. He also made a smaller drum, which he called *Timba*. The top section of the tree was given to Mugungu of the Mubwijwa clan, out of which he also made a drum and called it *Kanumi*.

Thereupon the Babiito began their journey to Kitara. There were four of them. They were accompanied by their Katikiro [Chief Minister], Mugungu, their doctors, Nyakoka and Karongo, the messenger [of the Bachwezi], Kanyabugoma of Nsinga, Kasaru, their Secretary [literally, who made their wishes known to the people], a servant carrying Rukidi's spear, known as *Goti Ati*, and Katanga of the Muchwa clan carrying another spear, known as *Karazankamba*. Rukidi himself was carrying a sword called *Kasutama* and a spear known as *Kaitantahi*. The servant of Rukidi's who filled the position of *Omweganywa* was carrying a spear called *Kaizireigo* and another servant, the *Omuhangane*, was carrying the spear *Nyakatoto*. There were others who accompanied them carrying many other things. Some of these things are still extant.[1]

When they reached the lake [Victoria Nile] the *abafumu* [diviners][2] advised the Babiito that in order to enjoy security and prosperity in their new country, they should make a sacrifice to the gods in the form of a baby, money, beads, and a cow. And these should be thrown into the lake. This advice was accepted but it was not easy to determine whose baby to sacrifice. It happened, however, that as the beads were being thrown into the lake as part of the sacrifice, Nyarwa's [the eldest Biito's] baby, who was starting to walk, swallowed one of them. Thereupon the *abafumu* concluded that the lake had chosen its victim and that bad luck would befall the Babiito if they refused to sacrifice the baby. The Babiito, not wishing to take any chances, cut the baby open, removed the bead, and reluctantly threw it into the lake. This was a majority decision and Nyarwa was furious at what he regarded as an unnecessary murder. To appease him, or perhaps to strike some sort of curious balance, Rukidi got hold of another baby [belonging to a peasant] and hurled it into the lake. The child's mother was heartbroken and pronounced the following bitter curse on the Babiito: "You have murdered my child after murdering your own. These murderous acts will never cease and you will always be killing one another." The subsequent history of the Babiito dynasty would seem to suggest that this curse came true, for the Babiito were engaged in endless quarrels and conflicts, either fighting against rebellions or fighting for the throne. During these wars numerous lives were lost and many murders committed.

The Babiito were so deeply touched by the woman's curse that despondency and fear came upon them. They became very quiet and unusually thoughtful. But Nyakoka cheered them up and prayed them not to fear and worry about an enraged woman's words but to continue their journey.

They bought a boat called *Nyakacaki* and having crossed the lake in it reached Kitara. They were rowed across by men of the Bahinda clan.[3] After they had crossed the lake, Rukidi and his brothers engaged in an animated discussion about something and it happened that while thus occupied a man of the Sese clan intruded into their discussion. The man was admonished by the brothers for this presumptuous intrusion and roundly warned to refrain from interrupting any conversation which he did not understand and which did not concern him. Out of this originated the Bagweri clan, which means the clan of "interrupters."[4]

The Babiito now engaged a man called Muhanguzi as their messenger and ordered him to announce their arrival to the people of Kitara. They then headed towards Buruli and having reached there proceeded through Kijaguzo, Buhemba and Rwembuba, and then on to Busesa, Rwanjali, Bucubya, and Kahanga, before finally reaching Bwera, where Wamara had built his palace.

While in Wamara's Palace

Their first task was to find out if there were some people left behind by the Bachwezi to look after the palace. As they had anticipated, they found two of the king's wives [abago]. These were Iremera of the Balisa clan and Bunono of the Baitira clan. They also discovered that there were royal drums which Wamara had left in the charge of a man called Mubimba of the Abasita clan, who had been the Chief of the Royal Drums. The Bachwezi had followed the custom of the kings before them by leaving these drums behind. It will be noted that Isaza, the Mutembuzi king, had also left them behind when he and his fellow Batembuzi vanished from Kitara. These drums were left on a hill called Mujungu [in Bugangaizi]. When these drums were recovered it became the practice to move them to the capital only on big royal occasions such as the coronation ceremony.

Up till now the foreigners had not exchanged a word with the local people. Then Rukidi asked: "Isn't there someone that we can speak to?" Thereupon Nyakoka summoned Kasoira, the leader of the abafumu who had served the Bachwezi. And Rukidi asked him: "Where did the rulers of this kingdom go to? And why did they leave it?" Kasoira answered: "I will tell you everything, sir." Then he went on to explain how the Bachwezi had lost prestige and respect among their subjects, a development which he attributed to the curse of Kantu. The Bachwezi therefore, finding their position intolerable, decided to destroy themselves by throwing themselves into the lake. Then Rukidi inquired from Kasoira who Kantu was. He replied: "Nyakoka knows who Kantu was." But Rukidi insisted that he would rather Kasoira told him about Kantu himself and advised him to leave Nyakoka alone. Thereupon Kasoira demanded to be given some tobacco to smoke before he could proceed with his story. Rukidi dispatched Nyakoka to his mother to collect the necessary tobacco. When this was handed to Kasoira he thanked Rukidi and proceeded to explain how old Kantu had been Wamara's friend and how he had been ill treated by the king's house-

hold. He expanded on Kantu's curse and its consequences.
Rukidi made Kasoira swear that the Bachwezi would not return. He then sent for Wamara's two wives, from whom he
wanted to ascertain if there were other versions as to why
the Bachwezi vanished. Nyakoka, however, warned Rukidi
that these ladies were *Bahumakati* [female Bahuma] and
were likely to be obstinate if not handled with civility, care,
and grace. Rukidi interrogated them tactfully. "My dear ladies," he said to them, "I wish very much to know the reasons
why your dear husband, the king, and his people decided
to leave their kingdom. Please, ladies, do not hide anything
from me." The two ladies looked at each other not knowing
who should start the story. Then one of them repeated what
Rukidi had already heard from Kasoira. They were dismissed
after they had been made to confirm and swear that the
Bachwezi would never return. Then Mugungu and Nyakoka
teased Rukidi, saying: "When are you going to mount the
throne? Make up your mind before we decide to give it to
your younger brother, Kato, on the assumption that you are
afraid to take it up." Rukidi retorted: "What do you want
me to do to demonstrate to you that I am very anxious to be
the King of Kitara?" He then inquired from Kasoira if the
Bachwezi had taken the royal regalia with them. He replied:
"No, my lord, they left the royal drums behind in the charge
of Mubimba of the Abasita clan. These particular drums did
not belong to them but had been left for them by Omukama
Isaza, who got lost in Nyamiyonga's kingdom." Rukidi issued
orders that these drums should be brought forthwith.

The Insignia of Office Handed over to the Babiito

A man called Kabahita of the Abazima clan was sent to
summon Mubimba, Chief of the Royal Drums, who lived on
the hill called Mujungu, to appear before Rukidi. When
Kabahita arrived at Mubimba's house he announced the object of his mission: "I have been sent to collect the royal drums
the Bachwezi left in your charge." But Mubimba happened
to be in a depressed mood at that time and was not inclined
to see anybody. He asked the royal emissary to leave him
alone and complained of the lack of food [millet] in his household because of a severe famine. His wife, he said, had given
birth and there was nothing for mother and child to eat. "If
he [Rukidi] is a true king," he remarked, "why doesn't he

send me some food and save my wife?" Kabahita hurried back
to Bwera and reported to Rukidi, who immediately dispatched
him to Mubimba with some food. Mubimba was overjoyed
at Rukidi's accession to his request and thanked him grate-
fully. He handed over to Kabahita the smaller drum
[*Nyalebe*] while he himself carried the bigger one [*Kajumba*]
and both set out for Bwera. On their arrival they were announced to Rukidi by Nyakoka. Mubimba was very glad to
see the new ruler of Kitara and exclaimed: "So this is the king
who has come to rule us!" Rukidi, too, was very glad to see
Mubimba and thanked him for preserving the drums.

Rukidi thereafter gave instructions that preparations for the
coronation ceremony should be started. Mugungu was asked
to produce those royal insignia of office left in his charge.
These included spears, shields, royal chairs, and royal drums.
Another man, Omunyunya, was also asked to produce the
spears and royal chairs left in his care. So did the others who
had been placed in charge of one thing or the other by the
Bachwezi. Iremera, Wamara's *omugo* [queen], produced a
cup made of beads, a milk cup, and a milk pot, while Bunono
brought other things. To these Rukidi added what he had
brought with him from Bukidi. From that time onwards these
things assumed great importance. They were covered with
beads and cowrie shells.[5]

Some of these things are still preserved while others were
destroyed primarily during Kabalega's conflicts with the Europeans. Important positions—which became hereditary—were
given to those who had looked after the royal insignia for the
Babiito.

Now, after all these things had been assembled, Rukidi
ordered the houses to be cleaned and their floors decorated
with beautiful grass before the coronation would take place.
Throughout all these developments, Rukidi, his brothers, and
their followers had camped outside the palace and did not
dare to live inside it. Meanwhile a continuous stream of people
had been gathering to welcome the new king. Rukidi also
ordered the royal Bachwezi fireplace to be covered with earth
until it stood out like an anthill. It was erected in front of the
palace and from then it became the practice for every king
to erect such a fireplace in front of his palace. It is around
it that the coronation ceremonies take place. In Buganda,
such a fireplace exists in front of the Kabaka's palace but is
not filled with earth. It is called *Wankaki* [*Mugabante*].

Isingoma Mpuga Rukidi Is Crowned

Before the coronation took place Rukidi had his head shaven, his fingernails well manicured, and his toenails well treated. Beads were put around his arms, ankles, and neck. His body was smeared with some sort of vaseline. Each member of the *ebikwato* [regalia men] carried the *ekikwato* [singular] allocated to him. Then Nyakoka, Mugungu, and his younger brother, Bamuroga, knelt down worshiped and praised Rukidi, and uttered the following words: "May the royal drums refuse to speak if this man is not a true son of the royal family and consequently not a worthy heir to the Bachwezi, his forefathers! And may he be hated by his subjects if he is a pretender!" Then Ruhaguzi took the big drum —*Kajumba*—and placed it on the raised earth of which we have spoken earlier. Rukidi beat it nine times and it produced good sound. Then he was given the smaller drums—*Nyalebe* and *Kaijuire*—and they also produced good sound. The crowd cheered, shouted with joy, and danced to music from the royal drums and other royal musical instruments. The king led the procession into the palace and sat on the royal chair which was placed in the sitting room.

Throughout this ceremony Rukidi delivered his speeches in a foreign language [Rukidi—the language of the Bakidi] because he did not know the Kitara tongue. Mugungu gave him a royal name, Winyi, and also a pet name [*empako*], Okali, which must be used when addressing the king. This pet name is only used by kings, not even by the royal family [Babiito].

The *empako* is used in Bunyoro-Kitara as a second name by many people. These names are of great importance in the culture of our people. They are used for greeting. It is inconceivable that one would call one's neighbor by his first name (it is considered rude to do so), but by his *empako*. If one did not know another's *empako* one would ask: "What is your *empako*?" and only after this would one greet one's neighbor. Below are only a few of these *empako*:

1. Amoti	5. Abwoli	9. Apuli
2. Akiiki	6. Adyeri	10. Acali
3. Aboki	7. Atenyi	11. Bala [for chiefs only]
4. Atwoki	8. Arali	12. Okali [only for the king]

CHAPTER 2

Babiito Kings of Kitara

LIST OF NAMES OF KINGS
WHO SUCCEEDED THE ABACHWEZI

So far we have discussed how the Babiito and Bahinda (of Nkore) came to Kitara. We hope therefore to go on to examine each of the kings of Bunyoro-Kitara and discuss their achievements.

First of all, here are the names of the kings of Bunyoro, Buganda, Nkore, Kooki, and Tooro:

BUNYORO	BUGANDA
1. Rukidi I Mpuga	1. Kato Kimera
2. Ocaki I Rwangirra	2. Ttembo
3. Oyo I Nyimba	3. Kiggala
4. Winyi I Rubembeka	4. Kiyimba
5. Olimi I Kalimbi	5. Kaima
6. Nyabongo I Rulemu	6. Nnakibinge
7. Winyi II Rubagiramasega	7. Mulondo
8. Olimi II Ruhundwangeye	8. Jembe
9. Nyarwa I Omuzarra Kyaro	9. Suna I
10. Chwamali I Rumoma Mahanga	10. Sekamanya
11. Mashamba I	11. Kimbugwe
12. Kyebambe I Omuzikya	12. Katerega
13. Winyi III Ruguruka	13. Mutebi
14. Nyaika I	14. Juko
15. Kyebambe II Bikaju	15. Kayemba
16. Olimi III Isansa	16. Tebandeke
17. Duhaga I Chwa Mujwiga	17. Ndawula
18. Olimi IV Kasoma	18. Kagulu Tibucwereke
19. Kyebambe III Nyamutukura	19. Kikulwe
20. Nyabongo II Mugenyi	20. Mawanda
21. Olimi V Rwakabale	21. Mwanga I
22. Kyebambe IV Kamurasi	22. Namugala
23. Chwa II Y. Kabalega	23. Kyabagu
24. Kitahimbwa I Y. Karukara	24. Jjunju
	25. Ssemakokiro

25. Duhaga II A. Bisereko, M.B.E.
26. Winyi IV Tito Gafabusa, C.B.E.

26. Kamanya
27. Suna II
28. Mukabya Mutesa
29. Mwanga II
30. Chwa Sir Daudi, K.C.M.G.
31. Edward Mutesa II

NKORE
1. Ruhinda
2. Nkubayarurama
3. Nyaika
4. Nyabwigara
5. Rusango
6. Kagwijagirra
7. Rugamba
8. Kasasira
9. Kitera
10. Lumonde
11. Mirindi
12. Ntare I Kitabanyoro
13. Macwa
14. Rwebirere
15. Karala
16. Karaiga
17. Kahaya I
18. Nyakasaija
19. Bwalenga
20. Rwebisengye
21. Gasiyonga
22. Mutambuko
23. Mukwenda
24. Ntare II
25. Kahaya II E. S., M.B.E.
26. C. G. Gasiyonga II

KOOKI
1. Bwohe
2. Kitahimbwa I
3. Mujwiga
4. Mugenyi
5. Ndahura I
6. Kitahimbwa II
7. Isansa I
8. Rubambura
9. Ndahura II
10. Kabumbuli Isansa II

TOORO
1. Olimi Kaboyo
2. Nyaika Kasunga
3. Kyebambe I, M.B.E.
4. Rukidi G. Kamurasi

NOTES

1. *Kings of Bunyoro-Kitara*

The number of Bunyoro kings appears smaller than those of Buganda and Nkore because of the time lag before one king succeeded another. This time lag was caused primarily

by the numerous succession wars between the princes.[1] Moreover, a prince who spent less than nine years on the throne
is not counted.[2]

2. *Kings of Buganda*

We shall ignore Kintu and Chwa Nabaka since they were
Batembuzi rather than Babiito kings. The list of the Babiito
kings of Buganda is long because the Ganda count the name
of every prince who sat on the throne regardless of the length
of time he was king. For example, Mwanga I spent only nine
days on the throne. We will also ignore Kiwewa and Kalema
because they were not kings but were usurpers while Mwanga
II still lived.

3. *Kings of Nkore*

We will only deal with the Bahinda, the descendants of
Ruhinda, son of Muchwa, who was the first *Mugabe* [king]
of Nkore, after the Bachwezi had left the country. We shall
also leave out Ruhanga, Rugaba, Nyamata, Isimbwa,
Ndahura, and Wamara because these were either Batembuzi
or Bachwezi and therefore not Babiito. These kings ruled
Nkore while it was still part of Kitara and ought therefore to
be considered as chiefs rather than as kings of Nkore.

4. *Kings of Kooki*

I have included the names of the Kooki kings because this
area was a separate and sovereign kingdom before the coming
of the Europeans. These Kooki kings were the descendants
of Mpuga Rukidi and ruled Kooki until 1894, when the British annexed it to Buganda.[3]

5. *Kings of Tooro*

I have included four names of the kings of Tooro because
these are the only ones clearly known. But the true Babiito
kings of Tooro started on 14 August 1891 with the accession
to the throne of Daudi Kasagama Kyebambe I, M.B.E.[4]

6. *Nota Bene*

I have included such men as Mashamba, Nyaika, Olimi
Kasoma, and Olimi Rwakabale in the list of Bunyoro kings
though they are normally referred to as *"baragwa ngoma"*
because they did not stay on the throne for a long period,
and because they did not die natural deaths. But I have included their names, however, for the following reasons: First,
they buried their fathers and succeeded them. Second, they
sat on the throne for not less than four or five years and were

honored with the title of *Okali*. And lastly, they met their deaths while defending their thrones.

Their vanquishers were called "Kyebambe"—meaning "usurper"—because they had seized by force the throne which did not belong to them but to their brothers. There was one man, Kabigumire, who is not counted as a King of Bunyoro-Kitara because he did not bury his father and was not honored with the title of Okali. Moreover, he was not given any kingly name. I have allocated the three years he spent fighting with his brothers to his younger brother and victor, Chwa II Kabalega, about whom we shall go into some detail later on.

Now, we shall commence our discussion of the achievements of the Babiito kings from the reign of Isingoma Mpuga Rukidi I to that of Winyi IV, Tito Gafabusa, C.B.E., the reigning Omukama.

1. ISINGOMA MPUGA RUKIDI I

Rukidi I was honored with the title of "Kyeramaino" [because he had very white teeth], and "Mpuga Isamba, son of Nyatworo." He was called "Mpuga" because he was multicolored, one half of him being white [indicating his Bachwezi descent] and the other black [because of his Bakidi descent on the side of his mother].

Rukidi Establishes His Capital in Bugangaizi

After the coronation ceremonies, Rukidi transferred the capital of his kingdom from Bwera [Buddu] to Bugangaizi. Bwera was left in the charge of a man called Baralemwa Kihesanantomi [he who works iron with his fist] of the Bamoli clan. He was to look after the town and cultivate the cult of Wamara, the last of the Bachwezi kings.[5] Rukidi left Bwera because he was anxious to move further away from Ruhinda, the rebel Muhuma chief who had declared himself king of Nkore [Karokarungi][6] and turned the area into a separate and independent kingdom. Rukidi had no wish to engage in any struggle with Ruhinda because he had not yet established himself firmly on the throne. He therefore moved the capital to Haburu in Bugangaizi and Haburu thus became the first capital of the Babiito kings. He ordered Bamuroga, the younger brother of Mugungu, of the Mubwijwa clan, to build his

palace on the model of Wamara's at Bwera. And Bamuroga
said to him, "My Lord, from where can we get the number of
people required for such a massive task?" The king advised
him to get all the help he could, including his own household
and his own brothers, because the palace belongs to the
crown. To the king's brothers, therefore, Bamuroga delegated
the job of building a house known as *Kasenda*. They were to
build a hedge around it. The job of plastering and smoothing
the house was given to the *Bahumakati* [palace ladies]. Ruswa
of the Mubwijwa clan was to build a fence around the palace.
He was also to build a house called *Kamurweya* near the
king's gate. Munuma's job was to build three houses—
Kyamunuma, Kyakato, and *Kyakatamura*. Bikanye was to
build a house called *Muchwa* [where the royal ladies held
their meetings]. The compound was cleared and many other
houses in addition to these were built. Among these other
houses was *Kagondo*, which was very big and had three big
passages. A man called Ruzika, a Muiru, built the *Karuzika*
[of Ruzika] House, named after him. The *Karuzika* House is
the main royal house, on top of which the royal spear
called *Galengera* was kept. The first of the three passages was
called *Rwemisanga* [of ivory] and here *enkorogi* were milked.
The second was called *Ijwekero*, and the third, *Ihundiro*.
Among the other houses were those built by Igisi [*Rwengo*]
and Abanywagi [*Kapanapa*]. This last was used for making
millet beer [*amasohi*]. Rukidi gave it to Wanyana, maternal
aunt [*nyinento*], to look after. Trees were even planted inside the palace with the intention of nursing them into a small
bush where Rukidi would worship his god, Rubanga. When
all these things were completed, Bamuroga called on the
king and said to him: "My Lord, everything is ready."

It was at the time of the New Moon[7] that Rukidi entered
the new palace. The coronation ceremonies were repeated
to mark the occasion of the opening of the new capital. Rukidi
wore the royal crown and the procession was led by Nyakoka.
Many people uttered the following words of praise as they
proceeded to the new palace:

Hamya	ha	kyaro	Mbaire.
"	"	"	Lyogere.
"	"	"	Nyamunyaka.
"	"	"	Agutamba.
"	"	"	Mujurambi.
"	"	"	Mbumba.

[Stay   on   village   Lover.
"   "   "   Mbaire (Love name).
"   "   "   Nyamunyaka (besiege).
"   "   "   Omukama (king).
"   "   "   Mujurambi (?).
"   "   "   Omukama (king).]

The king first entered one of the palace houses called *Mukanaiguru* and here everyone knelt down and honored him. From here he proceeded to the main royal house—*Karuzika*—where he spent a short time and then walked back to the sitting room and sat on the throne. He delivered his speech, which was interpreted to the people by Kasaru, who introduced Rukidi to them thus:

> This is your king who has succeeded to the throne of his fathers. He is not a bastard as you can see the resemblance yourselves. All of you and all the various ethnic groups from different countries gathered here must obey him and must always feel free to come to him whenever you are in trouble or in sorrow and he will help you.

The King's Dancers

Then Mugungu brought forward a performer called Nyakwehuta of the Muyaga clan. He was a great singer and dancer and sang the following song before Rukidi:

Rukidi rwa Nyatworo akazarwa engoma emukubire,
Kisusuna Njoka ndikafa Omutenkwa nk'ayakalimu oli;
Oli nkuba egwire obutiti obw'olikaimuka obatere;
Oli Mpango Nyamutema abatarwaire orabaire Nyaibutika.
Bite ebyemi obimale n'akalimi kagamba mbalimu;
Ab'oisire obahumulize ebibi babyeserekere.
Nzinire Dabongo erihango na Kirazankamba nditeho.
Kimuli kyokya amahanga, numwo amazoba gararra
Akwagura obuhere yali w'okuhera; otyo otyo buli n'ojwerwa.
Kaganda ka Mwanami tiyali w'okurugaho yahesaga erihango
     akalinga nananisiriza.

Rukidi was very pleased with the man's performance and made him the royal dancer [*Nzini*]. He was also given land [a village] on which to settle. From then this position became officially established and also hereditary. As this book is being written there is a man known as Tera Kabonerwa, who says he is the twelfth royal dancer since the time of Nyakwehuta, son of Odigo. They were normally resident in Mwenge (now in Tooro) but the land given to Nyakwehuta by Rukidi was in Buligira in the saza of Buyaga. Today Tera Kabonerwa still owns this place as his *mailo* land.

Administrative Arrangements

As soon as he was settled on the throne Rukidi divided Kitara among his brothers and his followers. To Nyarwa, his eldest brother, he gave Mwenge. Buganda went to Kato, and Busoga to Kiiza, his youngest brother. He advised them, however, against settling in their respective sazas because he wished the family to stay together. But the brothers interpreted this advice as a clever move by Rukidi to keep them in subjection. One of Rukidi's servants, who happened to overhear what the brothers were saying, went straight to his master and told him about it. But he paid no attention and merely told the servant to ignore his brothers, because they were used to behaving in such childish ways. He made Mugungu the Chief of all the Royal Drums [a post held by Mubimba under Bachwezi rule] as well as chief of Kijagarazi, where the drums were kept. Bamuroga, Mugungu's younger brother, was made ruler of Kijaguzo and Kisuna. He was also put in charge of the palace gate. Kisenge of the Abacaki clan became chief of Bugahya [the area around Hoima], while Nyakoka, his *omufumu*, and counselor, became chief of Kikonda and Sweswe. Rukidi forbade Nyakoka to settle in his counties because his advice was needed at the capital.

Kato Kimera Rebels in Buganda

After a short period Kato asked for permission to go hunting as well as to see what his *saza* of Buganda looked like. Rukidi allowed him to go. Suspecting that Kato might decide to settle in Buganda and not come back to Bugangaizi, Rukidi ordered many old men—faithful and trustworthy men—to accompany him. They included Katumba [of the Muhinda clan], Kahira [of the Buffallo clan], Balitema, Mpinga, Mazige, Gunju, Kaswija, and many others.[8]

Kato took a lot of salt with him, the salt being used in addition to the other obvious purposes to preserve the meat with which to feed his people. At the back of his mind, however, he was scheming to rebel against his brother and set up a separate kingdom in Buganda. Nevertheless, Rukidi accompanied him up to a hill called Kiburara, where he bade him farewell. It is said that the marks which they made on a stone at the spot where they said good-by to each other are still visible.

Kato proceeded to Buganda for good. He arrived at the house of a man called Ssebwana, who behaved like the *saza* chief of Buganda at the time. Ssebwana was not at home but his wives were. These ladies, struck by Kato's good looks and majesty, fell in love with him at first sight. They conspired with the servants to murder Ssebwana and marry Kato. When their plan was executed, and Ssebwana safely dead, Kato declared himself the King of Buganda and performed all the necessary ceremonies, following what had happened at Rukidi's coronation. He assumed the name of Kimera—signifying a branch which, having dropped from the parent tree, grows into another tree. He also sent a message to Rukidi telling him that he would never come back to the capital and that he was now king in his own right. Rukidi ignored Kato's rebellion and did not lift a finger to reduce him once more to obedience.

The Kitara Empire had now split into three different sections. There was Nkore, which had broken away under Ruhinda. There was Bunyoro-Kitara [which now claimed to be the legitimate bastion of that empire]. And there was Buganda. Originally Buganda was known as Muhwahwa[9] and came to be called Buganda after the name of the saza chief appointed to govern it by Wamara. This chief's name was Kaganda Rusirri s/o Ntege s/o Koyo. Bakitara used to despise the people of Muhwahwa and used to describe them jocosely as "Kaganda's little men, Obuganda." This nickname slowly took root and the name Muhwahwa disappeared.[10] Indeed all the three kingdoms assumed new names. Nkore [Ankole] was previously known as Karokarungi [meaning a beautiful village]. The remaining sections of Kitara gradually came to be known as Bunyoro. Originally these people referred to themselves as Abakitara. It is said that there is a region in Abyssinia called Nyoro and that the name Bunyoro may have developed out of this.[11]

Such successful rebellions tend to encourage other rebellions, especially if no efforts are made to suppress them. If Kato was allowed to secede, why should not the others follow his example? This question must have been in Nyarwa's mind when he sought permission from Rukidi to pay a visit to his *saza* of Mwenge. But Rukidi, determined to take no more chances, refused to grant him this permission. For one reason or another Nyarwa was not disposed to flout his junior brother's authority.

Rukidi ruled Kitara for a long time. He married the two ladies Wamara had left behind to look after the palace. Iremera bore him two sons, Ocaki and Oyo, both of whom later became kings. It was Iremera who taught Rukidi to like milk and to love cows. Previously Rukidi hated milk and used to be disgusted whenever it was offered to him. But one day when Rukidi was ill Iremera offered him milk, disguising it as medicine. He drank it and from that day Rukidi started to like milk and used to ask for it whenever he came back from his hunting expeditions.[12]

When Rukidi died he was buried at Dyangi; but his garments were buried at Masaijagaka in Chope. [The author gives no special reason why his garments were buried in such an outlandish place as Chope. This suggests, however, that Rukidi's influence extended as far as Chope.] Rukidi's mother was the lady Nyatworo of the Mukwonga clan.

2. Omukama Ocaki I Rwangirra

Rukidi was succeeded by his son Ocaki. There were no wars during his reign. This may have been due to the fact that the Babiito had not yet started to hate one another and the people of Kitara appeared to be contented with the state of affairs. Indeed Ocaki was on good terms with his uncle [*isento*] Kato Kimera [Kabaka of Buganda], and corresponded [exchanging messages] with him now and then. He ruled for nine years and died. He was buried in Keci while his garments were buried in Irangara. His mother was the lady Iremera [former queen of Wamara] of the Balisa clan.

3. Omukama Oyo I Nyimba Kabambaiguru

Oyo succeeded Ocaki, his elder brother. He was called Kabambaiguru because he had many children—more than two hundred in all. He ascended the throne as a very old man, succeeding his brother, who died without a son. There were no wars during his reign and he died a very old man. He was buried in Bukidi[13] while his garments and other personal belongings were buried at Kinogozi [Masindi]. He was also the son of the lady Iremera.

4. OMUKAMA WINYI I RUBEMBEKA NTARA

Oyo was succeeded by his son Winyi. The new king was of a playful disposition and one day sent a message to the King of Buganda demanding that porters should be sent to him from Buganda. This may have led to ill feelings between the two countries because it was during Winyi's reign that Baganda began to annoy Bakitara in many ways. Indeed on one occasion Kabaka Kaima [of Buganda] attacked Bwakamba, son of Mukwiri who was Saza Chief of Bwera. This developed into hostilities between Bakitara and Baganda. Winyi himself led the campaign in defense of Bwiru. During the battle Kaima was wounded and died in Isunga, a village in Bwiru. It was Winyi, too, who made Omubiito Kaganda, also called Kibi, ruler of Kiziba. [But during the reign of Duhaga I, Kiziba was to secede from Kitara.] Winyi I is still remembered in Bwiru, where he had built his capital. The site of that capital is still known as "Winyi's Village." It is situated near the Roman Catholic mission at Kitovu.

He also ruled for a long time. When he died his body was taken to Bukidi for burial but the Bakidi people refused to allow their territory to be turned into burial grounds for Bakitara kings.[14] His body was therefore brought back and buried in Kiburara in Ssingo. Winyi's mother was the lady Nyaraki of the Mukwonga clan.

5. OMUKAMA OLIMI I RWITAMAHANGA KALIMBI

The *obuwali* name of this king was Rukidi. Olimi succeeded his father, Winyi I. Because of his courage and bravery Olimi I was honored and respected throughout the country. He was addressed as follows: "Olimi Rwitamahanga Omwitabyaro wa Kalimbi [Olimi, the scourge of nations]." During his reign Baganda invaded the Bwiru [Buddu] and Bulemezi sazas of Kitara. Olimi moved against them at the head of his army and at the battle of Mulago defeated and killed Kabaka Nyakibinge. It was a fierce battle, and at one time Nyakibinge, being hard pressed, prayed for the assistance of the *embandwa* [spirit] Kibuka [flyer], who was supposed to fight from the clouds. Kibuka is said to have killed a Munyoro man called Nsembukya, son of Kwezi, with one arrow. Baganda, however, lost the battle and, for one year, the Kiganda throne was occupied by a woman called Nanono, who acted as regent.

Olimi's intention was to annex Buganda, thereby restoring it to Kitara. But his ministers and advisers warned him against the adoption of such a policy.

> Do not do such a thing [they admonished him], because one throne should not swallow another. Moreover, Kato, the founder of Buganda, is your relative. An annexation policy may result in the country rising against you. And a curse may descend on you with disastrous consequences.

Olimi accepted their advice. But having an aggressive spirit, he turned his attention to Nkore. He attacked and defeated Nyabigwara, the Omugabe [king] of Nkore. He transferred his capital to Nkore and made his home there.[15] He took pity on the king and spared his life. People of Nkore speak of the great event which happened at this time—how darkness engulfed the world, and how the sun fell from the sky to the ground. [But this was not so. The sun did not drop onto the ground. The event refers to what Europeans call *eclipsis solaris* or solar eclipse.][16] This terrible event nevertheless filled people's hearts with fear.

Olimi reigned for a long time. He was buried in the royal cemetery at Kalimbi, in the *Gomborora* [sub-county] of Mutuba II in Ssingo. His mother was the lady Nyagiro of the Banywagi clan.

6. OMUKAMA NYABONGO I RULEMU

The *obuwali* name of this king was Chwa. He succeeded his father, Olimi I, at a period when the country was at peace —a situation which his father had worked all his life to establish.

Nyabongo led several expeditions into many neighboring states. His first inclination was to move against Madi. He was, however, strongly advised not to undertake this venture by his *abafumu*, who warned him that it would cost the life of one of his sons. But Nyabongo's eldest son, Kabakangara, encouraged his father to ignore this advice, arguing that the loss of one individual was not the end of the world. He pleaded with his father that the fear of the loss of a son ought not to prevent them from undertaking an expedition which would lead to an increase in their flock of cattle. Moreover, the loss of one son would not deprive the country of an heir. Having heard these encouraging words, Nyabongo made up his mind to undertake the expedition. He ordered the war drum to be beaten and his soldiers summoned.

The attack on Madi—which is called Orwekyeteme—was led by Nyabongo personally. The warning of the *abafumu* did, however, come true; and Nyabongo did lose his son Kabakangara, the very one who had persuaded him to undertake the expedition. It is said that Kabakangara, who was the leader of one of the contingents of the army, was swallowed up by the lake while attempting to cross it. It is also stated that after this unfortunate incident the lake split itself in two, leaving a piece of land in between. This enabled Nyabongo and the rest of his men to cross over to Madi country. This was how the name Orwekyeteme came to be given to this expedition. This was also how Nyabongo got the additional title of Kyambukyankaito [one who crosses a river with shoes on].

When Nyabongo reached Madi he discovered that the ruler, King Muzibuyecumita, was not at home, having himself gone on a raiding expedition. Muzibuyecumita's mother gathered together some soldiers and offered battle but was defeated. She was captured and taken to Nyabongo. In their interview the king's mother said defiantly to Nyabongo: "You must be some king who engages in battle with women! My son would have thrashed you if he were here." Nyabongo, infuriated at this insolence, decided to stay put in Madi until the king returned so that they could have a trial of strength to discover who was stronger. He dared her to send for her son. Muzibuyecumita hurried home as soon as this news reached him. The following day, at sunrise, the two kings fought a fierce battle. The fight lasted until evening, by which time Nyabongo's men had grown so tired that they were on the point of fleeing. Just at that moment, however, Nyabongo uttered the following prayer: "You who resides in the heavens, help me or I bring shame on myself." Suddenly, there came a very strong blast of wind which almost blinded Muzibuyecumita's soldiers and scattered them. Muzibuyecumita himself was captured and Nyabongo took him to his mother

and said: "Here is your son." Afterwards he put mother and
son to death and seized their cattle. Nyabongo annexed Madi
to Kitara.[17]

Nyabongo set out to return to Kitara loaded with booty.
When they reached the lake they uttered some prayer and
it split itself once more into two parts to make way for them
to pass. After they had crossed, the lake became one once
more. Meanwhile, from the other side of the lake, Muzibuyecumita's men were heard shouting:

> Do not delude yourselves. True, you have captured our
> cattle but we warn you that you cannot manage them.
> They are a ferocious breed and do not belong to our
> country. We captured them after long raiding expedi-
> tions and have found it difficult to keep them under
> control. They are called *Enewere* cattle.

The Madi men were perfectly right, for on reaching home
the new cattle fought with those of the king and killed them
all. After some time, however, Baganda raided Kitara and
carried off these very cattle. This occurred during the reign
of Kabaka Mulondo.

Nyabongo ruled for a very long time. When he grew very
old he decided not to fight any more. But in his prime he
was a warrior king who fought against many countries and
thus acquired the title of "Rulemu." He was buried at
Muyenje, now in Buganda. His garments and other personal
belongings were buried at Busesa in Buyaga. His mother belonged to the Muchwa clan.

7. WINYI II RUBAGIRAMASEGA

The full title of this king was "Winyi Rubagiramasega
Katamikundi of Lapenje, Emparangani, son of Chwa." He
succeeded his father, Nyabongo Rulemu. He fought for the
throne with his elder brother Kalirahaiguru.[18] This succession war lasted for a long time and caused many deaths and
miseries. In the end Winyi II emerged victorious and because
the war was long and bloody he was nicknamed Rucwerabazaire [one who brings grief on parents]. It is said that during
his reign ghosts frequently appeared, anxious to know "who
succeeded to the throne in the end"; and that people used
to say to them: "It was Winyi"; and the ghosts used to retort:
"That's what we thought too."

Okukama Winyi II was a very cruel man [*witima muno*] and used to murder people for no reason. And for this reason he was called Rubagira Masega [one who provides nourishment for the eagles]. Indeed he could not bear to see his eagles going hungry. And whenever he heard the sound of these eagles he would exclaim: "Poor ones! They are asking me to give them food." Then he would straight away order the execution of some innocent people to provide food for them.

It was during the reign of this king that Buganda extended its border to the river Wabiruko in Mityana. This area was captured from the Kukwenda [Mukwenda]. Winyi does not appear to have bothered to defend Mityana. Indeed throughout his reign he made neither raids nor wars against other countries. The people of the Mityana district simply went over to Buganda quietly and offered no battle even after Baganda had killed some of them. They seem to have seen Buganda as the lesser of two evils. Winyi did not undertake foreign expeditions because there was no need for them and the country was quiet and peaceful. [The obvious reason would seem to be that only a few people were prepared to fight for a cruel king—a fact implicitly admitted by the author in the next sentence.] Winyi II was very much hated by his subjects. He was buried at Lapenje in Ssingo. His mother belonged to the Balisa clan.

Many of the royal tombs in Buganda have now disappeared either due to devastation by wars or due to neglect because of their being in a foreign land.

8. OLIMI II RUHUNDWANGEYE

Olimi II was given the following titles: "Ruhundwangeye Mirundiegoroire, Magurugagenda Omurucuba." He was a very handsome man and came to the throne when he was still very young. There were no wars during his reign because his grandfather had pacified the country. He is mostly remembered for his handsomeness and love of cattle. He is said to have loved cattle more than any Mubiito king before him and even used to attend to the cattle himself just like the herdsmen. One day he got hurt as he was attending his cattle and from then onwards Babiito kings were forbidden to herd cattle. This action was considered necessary because a king sometimes could be wounded by a stick and shed some blood. But Kitara kings must not shed their blood [as this would disqualify them from office].

Olimi II was buried at Burongo in Ssingo. His mother belonged to the Bakwonga clan.

9. NYARWA OMUZARRA KYARO

Nyarwa was called Omuzarra Kyaro because he remained on the throne for a short time. He was cheated out of the kingship by his young brother (who later became Chwa I) in a manner that does not appear clear to tradition. Nor is the manner of his death known.

Some people say that he was ensnared by his brother during a raiding expedition in Nkore, taken to Kyaka [now in Tooro], and murdered, after which Chwa seized the throne. Another version of this story states that Nyarwa was so grieved by his betrayal that he vanished into the heavens. Following this incident, succeeding Babiito kings used to sacrifice cows at Nyarwa's hill in Kyaka. They would throw the meat up in the air, uttering the following words: "This is for Nyarwa, who has gone up to the heavens." Then the bones would fall to the ground. They performed this antic to calm the anger of Nyarwa, who might be hungry up there. Nyarwa was supposed then to have been buried in Kyaka. His mother was the lady Runego of the Bagweri clan, who was also the mother of Chwa I.

10. OMUKAMA CHWA I RUMOMA MAHANGA

This king was praised as "the true Chwa [cutter], the scourge of the cows of Nkore."

The Attack on Nkore

A short period after Chwa I had usurped the throne from his brother Nyarwa, a cattle disease called *Kisotoka* [*nsotoka*—rinderpest] descended on Kitara and killed off all the animals. Chwa I was therefore advised to replenish his flock of cattle by invading Nkore, which had a lot of cattle at this time. He suddenly mobilized his men with himself as leader. And the Nkore campaign had started. At Rulembo he confronted Omugabe Ntare Kitabanyoro [the scourge of the Banyoro] of Nkore and offered battle. Ntare, defeated and badly hurt, fled to the island of Kagera and remained there for the rest of his life. Chwa I established his capital in Nkore on the hill called Kakunyu.

The Attack on Rwanda and Other Countries

After three years in Nkore Chwa was persuaded by the people of the Bachwezi clan—the Abafumura—to invade Rwanda, where many cattle also existed. Thereupon he mobilized his men and moved against Rwanda. But, suspecting during the march that some of his men had deserted and had bolted back to Kitara, he decided to estimate their number by ordering everyone to be in possession of a stone. This incident took place at Birenga hill. When they arrived at a sandy river in Nyaruyanja village he ordered them to throw down their stones. The stones thus thrown down formed three big heaps and two small ones. He ordered this exercise to be repeated in order to make sure that he had sufficient men for the invasion.

At dawn he encountered King Kahindira of Rwanda [Ruanda] and a battle was fought. Kahindira was beaten and his cattle captured, many of which Chwa I sent to Kitara. Chwa himself settled in Rwanda for four years and Rwanda thus became the main center for his raiding expeditions. He attacked many countries to the west of the lacustrine region and even went beyond Lake Kivu. He died in Rwanda. (Usually when an Omukama died, his officials tried to hide the fact. From this developed the custom of saying that the king has been lost or has been swallowed up.)

During the four years he ruled Rwanda, Chwa I gave that country a taste of good administration. He reorganized it after the pattern he was used to in Kitara. In the Chronicles of Rwanda, the Kitara occupation of that country is said to have been of great importance because Chwa I left a legacy of good administration.[19]

After the death of Chwa, his men decided to return to Kitara. [This would seem to suggest that their hold over that country was very precarious. It would even suggest that they might have been driven out of the country]. During their return journey they passed through Nkore, where they were challenged by Omugabe Ntare. Apparently Ntare had learnt of the death of Chwa and the decision of his followers to return to Kitara. So he ambushed them and killed some of

them, thus avenging his earlier defeat. The defeat of the Bakitara was primarily due to the lack of a leader in the absence
of Chwa, to give them inspiration. It is not surprising therefore that many of them fled in the heat of the encounter
and many of those who stood their ground were cut to
pieces.[20] Ntare captured Chwa's palace, including his household.

In Bunyoro-Kitara Chwa did not leave any heir. And because of his prolonged absence, a lady called Mashamba was
put on the throne as regent. Mashamba was a *Mubiitokati*
[princess] as well as the *Batebe* [the official sister of the
king].[21] The kingmakers were not disposed to offer the throne
to a prince of a distant relation to the ruling line [lest he
might make his position permanent]. The elevation of
Mashamba was therefore a temporary measure [necessary to
avoid a breakdown in administration]. Meanwhile concerted
attempts were made to find an acceptable successor to the
throne.

The search soon switched to the captured ladies in Chwa
I's household who had become his queens [*abago*]. It happened that there was one called Ihembe, who belonged to
the Babiito clan. Ihembe had been at the last stages of pregnancy when she disappeared. Thereupon the kingmakers secretly sent out people to look for her and the child.

Omukama Chwa I was not buried in Kitara, but in Rwanda.
His mother was the lady Runego of the Bagweri clan. Her
other son was called Nyarwa, as we saw. For the weeping
of lady Runego after the disaster at Karokarungi, that kingdom's name became known as Nkore[22] and Kitara became
known as Kyaka.[23]

11. OMUKAMA (REGENT) MASHAMBA

Omukama Mashamba, formerly princess and daughter of
Winyi II, became regent [as we saw] when there was no
direct heir to succeed Chwa I, who was living in Rwanda
at the time when the kingmakers were looking for Ihembe.

An Omubiito Is Found

The search for Ihembe, who was suspected to be with the
king's son, continued in earnest. Finally she was found, together with Prince Winyi, and they were persuaded to come

back to Kitara. The party traveled during the night and went into hiding by day because they were afraid that they might be identified and killed.

After some time they reached Kitara. The prince was at first hidden from his aunt [*isenkati*] the Queen Mashamba for some time. This was done to ensure his safety at least until the elders of the clan and the important chiefs had assembled and confirmed his true identity. It is worth noting that there were those who believed that Winyi was a pretender to the throne, that, in fact, he had been captured with his mother after his birth, and that it was Chwa who gave him the name of Winyi before he left Kitara. Nevertheless his true identity as the son of Chwa I was confirmed by those who ought to know. They were particularly struck by his resemblance with his father. He was then brought to Mashamba, who also confirmed his identity. She requested them to leave the prince with her. It transpired, however, that a servant, who belonged to the Basegu, was in possession of Mashamba's secret plan to kill the prince. Some of the elders were in collusion with her. This plan was disclosed by the servant and the majority of the elders therefore said to Mashamba: "Our Lady, let us first present him to the people so that they, too, can confirm his identity, after which we will return him to you." And Mashamba, not suspecting that her secret plan was now exposed, agreed with this suggestion but warned them to bring him back soon.

Mashamba Is Assassinated

It was the elders' turn now to plan to get rid of Mashamba, especially as they hated the thought of being ruled by a woman. A message was consequently sent to her that the prince was being brought back to her in honor of their promise. The following morning the prince was brought to the palace, accompanied by these elders and some important chiefs. Some of them hid their swords in their garments, while those who carried spears hid them outside the palace gate [*Mugabante*]. As soon as Mashamba appeared, the agreed signal was given, and one of them pulled out his sword and plunged it into her, killing her instantly. Then the others fell on her household officials and liquidated them.

Afterwards the young Prince Winyi was crowned as Kyebambe I. He was called Kyebambe because he had usurped the throne of his aunt, Mashamba;[24] and he was called Musikya because he killed his aunt, thus decreasing the number of people in his clan.

Mashamba was buried at Rwembuba in Bugangaizi. She spent more than four years on the throne and was married to a Mubiito called Iguru, son of Murro. Iguru was a cruel man who put innocent people to death. This was one of the reasons why many people hated Mashamba.

12. KYEBAMBE I OMUZIKYA

During Kyebambe's reign the Basegu clan came to assume the same importance as the Babiito clan. It will be remembered that the man who had warned the elders of Mashamba's conspiracy against Prince Winyi belonged to this clan. As a reward for his loyalty the position of his clan was elevated. The *Abatimbo* [king's dancers and singers] also became very important during Kyebambe's reign because the king had been a music lover from childhood.

Kyebambe fought no foreign wars. Peace reigned in Kitara. And even though civil war was raging in Buganda—between the supporters of Kabaka Juko and those of Kayemba— Kyebambe failed to exploit the situation [as Buganda could easily have done].

Kyebambe reigned for a long time and died a very old man. His tomb is at Kijaguzo, in the Nyakabimba area of Tooro. His mother was the lady Ihembe of the Babiito clan.

13. WINYI III RUGURUKA MACOLYA

Winyi III succeeded his father, Kyebambe. He was renowned for his sportsmanship, especially in long-distance running and in hunting. We have no tradition of any wars fought during his reign. He had eight children and here are their names:

1. Rucwerabazaire
2. Bikaju
3. Karamagi
4. Nyaika
5. Mulali [whose mother was Kuhunda]
6. Ruteba [whose mother was Kapapa]

7. Muganda [whose mother was Mworobi]
8. Onyiri [whose mother was Munyunki]

Winyi III died from a snake bite while he was on one
of his hunting expeditions in Miduma. He left the throne
to his favorite (and fourth) son, Nyaika, who was also acceptable to the people at large. Winyi's tomb is at Miduma
in the Sabairu Gombolola [sub-county] of Buruli [now in
Buganda]. His mother was the lady Gawa of the Bakwonga
clan.[25]

14. OMUKAMA NYAIKA I

Winyi III, as we have seen, was succeeded by his son
Nyaika. But Nyaika I, however, is not really counted among
the line of kings of Kitara on the technical grounds that, first,
he ruled for about two years; and, second, he was not regarded by the kingmakers as the true heir to the throne.[26]

When Winyi III died all the important Babiito including
Nyaika's elder brothers were away in their respective areas
of jurisdiction. Nyaika therefore happened to be the only
available candidate on hand. [Moreover, he was his father's
nominee.] It is not surprising therefore that when his brothers
heard that he had seized the throne, they defied his authority
and refused to pay their respects to him. Omubiito Bikaju
of Bugungu was the first to raise the standard of rebellion.
Almost immediately the others followed his example.

One day it happened that while Nyaika was playing with
some of his court favorites, Mugungu and Mugasa, Mugasa
accidentally hurt Mugungu's eye, destroying it in the process.
Fearing that he would be killed by the king, Mugasa fled
to Bugungu and sought refuge with Bikaju. When Bikaju
saw him he inquired about the condition of affairs in Kitara.
From Mugasa he learnt first hand how Nyaika had succeeded
to the throne and how the other princes had refused to recognize him as king. Bikaju then decided to go to the capital
and pay his respects to his younger brother, but was dissuaded
from doing so by his wife, who taunted him as follows: "You
failed to succeed to the throne in spite of the fact that you
are the elder brother of Nyaika. Now you want to curry favor
and crawl before your younger brother, who is a mere child.
It will be better for us to remain here in our bush."

Bikaju's pride was hurt by his wife's scornful words. This

determined him to march to the capital and attempt to seize the throne from Nyaika. First of all, however, he sent a secret messenger to Mugungu requesting his support in this venture. Mugungu immediately sent a message to Bikaju encouraging him to proceed with his plans because he regarded the king as too young to rule the kingdom effectively. Mugungu also called a secret meeting of some of the elders of Kitara and won their support for Bikaju. Here are their names:

1. Kapapa Omutaseka
2. Omukama w'Abatwanga
3. Kihuka of Nyarukondo
4. Kihyo Omutaseka
5. Butyoka Kyokora, etc.

Another message was despatched to Bikaju to explain to him the plan for this coup d'état. He must invade the capital at night bringing as many people as possible. These men must carry leaves to hide their number. When they reached the capital these leaves would be thrown onto the roofs of the houses in such a way as to make them rustle and produce the noise *pa—pa*. The aim was to frighten the inhabitants of these houses and thus keep them inside. The noise would also act as a signal for the plotters that the coup was on. The task of surprising the king and killing him would be left to them.

Bikaju did as he was told and the coup succeeded without a hitch. The people were terrified when they heard the rustling of the leaves and locked themselves up. When they woke up in the morning, they discovered to their surprise that the king had been murdered by a group of men acting for the elders and that Bikaju was now their king. Nyaika's body lies in the royal cemetery of Kihwera in Bujenje. It is worth remarking that although Nyaika ruled for a short time, he buried his father and was hailed as Okali by his subjects. It is for these two reasons that we have regarded him as a true king in this book.

15. Omukama Kyebambe II Bikaju

Bikaju was called Kyebambe because he killed his brother Nyaika I and usurped his throne.

The following day after his coup Bikaju performed his coronation ceremonies. There was music and merrymaking and the population, surprised at what they knew was going

on, gathered to see who the new king was. "Why," they exclaimed, "this is Prince Bikaju! Where is Omukama Nyaika?
Has he been murdered without a war being waged?" Some
of them, however, were delighted when they learnt that
Bikaju was now their king. They cheered and greeted him
and gave him the name of Kyebambe [usurper]. They ad-
mired him particularly because he was a brave and cou-
rageous man. His father, they knew, had not nominated him
as his successor because his mother had been a servant in
the king's household.

Kyebambe II had a wife, the lady Kitanire, who belonged
to the Babiito clan [Omubiitokati]. Kitanire was in love with
Katenga, son of Rulya, of the Basaiga clan, who was also
the king's uncle. One day the king dropped into Kitanire's
house and there found his uncle, Katenga. But the queen,
spotting her husband, warned her lover to defend himself
and gave him a sword. "Kill the king," she told him, "because
he comes with an intent to kill you." He hid himself behind
the curtain and prepared to surprise the king. As soon as
the king entered the house, Katenga attacked him with the
sword, wounding him seriously. The dazed king cut himself
loose from his assailant and made for the house in the palace
called *Kabagarama* and summoned his sons—Byakaya,
Isingoma, Runywambeho, and Isansa—to come quickly to his
aid. When they rushed to the scene, Kyebambe chose Isansa,
the bravest of them all, to seek out his assailant and kill him.
He handed him the royal spear [*erihango*].

Isansa sought out Katenga and killed him. He also set upon
all members of the Basaigi clan—Katenga's clan—he could find
in the palace and killed them all. He also issued orders that
all Basaigi throughout Kitara should be liquidated. His order
read: "I do not want to see any Musaigi [singular for Basaigi]
left in this country. The entire clan must be liquidated." It
happened, however, that Isansa's wife, the lady Kindiki, belonged to the Basaigi clan. And although she was expecting
a baby at the time she was also ordered to be killed. But
when the executioner, a man called Mukerenge, a Mutonezi
chief, saw her condition, he refused to carry out his order
and hid the lady instead.

Meanwhile Kyebambe II had taken poison and died.[27] He
was the son of a woman called Kacubya, who had been the
maid of Winyi III. He was buried at Nyamiryango in Kihukya
County. Before his encounter with Katenga, he had already

ruled for a long time. He was a very brave man who fought and defeated the Baganda in several engagements. It is thought, however, that it was during his reign [about the beginning of the eighteenth century] that the county of Kyaigwe [Kyaggwe] was lost to Buganda. At that time Mawanda was Kabaka.

CHAPTER 3

Babiito Kings of Kitara (continued)

16. OMUKAMA OLIMI III ISANSA (c. 1710–30)

Isansa took the royal name of Olimi III when he succeeded his father, Kyebambe II Bikaju. His full title was: "Gabigogo Gabohwa Enkya, Omukwata Galemire Birali Mpanja, Mikundi Nyaraki."

Olimi III is counted among the hero kings of Kitara. He built his capital in Isingo-Kyenkwanzi (Ssingo), which is now Mukwenda's[1] county of Buganda. From here, he waged wars and carried out raids into other countries. After he had established himself on the throne, the executioner Mukerenge, who had been detailed to execute Isansa's wife, Kindiki, during the purge of the Basaigi clan, brought before him Kindiki and a baby of four months and said:

> My Lord, when your father was exacting revenge on the Basaigi clan, I was given the task of executing my lady, your wife, but I had not the heart to carry out my orders because she was expecting a baby. So I hid them in some safe place. I have therefore brought her back with your little son and beg your forgiveness.

Olimi was very pleased to see his wife and son. He gave the child the *obuwali* name of Mujwiga and many other names besides. He called him Muherere because he had very light skin; and Mujwiga because he was very hairy.

Wars with Nkore, Kyaihangiro, and Buganda

During the reign of Isansa, Buganda extended its borders to Mubende up to the river Nyabakazi/Omukitengeza [mile 84 on the Kampala-Mubende Road]; and to Ssingo up to the river Mayanja [mile 36½ on the Kampala-Hoima Road]. Nkore, too, extended its border at Kitara's expense as far as the Katonga River in the region of Rwamwanja to the west.

Isansa was at a loss as to how to deal with this impudence of Buganda and Nkore. Being a brave man, however, he summoned his soldiers, called up the reserves, and at the head of them decided to move against his adversaries. Nkore was his first target. He decided to travel through Kyenkwanzi, Parajwoki, Bugahya, and Bugoma. He then crossed the river Nguse, passing through Buyaga and Bujogoro, and arrived at Mulongo [Lwomulongo Muzizi] and on to Kikankana. He crossed Kakumbirirwa and was challenged by the Abagesera at Kijumba [Nyantungo Mwenge]. Isansa defeated them and chased the rest before him. The way was now clear to Nkore. He encountered Omugabe Karaiga at Rulembo [his capital] and beat him decisively. Nkore was captured and the country raided.

Having consolidated his hold on Nkore, Isansa was tempted to cross over to Kyaihangiro and Rwanda and conquer them too. Indeed, he had already dispatched his son Mali, who was commanding a group of soldiers called the Ekikwekweto to accomplish this mission. After Mali had traveled for two days, Isansa mobilized his soldiers and decided to follow his son. When the people of Nkore heard that terrible military drum of his they said one to another: "That drum sounds like that of the Omukama of Kitara." And those who were accustomed to the sound of this drum concurred: "Yes, he is the one; and he is going to raid Kyaihangiro." The people of Kyaihangiro sent a message to him urging him to turn back because it was not customary for the Abakama [kings] of Kitara to invade their country. Isansa was inclined to ignore their warning until his *abafumu* warned him not to conquer or raid Kyaihangiro because that was where the Muchwezi king Ndahura was captured and mysteriously disappeared and where Chwa I got lost. He changed his mind and accepted their advice.

Just at that juncture some messengers arrived post haste
from Kitara and reported to him that the Baganda were devas-
tating his kingdom. Thereupon, Isansa beat the retreat, reorganized his army, and hurried back to Kitara. At the same
time he sent messengers to recall his son Mali. But the messengers were too late. Mali had already encountered the King
of Kyaihangiro, who defeated his army and captured him
after a fierce battle.

When Isansa reached Kitara he turned his army on the
Baganda and defeated them. He drove them back to their
original boundaries. He put Kitara in order and restored its
lost provinces.

Isansa Is Deceived by the King of Kyaihangiro

The King of Kyaihangiro, who had defeated Mali, the son
of Isansa, one day asked his captive: "How did you come
this way?" Mali replied: "We came together with my father,
who remained in Nkore." The king then went on to ask:
"But how do you manage to conquer all those countries?"
And Mali replied: "We conquer them by the spear called
Kimuli belonging to Wamara of Bwera." This conversation
caused the King of Kyaihangiro some uneasiness. He was
afraid that Isansa would certainly prepare to avenge his son's
defeat. Thereupon he thought up a great idea. The whole
scheme was intended to cause enmity and hatred between
Kibandwa Wamara [one who was possessed by the spirit of
Wamara and therefore represents that god in this world] and
Isansa, thus dividing Kitara's ranks. The King of Kyaihangiro
therefore asked Mali to give him his charm [*orugisa*]. He
promised to send it to Isansa to convince him that Mali was
still alive. He was sure that if Isansa got this message, he
would send men to bring Mali back. Mali saw nothing wrong
with this idea and therefore handed his charm to the king,
who, contrary to his promise, sent it not to Isansa but to
Kibandwa Wamara of Bwera. He said to his messengers:
"Take Mali's charm to Wamara of Bwera and tell him to
preserve it for Mali, who will collect it on his way to Kitara
to succeed his father, Olimi III Isansa, as king." *Kibandwa*
Wamara did as he was instructed.

Now, to complete the plot, the King of Kyaihangiro secretly
sent messengers to Isansa and said to them: "Go and ask
the king of Kitara why he refused to send me my reward

for releasing his son Mali. He was handed over to *Kibandwa*
Wamara of Bwera, to send on to his father." He implied in
the rest of the message that Isansa was not to blame him
if he had not yet seen his son, in which case it would be
assumed that he had been murdered by *Kibandwa* Wamara.

Isansa was furious when he got this message and was convinced that *Kibandwa* Wamara had murdered his son. He
was also convinced that the King of Kyaihangiro had actually
released his son and had handed him over to *Kibandwa*
Wamara. He therefore decided to avenge his death. But he
wanted to be convinced beyond doubt that Mali was really
dead. So from among the maids in his household he chose
the most beautiful and sent her as a spy on *Kibandwa*
Wamara. She was to ascertain that Mali was dead and she
would know this by listening carefully to conversations or
if she discovered Mali's charm at Bwera. Her first task, however, was to lure *Kibandwa* Wamara into marrying her.

With these instructions the maid proceeded on her mission
to Bwera. At *Kibandwa* Wamara's palace, she was announced
as an eligible young lady and a possible bride to be. The
announcement did not indicate that she had been sent by
Isansa. [As tradition is silent as to what happened after this
announcement, we shall assume that she was eventually married to *Kibandwa* Wamara.] Nevertheless, during the New
Moon ceremonies, all *Kibandwa* Wamara's bags were opened
and the charms and beads were brought out to be worn for
the occasion. It was only then that Isansa's maid was able
to recognize Mali's charm, which had been included among
the treasures. She immediately picked it up and said: "I will
wear this one." The following morning she asked her maid
to prepare water for her and to put it in the bathroom. She
was using this as a blind to enable her to get away unnoticed.
When this was done, she used the opportunity to disappear
through a hedge, taking the charm with her. When she arrived back at Isansa's palace, she produced the charm and
said: "My Lord, here is the charm. It is the only one I recognized that may possibly belong to Mali." Isansa ordered the
charm to be taken to Mali's mother as well as to his other
wives for identification purposes. They all wept when they
saw this charm and there was no doubt now in their minds
that Mali had been killed by *Kibandwa* Wamara.

Isansa's rage was unbridled and he swore to avenge his
son's death. He issued orders at once to Chief Ngambangani,

son of Runyamunyu Omukada, to go to Bwera and raid
Kibandwa Wamara's palace. Accompanied by a detachment
of soldiers Ngambangani raided *Kibandwa* Wamara's household. Some of his children were killed while others were captured. Tradition records that the trees wept and bled when
cut open as a result of this sacrilege. *Kibandwa* Wamara himself was not captured because he was the representative of
a god on earth. He was furious at Isansa's unwarranted action.
"Am I not Isansa's servant, and why therefore should he attack me?" he complained. Then he seized the royal spear
called *Kimuli* [*Kyokyamahanga*] and held it upside down and
pronounced the following curse on Isansa: "Your kingdom
will be swallowed up by the shield of your young brother,
the King of Buganda." Ngambangani returned to the capital
and gave Isansa a full report of all that had transpired.

Prince Mali, however, never left Kyaihangiro. He grew into
an old man and had children there. It may be that his descendants are still living in that country. After a short period
Omukama Olimi III Isansa died and was buried at Kiguhyo
in the Mutuba I Gombolola in Buyaga. His other burial place
[for his garments and other personal belongings] is at Bu-
honda in Bugangaizi. He was the son of Lady Mpanga
Omwangamwoyo, Omubiitokati [of the Babiito clan].

17. OMUKAMA DUHAGA I CHWA MUJWIGA (c. 1731–82)

When Isansa died he was succeeded by Duhaga I. His
other name [military name] was Mujwiga. Physically he was
a very small man and for this reason he was given another
name—Ruhaga [expansion]—signifying that he would expand
in size after he had remained on the throne for some time.
He was also greeted with the title of *"Maherre ga Isansa,
Mujwiga, Matamancwera, Engundu y'ekisiha"* because he was
very light-skinned [*maherre*]; he was very hairy [*mujwiga*];
in moments of anger his temper was uncontrollable [*matamancwera*];[2] and because he was a very difficult man to deal
with [*ngundu y'ekisiha*].[3] The additional name of Chwa was
conferred on him by the Banyankore [people of Nkore] because he fought with them very much and they likened him
to the celebrated Chwa [Chwamali] of long ago.

When Duhaga became king he discovered that there was
no Musaigi to succeed to the position of the king's mother
because his father, Isansa, had killed all members of the

Basaigi clan in the country to avenge the death of his father, Kyebambe II Bikaju. The Basaigi, however, were still in Nkore. And from there a queen was got to fill the position of the official mother of Omukama Duhaga I.

In the beginning Duhaga had no children. And after he had spent some time on the throne, he sent a messenger to *Kibandwa* Wamara of Bwera requesting him to give him children [make him fertile]. He also asked him for the famous royal spear that conquers the world. *Kibandwa* Wamara's reaction can be easily imagined. His reply was provocative:

> How can you have the nerve to ask me for children and the famous spear? You were certainly not too young to remember how your father killed all my children! I will nevertheless give you children. But I will give you the spear only on condition that you give me ninety menservants, ninety maidservants, ninety cows, ninety sheep, ninety goats, ninety chickens, ninety beads, and ninety cowrie shells [used as currency at the time]. Without receiving these items, I will not give you the famous spear.

Duhaga felt insulted by his demands and refused to accept them on the ground that it was customary that kings were never asked to pay for anything. He dispatched a message to *Kibandwa* Wamara at once asking him only for children without the spear. "Children, he shall have," said *Kibandwa* Wamara, "but how will he defend these children without the spear?" He therefore chose a small basket and filled it with *enjogera* [made of copper] and sent it to Duhaga with the following instruction: "Let each child that is born wear one of these around its ankle." From this moment Duhaga's fertility was restored and he produced so many children that all the *enjogera* contained in the basket were used up. Among all the kings of Bunyoro-Kitara, Omukama Duhaga I had the second greatest number of children.

Wars against Nkore, Kooki, and Bwera (Buddu): Kooki and Bwera Secede from Bunyoro-Kitara

After the death of Duhaga I, his young brother, Bwohe, rebelled and declared himself King of Kooki. [A detailed account of this story will be found in a subsequent chapter dealing with the kingdom of Kooki.] Suffice it to say at this stage that the rebellion eventually succeeded and Kooki became separated from Bunyoro-Kitara.

To return to Duhaga's reign. Duhaga was not unduly dismayed by the reaction of *Kibandwa* Wamara regarding the famous spear that conquers the world. He continued his raids into neighboring countries. His first expedition was against Nkore. At that time Karaiga was Omugabe. Duhaga defeated him and destroyed his royal drum—*Bagendanwa*—by cutting it to pieces.

His second expedition was against his own son, Kitehimbwa of Bwohe, now nominal master of Kooki, but in reality under the protection of Kabaka Jjunju of Buganda. Kitehimbwa was killed and Kooki restored to Kitara. Jjunju was very much angered by this incident, especially as Kitehimbwa's son [Duhaga's grandson] had arrived at his palace and had asked him to restore Kooki to him. Jjunju therefore invaded Kooki, defeated Duhaga's army, and installed Mujwiga as Omukama of Kooki. Jjunju next moved against Bwakamba, son of Mukwiri, and head of the Babiito clan as well as being the Saza Chief of Bwera. Jjunju defeated and killed him. The Bwakamba family had been rulers of Bwera since the time Omukama Isaza Waraga [Omuchwezi] had allotted this area to them. Jjunju annexed Bwera to Buganda and appointed Ruziga of the Basiita clan, as its saza chief. Kooki, on the other hand, became Mujwiga's kingdom. But even today Bwera [Buddu] exhibits many characteristics which denote that it was for a long time a province of Bunyoro-Kitara. Such personal names as Katabarwa, Kagoro, Kajerre, Bwigara, Mukwiri, Kasumba, Komungoro, Kigemuzi, and so forth found in Buddu, are all authentic Kinyoro personal names.

Ekya Kaborogota

The loss of Kooki and Bwera determined Duhaga to declare war on Buganda and recover his lost territories. But before he declared this war, he asked the advice of his *abafumu*, since he had just performed the *enjeru*[4] ceremony. One of them, Kakyali, advised him to proceed with his plan, while the other, Nyakoka, warned him against doing any such thing. This discrepancy in expert opinion led to a furious debate between the two *bafumu*, especially as each claimed that his own advice was the right one. The king himself grew impatient and angry over these wrangles and decided to follow

Kakyali's advice of war against Buganda. Consequently, he mobilized his men and prepared for war. But as he was coming out of his palace, Nyakoka begged the king to rescind his decision. He said: "I pray you, my lord, stay in your palace, because the gods are against your going to this war." But because of the jealousy and rivalry between the two *bafumu,* Kakyali insisted that the king should undertake the expedition. Duhaga once more accepted Kakyali's advice and went to war against Buganda. When Nyakoka heard of this final decision, he threw down his spear, *Binyomyo,* and hopping up and down declared: "If the king conquers Buganda, then let me and my children never be his *bafumu* any more." Tradition records that Nyakoka's spear ascended into heaven and got lost.

Nyakoka's prediction, however, came true. Duhaga was decisively beaten by the Baganda after a big battle which was fiercely fought. Many Babiito lost their lives in this war. Duhaga alone lost seventy sons, and suffered the humiliation of fleeing and being pursued by Baganda. He fled into the papyrus swamps of the river Kaborogota and hurt himself in the process. Some people suggest that he was cut by papyrus; others say that he fell on his own spear and was wounded in the thigh. Whatever was the case, he was carried away by his followers to Nkwali market and died there. It must be pointed out that he did not die of the wounds he received. He followed the custom of Kitara kings and drank poison. Before he died, however, he managed to send for his son Kasoma, who had survived the massacre, and bequeathed the throne to him. He also instructed him in the details of governing the country. It is stated that Kasoma wept when he realized that his father was on the point of taking poison. Thereupon the king admonished him: "How will you be able to keep the throne and control your people if you weep so easily? How can you resist your elder brother's [Nyamutukura] attempt to oust you from the throne?" After uttering these words, he took poison and died. He was buried at Irangara in the gombolola of Mutuba III in Bugangaizi. He had very many children.

During his reign food and clothing were mostly got from his raiding expeditions. Out of this grew the saying: "Are you Duhaga who robs and takes away things he did not work for? [*Nonyaga, nogonza kulira, oli Muhaga?*]" Today, the Babiito belonging to Duhaga's sub-clan have ceased to be of great importance and many of them have become *bairu*, only retaining the name of Babiito. Omukama Duhaga I ruled for a long time. He is counted among the hero kings of Kitara. His mother was the lady Kindiki of the Basaigi clan.

18. Omukama Olimi IV Kasoma (c. 1782–86)

Kasoma assumed the royal name of Olimi when he became king. But after a few years he was deposed by his elder brother, Nyamutukura. For this reason he is not technically counted among the kings of Kitara. We hope to show, however, that he was king in the true sense of the word.

After spending a year in Irangara, and having completed all the customs pertaining to the coronation, he moved his capital to Kijagarazi Nsonga in Bugangaizi. After some time he moved his capital to Kiboizi. At this time Nyamutukura was living at Kisunga Rugonjo. But he was unhappy at Kasoma's elevation at his own expense. He therefore planned to seize the throne through a coup d'état. Having mobilized his army, he sent a message to Kasoma that he was coming to pay his respects to him. But Kasoma, being wise to his brother's dark scheme, also mobilized his own army and waited for him. When Nyamutukura had crossed the river Nguse, Kasoma, accompanied by his men, went to meet him. As they approached near to Nyamutukura, Kasoma said to his men: "Now, boys, show your shields to my brother and it will be left to him to demonstrate whether he has come on a peaceful mission or to fight." Nyamutukura, aware of what was going on, ordered his men to fix their sharp blades on to their spears and attack. A big battle ensued and ended with Nyamutukura's defeat and flight. Tradition records that so many people were wounded in this battle that the river Nguse turned into blood.

Kasoma chased him across the river. And as Prince Nyamutukura fled through the papyrus covering the swampy river of Kairabya, there came a time when he was deserted by all his men except one. The man was his servant called Kanyaihe. The prince also had only one shield left with which to defend himself. At a certain stage the papyrus became so thick that he could not make his way through it with this shield. So he prayed his servant to cut down some of the papyrus so that he could go through. This was done with some difficulty. And after crossing this swampy place they

arrived at the home of a man called Mutaikanga, who turned
out to be a chief. When Mutaikanga's mother saw the fleeing
prince, she said to her son: "Isn't this the animal being hunted
by the king? Send him away lest he would bring you trouble."
It happened that Nyamutukura overheard what the lady of
the house was saying. Thereupon Mutaikanga said to the
prince: "Sir, it would be better for you to get away from
here. My house is well known in this country and the chances
are that the king's men will search here and arrest you."

But as the prince turned away to go, Mutaikanga was so
overcome with emotion that he took pity on him and requested him to come back. Nyamutukura was afraid that
Mutaikanga's mother was sure to give him away and so refused to accept his offer. He moved on and arrived at a house
which belonged to a man called Kataba of the Bahinda clan.
Kataba's mother was very glad to see him and welcomed
him into the house, saying: "Oh, this is the son of my king
who is being pursued by his enemies. I am glad that you
have not been killed by their spear." Kataba himself was also
pleased to see the prince. He said: "Oh, he looks like the
son of our dear king. Welcome to our humble home." Thereupon they led the prince to the back of the house, plucked
the nettles and briars from his body, and prepared a bath
for him. After which they smeared his body with balm and
then prepared him a bed. Kataba and his mother indeed were
preparing to kill a goat in his honor but the prince objected
to this hospitality because it was not customary for princes
to feast while fighting was going on. He asked them to prepare
him some green vegetables instead. At nightfall Kataba and
his friends escorted the prince safely out of the house and
he continued on his journey. When he reached his own area
of Kisunga he swore never to go back to the capital because
he nearly lost his life there.

Nyamutukura Defeats Kasoma

For some time Nyamutukura lived a private life and seemed
to have given up every hope of fighting for the throne as
a worthwhile proposition. But something, however, happened
which disturbed the existing calm. One day, two important
and influentual Babiito, the *Okwiri* [head of the Babiito clan],
Rumoma, and Rabwoni, son of Bireju, who had come to pay
their respects to the king, got drunk and started a heated

argument. Then Rabwoni said to Rumoma: "Now shut up. You are always causing a lot of arguments!" Having said this he pulled out the straws from his bottle of beer and threw them at Rumoma's face and accused him of complicity in Nyamutukura's plot to overthrow Kasoma. He mocked him for the failure of this conspiracy. Rumoma was very hurt by this allegation and assured Rabwoni that if he had been on the side of Nyamutukura it would not have been possible for Kasoma to be king. When people saw them quarreling they went straight to the king and prayed him to come and prevent these important men from fighting each other. But he refused to intervene because he believed Rumoma and Rabwoni to be two sensible men who knew what was required of them to do. In the end, however, they were stopped from fighting each other. Okwiri Rumoma was so angry over this incident that he decided to depart for his own area. For the next two days, which he spent in the capital, he did not speak a single word to anybody. On the third day he left for Kihaguzi.

As soon as he reached his district he beat his war drum called *Runyanga;* and, having mobilized his men, headed for Rugonjo. Here he sent a message to Prince Nyamutukura which said: "Let us go to the capital and I will make you king." But Nyamutukura, suspecting foul play, refused to have anything to do with such a venture. He made it plain to the Okwiri that he was convinced that his offer was a sure way of putting him in the hands of Kasoma. Rumoma swore that there was no plot to destroy him and that his suspicions were totally unfounded. And to prove his point he sent his son to Nyamutukura as a guarantee for his word. This gesture cleared Nyamutukura's doubts, and having joined forces with Rumoma, they moved against Kasoma. But Kasoma was well acquainted with their plans and had also mobilized his forces to meet them. A big battle was fought and Kasoma, soundly beaten, fled the field.

Nyamutukura led his victorious soldiers into the palace and installed himself as king. After some time, Kasoma was captured and brought before him. Then he asked his vanquished brother, now the ex-king: "What post would you be happy to have—a chieftainship or an Okwiriship, or the Chief of the Royal Gate?" Thereupon Kasoma replied contemptuously:

I do not want any of these posts. I have been king,

and do you seriously think that I am going to crawl
and worship you? If it was I who had vanquished and
captured you, you could not be making use of those
eyes of yours. I would have smashed that abdomen
[*ebitundu*] of yours. Do not ask me such a ridiculous
question. Take the throne which you have seized from
me and do your worst.

Infuriated by such harsh words and by his brother's proud
and unbending attitude, Nyamutukura ordered his immediate
execution. Olimi IV Kasoma was taken to Kabale and executed near the lake. As a curious kind of vengeance, Nyamutukura later on killed those whom he had ordered to execute
his brother. Olimi IV Kasoma was buried at Ruhunga in the
gombolola of Mumyoka in Bugangaizi. His mother belonged
to the Muchwa clan and was a sister of Nyamutukura's
mother.

19. OMUKAMA KYEBAMBE III NYAMUTUKURA (1786–1835)

His original name was Musuga; but he was given the name
Nyamutukura [very light] because, like his father, Duhaga,
he was fair-skinned. He was given the name of Kyebambe
because he had killed his brother and usurped his throne.
It seems that this name was given to him by Kasoma before
his death. But whether this was so or not, the fact remains
that he would have been given such a name anyway.
Omukama Chwa II Kabalega was never called Kyebambe—
even though he defeated his elder brother Kabigumire, and
seized the throne—because Kabigumire was never greeted
with the royal name of Okali and did not bury his father.
Moreover, Kabalega became king while he was still alive.
What Kabalega did was to kill his younger brother, Kabu-
gungu, in the place of Kabigumire [who had fled to Chope].
We will deal with this in more detail in a later chapter. Now,
let us return to Nyamutukura.

After he had established himself on the throne, he remembered Mutaikanga's mother [the lady who had refused to
hide him when he was a fugitive]. He killed her as well
as all those who had sided with Kasoma against him. But
he also remembered those who had been kind to him and
rewarded them handsomely. For example, Kataba of the Bahinda clan [who had hidden him in his house when he was

a fugitive] was made an important chief. Indeed during his reign the Abahinda clan was called Ababiito.

Nyamutukura's first capital was built at Ruhunga. Then it was moved to Kikumbya, from where he sent his son Kaboyo to go to Tooro, count all the cattle there, and bring them to him. After some time he moved the capital to Kihayura Burambika, where he spent about seven years before moving the capital again to a place called Nyakitojo. It was from here that Kaboyo left for Tooro and proclaimed his rebellion.

The Rebellion of Nyamutukura's Sons: Tooro Secedes from Kitara

The principal reason for these rebellions was because Nyamutukura had reigned for a very long time and had become extremely old. His sons, too, had become old men and their natural desire for the kingship became so great that they decided on some drastic actions. That their father had given them their respective sazas even made their schemes easy to execute.

His son Karasuma Bugondo of Musuga, Saza Chief of Bugungu, was the first to scheme against his father. He went on a secret mission to Kabaka Kamanya of Buganda, asking him for soldiers with whom to attack his father and declare himself king. But Kamanya happened to be on friendly terms with Nyamutukura and therefore would have nothing to do with such a plot. On the contrary, he sent a message to his friend telling him of his son's mission to him but at the same time warning him to vacate the throne in favor of his children if he had grown too old to rule. Nyamutukura did not listen to this advice. Instead, he asked Kamanya to seize his son and kill him and wondered if an old man did not deserve a roof over his head and whether he was liable to be deprived of all his belongings while he was still living, on the ground that he was very old. It would appear that Kamanya was not happy with this reply, for instead of killing Prince Bugondo, he gave him a small army sufficient to escort him home. But Nyamutukura tricked his son and got him killed before he could reach Bugungu. His remains lie at Kitagi, in the Sabagabu Gombolola of Buhaguzi.

Kaboyo was the next to rebel against his father, when he proclaimed himself Omukama of an independent Tooro. He had been sent to Tooro by his father to count the cows and bring them back to him. He took the opportunity, however, to further his own political interests. While on this errand, Kaboyo got in contact with some influential people in Tooro and in Busongora and let them know that he planned to return to Tooro and declare it independent of Kitara with himself as king. He asked for their support in this venture and both the Batooro and Basongora expressed their readiness to support him.

It transpired also that the chiefs and other important people in Kitara were unhappy with the way Nyamutukura showered favors on Kaboyo, among all his sons. They therefore devised a means of separating both of them. Consequently, they advised the king to decorate Kaboyo—thereby elevating him above all his brothers—not only because he was the eldest of them all but also because he was the king's favorite son. The king took their advice and decorated Kaboyo. But then these advisers came up with another suggestion. They reminded the king that "one who has been decorated is not allowed to see his father"—that he must therefore be separated from him. Kaboyo was sorry to hear that he could not see his father any more, because he loved him too; but he was very angry to learn that the chiefs—particularly those of the Bahuma group—hated him and favored his young brother Mugenyi. This, in fact, made him decide to rebel. Then he sent his father a dog and requested him to give it a name which would indicate old age, after which he himself would give it a name indicating youthfulness. But the king sent the dog back to Kaboyo and asked him to give it a name first and then bring it to him. Kaboyo then named his dog Lyabaira [meaning, "it is high time the father made room for his sons"] and sent it back to Nyamutukura. In this way he demonstrated that he was fed up with the prevailing state of affairs. The king asked him to change the dog's name to Bigire Owakuhwa [literally, "they have gone to an end"].

Shortly afterwards, Kaboyo went to Tooro. The chiefs, warned of Kaboyo's intentions, let the king know that he was planning to make himself King of Tooro. But because of his great love for Kaboyo, the king ignored this warning and merely told them that Kaboyo had only gone to inspect the area under his jurisdiction. When Kaboyo reached Tooro, he was enthusiastically welcomed by the people of that county. He declared Tooro independent of Kitara, made himself king,

and performed the coronation ceremonies. His father did
nothing to punish him.

His next step was to raid his father's cattle at Myeri in
Mwenge County. When this news was reported to Nyamutukura, he gave the following order to his soldiers: "Go and
capture Kaboyo and bring him back to me." But because
he loved him very much he added, "If he runs away do not
give chase, because he has a weak heart; and if he gives
battle, do not engage him but retreat instead." He gave these
instructions because he did not wish to see his favorite son
killed.

When some Babiito saw these developments, they also decided to rebel in their respective areas. Kachope and Isagara
Katiritiri, who were the saza chiefs of Chope, rebelled and
declared Chope a separate kingdom. Nyamutukura had no
reply to this challenge either, because of his extreme old age.
So he left them alone. It has been stated by some writers
that Nyamutukura led his soldiers to suppress the rebellion
of Kaboyo in Tooro. This is not true because he had already
made *enjeru* and could not therefore go to war. If he did
so he would be breaking the custom of his ancestors which
stipulates that after the making of *enjeru*, a king must neither
kill a person with his own hand nor join the army. During
such a period, the king usually delegated such tasks to the
Bamuroga,[5] the Saza Chief Mugema[6] and two others. The
only king known to have gone against this custom was Duhaga
I. But Duhaga was also noted for his uncontrollable anger
and for this blunder he did not survive the war. Indeed, those
who believe that Nyamutukura led his army into Tooro, also
assert that he was wounded in the arm during this campaign.
But if this was so, why is there no record that he took poison
and died as custom prescribed in such an eventuality? No,
Nyamutukura sustained no injuries because he did not go
to the war. It was Kahibale, one of the king's delegates, who
was wounded by the Batooro and died on the spot. It is
probable that Kahibale has all along been mistaken for the
king. A further reason why he could not have gone to the
wars himself and personally suppressed the rebellions is that
he was too old and therefore physically very weak. He was
so old that he could not stand up on his own; he could hardly
walk and was therefore carried out every morning. Now, how
could such a person have led a campaign in Tooro with its
many hills and other physical barriers?

Many important people lost their lives during the Tooro campaigns. They included Igisi of Buziba, Dwangu of Buyanja, Wamara of Kitwanga, Kibego of Kihayura, and many others.

Because of these troubles the king moved his capital to Bugoma, where he died five years after Kaboyo's rebellion.

Nyamutukura had many children. Below are the names of those who are known and their respective sazas:

1. Kaboyo Omuhundwa was given the saza of Tooro.
2. Mugenyi was given the saza of Mwenge.
3. Isagara Katiritiri was given the saza of Kibanda Chope.
4. Kachope was given the saza of Kihukya [Chope].
5. Karasuma Bugondo Bwamusuga was given the saza of Bugungu.
6. Kagoro Majamba was given the saza of Kijumba.
7. Kigoye [son of Nyaika] received no saza.
8. Nyinamwiru, his daughter, was given the saza of Nkoni.
9. Kahibale lost his life in the Tooro campaigns.
10. Kabanyomozi [princess].
11. Kalyebara.
12. Ogena.
13. Kairagura.
14. Kahoza.

Kyebambe III Nyamutukura is counted among the most revered and respected kings of Kitara. He also spent more years on the throne than any other king before him; but his long reign brought disastrous consequences for his country because it gave rise to the breakaway of Tooro and several other rebellions. Had this secession not occurred, Kitara would have been strong and respected, for, as the proverb says: "Unity is strength." During Nyamutukura's reign the empire of Kitara was reduced to the status of a small kingdom. Buganda had expanded at its expense. Kaboyo's Tooro extended as far as the river Munobwa in Mwenge, while Buganda extended as far as Kiboga and Nyabakazi in Buhekura [Buwekula] County.

Omukama Kyebambe III Nyamutukura was buried at Kibedi-Nyamanunda, in the gombolola of Mutuba I Buyaga; his garments were buried at Bujogoro. His mother was the lady Kafunda of the Bachwa clan.

20. OMUKAMA NYABONGO II MUGENYI (1835–48)

Nyabongo succeeded his father when he was already an old man. When his father died he sent for his elder brother, Kaboyo of Tooro, to return to Kitara and succeed to the throne, but Kaboyo rejected his offer. Mugenyi's *ekikubyo* name was: Biranga of Mwenge. He was a typical Muhuma in appearance and character. He loved his cattle very much. He was a king of peace. He neither fought with Ssuna II of Buganda nor attempted to suppress the rebellions of his brothers, Kaboyo, Kachope, and Isagara Katiritiri. He was always moving around the country because of his love for cattle.

He first built his capital at Makara, where he lived for many years. Then he moved it to Rwenyenje, then to Kitemba, then to Galihuma Kijumba, then to Rwenkuba, and finally to Rwenkukuni, where he died. His body was taken from there to Kicunda. It was here that his son Rwakabale found it in the custody of Menya and brought it to Buhenda for burial. He appointed Ibona and Omugo [Queen] Kisabwa to look after the tomb.

Nyabongo may have reigned for twelve or thirteen years, succeeding to the throne around 1835 and dying around 1848. Few significant events happened during his reign. He is, however, reputed to have been a king of peace who loved his cattle dearly. He is also said to have had many children and below are the names of those who are known:

1. Dwetakya; 2. Nyakuhya; 3. Kweru; 4. Rwakabale; 5. Kamurasi [Saza Chief of Bugungu]; 6. Kamihanda Omudaya [Saza Chief of Kicwabugingo]; 7. Isingoma Rutafa, the father of Zeresire, Alifunsi [Alphonse] Ngasirwa and of Jesika [Jessica] Gafabusa and Kahimbara [daughters]; and 8. Kasami [minor chief of Bujwahya].

Nyabongo II Mugenyi was buried at Bukonda in the gombolola of Sabagabo in Buyaga. His garments were buried in Kitonezi, Mutuba I. His mother was the lady Kajaja of the Bafunjo clan.

21. OMUKAMA OLIMI V RWAKABALE (1848–52)

According to Kitara tradition Olimi IV does not count for much because he did not die a natural death. Nor did he take his own life. But although he spent only four years on the throne we must count him as a king of Kitara because he buried his father, Nyabongo II, and was given every honor due to a king. Shortly after Nyabongo's burial, Olimi's elder brother, Kweru, rose in rebellion. This rebellion was suppressed and Kweru killed at Buhango on Nyabinya stone.

Nor was he acceptable to his younger brothers, Kamurasi and Kamihanda Omudaya, who each gave their dogs revealing names to register their disapproval. Kamurasi called his dog Obuto Buseza [meaning that only his youth had denied him the throne]; and Kamihanda called his Kibi Kikumbwa Isemu [meaning that he and Kamurasi were prepared to face any danger in an attempt to overthrow Olimi V]. Thereafter they worked out their plan for the coup d'état. They sent a message to Olimi informing him that they had gone to Bugoma to look after their cattle. But when they reached Bugahya of Kasumba, Kamurasi instructed the inhabitants to shout loudly that "Kamurasi has rebelled." He then proceeded to Bugoma by way of Rubindi and Bugahya of Jawe Nyinekiringa, and arrived at the island of Karakaba, where he found supporters who rallied to his standard. Here he formed his own army, which included soldiers from Bukidi. Kamihanda also formed his own army, which was commanded by Kikwizi, son of Mulere of the Basaigi clan. He was assisted by Rugangura, son of Nyakojo Omusengya. The Bakidi contingent was led by Rugunjerwa Mpunde of the Balisa clan. Kamurasi therefore confronted Olimi with a very large and powerful army. Olimi's army was commanded by Nyaika Kigoye. Olimi V Rwakabale was defeated in this war and killed by Kamurasi.

Another significant thing which happened during Olimi's reign was the appearance of a strange group of people. They were representatives of a certain god. They carried neither spears nor sticks. They were called *Aba Busesega, aba Buyonga burokire, aba Busungu bwokya Ekitete*. There were not many of them. Their duty was to sing *Rwanyamurahya* and perform dances in the bush [areas of short grass] or in areas of flat rock. Instead of spears they were armed with reeds [*obusungu*] and instead of shields they protected themselves with leaves [*emiko*]. They predicted that the era of peace was at hand.[7] These people came from Bubango in the gombolola of Sabagabo in Buyaga.

Olimi V Rwakabale was buried at Kitonya in the gombolola

of Mutuba III, Buyanja, in Buyaga. His mother belonged to
the Bazira clan.

22. OMUKAMA KYEBAMBE IV KAMURASI (1852–69)

Kamurasi's praise names were as follows: "Rukanama of
Kanembe, Okukidi of Isaka, Mirundi egoroire." He came to
the throne in about 1852, when Ssuna II was still King of
Buganda. He succeeded his brother, Olimi V, whom he had
killed. He was given the name of Kyebambe because he was
a usurper. After becoming king, he moved the capital to
Kicunda Rwempango. Here he attacked those strange people
who claimed to be the representatives of gods on earth [the
Busesega people we have mentioned previously] and liquidated them.

After a short period on the throne, he was attacked by the
princes of Chope, Kachope and Isagara. Kamurasi fled to
Busesa, where his important chiefs happened to be at the
time and still celebrating his coronation. These invading
princes, having killed many people and raided the country,
marched back to Chope.

When Kamurasi came back from Busesa he moved against
other princes of Kitara who were threatening to rebel. He
dismissed Prince Kaliba, the Saza Chief of Kyaka [which
was called Kitara at that time] and replaced him with his
brother, Dwetakya. He also dismissed Mwanga from the saza
chiefship of Mwenge and appointed Materu in his place. He
then returned to his capital, which was at Kicunda. Later on,
however, he transferred this capital to Rwenyenje.

The Princes of Chope Invade Kitara Again

After eight months, news reached Kamurasi that the princes
of Chope had attacked Kitara once more. He mobilized a
large army and let it be known that his object was to attack
Buganda. He made up this story as a tactical move because
he did not wish the rebellious princes to take fright at the
size of his army and flee. His intention was to force them to
give battle. The expedition therefore set out, taking the
Busimbi road towards Buganda. They traveled as far as
Kyenkwanzi, then headed for Dusungu, and finally ended up
on the island of Karakaba, where they camped. Here he con-

fronted the enemy. On the following morning the Chope
princes shouted to Kamurasi:

> We are the true heirs to the throne of Kitara. You are a
> usurper because you come from Mwenge and are of Ba-
> huma stock. What do your kind know about fighting,
> you delicate drinkers of milk?

But Kamurasi said to his men:

> Do not waste your breath [*kujura akanwa*—literally, to
> wear the mouth] by shouting back abuse at them, but
> allow them to shout themselves hoarse. They are the
> same people as we.

Then they fought a pitched battle. Kamurasi was wounded
in the finger but Kachope and his men were overwhelmed
and fled the field. Nevertheless, they spread the false story
that Kamurasi was fatally wounded in the encounter. They
even sent a message to Prince Kamihanda Omudaya of
Rusunga and Saza Chief of Buruli informing him that the
king had been fatally wounded and was expected to die at
any time. Distressed by this news Omudaya collected his
soldiers and the next morning set out to the rescue of his
brother the king. After a long and tiring march he encountered
the forward position of the rebel forces at Kokoitwa, where
they had camped. This news was at once conveyed to Prince
Nsale [who was one of the commanders of the rebel forces].
But he and his soldiers underestimated the strength of Prince
Omudaya's army and, mocking the enemy, declared: "Let
him come with his little men and meet their death." At this
juncture one of Omudaya's men speared a man called
Kibokoire, an enemy soldier. He was a mutongole chief to the
Saza Chief Kato. He ran to his camp and fell in front of his
friends, who were intoxicated with *amasohi* [local beer].
"Sir," he said to his commanding officer, "things are getting
bad." Thereupon, the rebels, blinded with drink, managed to
pick up their shields and rushed out to offer battle. Omudaya
did not miss his opportunity. Nearly the entire rebel force was
destroyed. Of the princes only two survived—Ruyonga and
Mphuhuka, who fled across the lake and took refuge on the
island of Galibama. Among those killed were: Nsale, Kato,
Kwabigoye, Manyindo, Kabadima, Kabanyomozi, Fotoire, and
Mampohya. From this disaster at Kokoitwa arose the saying:
"*Ohumwire ekihumura babi Nsale eki yahumwire Kokoitwa!*

[You have rested the disastrous rest which Nsale rested at Kokoitwa]."

But Prince Omudaya was very depressed by the terrible deaths which he and his soldiers had caused during the battle. In his victory therefore he saw no joy and in fact declined to speak to his brother Kamurasi afterwards. And when the king sent him a congratulatory message, he said to his soldiers: "Let him not congratulate me for destroying all our family and our clan." To demonstrate his unhappiness about his victory, he ordered his soldiers not to beat his military drum during their return march. Omukama Kamurasi also ordered that all the bodies of the fallen Babiito should be gathered and properly buried. But Prince Nsale's mother, brokenhearted by her son's death, decided to seek vengeance. She is said to have gone to a foreign country [Sudan] to enlist help against Kamurasi. She brought back with her an army called Kotolya.

Meanwhile Kamurasi built a new capital at Kihigya. From here he raided Chope, capturing all the property of the princes of that region. He also attacked the two surviving princes—Ruyonga and Mpuhuka—and dislodged them from their stronghold on the island of Galibama. Once more they crossed the lake and retreated into Bukidi country. Thus did Kamurasi achieve the temporary pacification of Chope as well as the suppression of all those who had opposed him, and became the only recognized king of what was left of the empire of Kitara.

But he could not settle in a place for long. He moved his capital to Panyadoli, then to Kinyara, then to Kisuga, then to Kiswata, and then to Kiryandongo.

The Rise of Nyakamatura

There were not many wars during the reign of Kamurasi. Nor did he attack either Buganda or Tooro. But his reign saw the rise of a powerful man to eminence. This man was called Igwahabi, the son of Nyakatura, of the Bamoli clan. Igwahabi was not only a very strong man but also a very good dancer—for these reasons he was nicknamed "Mwijoro." But this gifted man happened to have wronged Prince Omudaya and almost met his death at the prince's hand. Luckily, he was ransomed by Kamurasi, who later gave him a position as one of his pages and named him "Nyakamatura."

After some time Nyakamatura was elevated to the saza chiefship of Bugahya, thus filling the position held by Jawe Nyinekiringa, who had been killed by Prince Nyaika, son of Kigoye, to avenge the death of his father, which occurred at Jawe's palace. Kigoye had been captured and kept under house arrest at Jawe's palace, where he suddenly died of smallpox. On the day he died, Jawe's enemies spread the rumor that Kigoye had been poisoned by him. Nyaika believed this story and planned to avenge his father's death. One day Nyaika was informed that Jawe was going to the capital to pay his respects to the king. He therefore ambushed Jawe and murdered him. And with the death of Jawe the saza chiefship of Bugahya fell vacant and this made it possible for Nyakamatura to be elevated to the post. He proved to be a very powerful chief, especially during the reign of Chwa II Kabalega. He was the father of the famous Paulo Byabachwezi, who also succeeded his father as saza chief of Bugahya [1893] and played a very important role in the government of Bunyoro-Kitara during the reign of Kitahimbwa and A. B. Duhaga II respectively.

Here are names of the children of Omukama Kyebambe IV Kamurasi:

Kabigumire	Kabagungu
Kabalega	Isingoma
Ntirri	Mubu
Kanyabuzana	Kabatongole
Kabasenya	Kabasuga
Kabagonza	Ndagano Rutakya
Mugizi I	Kanyamukono
Kabahukya	Kaikara
Beza Barongo	Nyakato
Kahamba	Kabasesera
Nyakaisiki	Kaijamurubi
Rutanana	Rukosa
Nyakaisiki II	Calimbwa
Kabahinda	Kalyegira
Komusenyi	Lakeri Mugizi II
Tibanagwa	Kasuzi Rwigirwa
Kafuzi	

Kamurasi died at Kiryandongo in December 1869. He was buried at Busibika [Kisubika] in the Mumyoka Gombolola of Buyaga. His mother was the lady Kigirwa Nyarwegendaho of

the Basiita clan, who was also the mother of Prince Kamihanda Omudaya. Omukama Kamurasi was loved and respected by his subjects. It was during his reign that the first
Europeans came to Bunyoro-Kitara.

The Coming of Europeans to Bunyoro-Kitara

The first Europeans to come to Bunyoro-Kitara were Speke
and Grant. They came in [September] 1862 and were followed by Samuel Baker [or Muleju—the bearded one] and
his wife, Kanyunyuzi [the little star—as Banyoro affectionately
called her] in [February] 1864.

1. SPEKE AND GRANT (1862)

On 25 September 1861, Speke and Grant left Zanzibar and
started their inland journey toward the lacustrine region of
East Africa. By 10 January 1862 they had arrived at the court
of King Rumanyika of Karagwe. They were well
treated by Rumanyika and they praised his hospitality and
wisdom. They regarded him as the most hospitable and wisest
of all the rulers they had met on their way from Zanzibar.
They noted that Rumanyika did not speak badly of the kings
of Kitara and Buganda but on the contrary regarded Omukama Kamurasi as the father of the kings of the lacustrine
region. Rumanyika did not delay his visitors unnecessarily.
In February 1862 Speke and Grant arrived in Buganda. At
that time Muteesa I was Kabaka, and a very young man. He
kept his visitors waiting for a long time before they could see
him; and after he had granted them audience he did not
permit them to leave Buganda until 7 July, when he provided
them with guides to lead them to the Kitara border. On 18
July Speke and Grant parted company, Grant taking their
luggage by land toward the lake side; and Speke set out for
Jinja [in Busoga], hoping to discover the source of the river
Nile in Lake Victoria. On 28 July he discovered the spot
where the Nile joins the lake and named it Ripon Falls. From
here he passed through Burondonganyi and reached Bunyara
[Bugerere] in Kitara. Then he returned to Buganda to look
for Grant and united with him once more on 20 August. It
was here also that they were found by Kamurasi's messengers
—Bitagurwa and Kijwiga—who were on a mission to Muteesa
of Buganda. Speke and Grant were told by these messengers

that Kamurasi wished to see them. They crossed the Buganda-Kitara border on 23 August and arrived at Kijwiga's area on 24 August. By 29 August they had arrived at Kyagamoyo and by the 30th at Kiratosi. Here they were intercepted by Muteesa's messengers, who had orders to call them back to Buganda because he did not want them to be received by Kamurasi. Speke had no intention of going back to Buganda because he was still angry over Muteesa's inconsiderate behavior in delaying their departure and practically taking them prisoners. Their Baganda guides left Speke and Grant on 1 September and returned to Buganda. Speke was left with only twenty men, a number which was substantially augmented by an additional fifty porters supplied by Kajunju. On 8 September the party reached Kihaguzi, the capital, lying to the north of where the river Kafo joins the Kiihira [Victoria Nile]. They waited for ten days before they were granted permission to see the king. This delay was caused by the fact that they had initially been mistaken by the local people because of their white skin to have been the Bachwezi who had reappeared to recover their throne from the Babiito. People were afraid of them. It was not until 18 September therefore that they were permitted to see Kamurasi. They were ferried over the Kafo in boats. They found him seated majestically in the reception room flanked by fifteen of his most important chiefs. The European travelers sat on their iron stools. They gave Kamurasi the following presents: 1 rifle, 1 iron box, 2 blankets, 10 rounds of ammunition, 4 bags of beads, 2 bags of big colored beads, 1 foldable pocket knife, 2 books, 1 handkerchief, a pair of scissors, 1 bottle, 1 padlock, gunpowder, 14 rolls of cotton material, 1 bag made of cloth, a pair of glasses, several boxes of matches, and many other small gifts.[8]

Speke told the king that their mission was motivated by a desire to establish trading relations between Kitara and Europe and requested Kamurasi's co-operation in this venture. They also gave him a Bible and explained to him the tenets of the Christian faith. This was on 20 October 1862. And the following day they offered to educate two of his sons in England. But Kamurasi was unwilling to hand over his sons to foreigners. He offered, however, to give them two of his pages, who were not princes. Speke and Grant rejected this offer.

While in Kitara, the explorers heard of the presence of

white men in Acholi country and sent their messengers to
investigate who they were. It turned out, however, that the
so-called white men were not Europeans but Arab slave
traders who had established a trading station at Faloro north
of Gulu, near the Nile.

The explorers remained at Kamurasi's court until 9 November 1862. They were then rowed across the Nile to Atura,
arriving in Bukidi country on the twenty-third. They joined
the slave traders and traveled with them up to Rejaf, where
they met Baker in February 1863.

At this juncture, their porters and guides returned home.
But on their way they had the opportunity of informing the
Arab slave and ivory traders in Rejaf and Debono about
Kitara. It was these people who led the Arab traders and
their soldiers into Bunyoro-Kitara. Afterwards these Arabs
allied themselves with Prince Ruyonga to attack Bunyoro-
Kitara. They killed about three hundred people and captured
many of the wives and children of the people of Chope.[9]

2. SAMUEL BAKER AND HIS WIFE KANYUNYUZI,
    FEBRUARY 1864–NOVEMBER 1865

On his way to Kitara, Baker had made the acquaintance of
a woman, the aggrieved mother of Prince Nsale, who had
been slain with his other brothers at the battle of Kokoitwa.
This lady, consumed with a burning determination to avenge
her son's death, tried to persuade Baker to team up with
Ruyonga in his fight against Kamurasi. Baker declined to offer
his assistance because he had been advised by Speke and
Grant to proceed to the court of Kamurasi.

Baker and his wife reached the Karume Falls in Chope at
the end of January 1864. Here they were met by Kamurasi's
chiefs, who were frightened at seeing Baker's large army of
porters. Among Baker's men was an Arab ivory trader called
Ibrahim. He commanded 112 soldiers. On seeing these soldiers
the local people thought that they belonged to the Arab slave
traders who had fought with Ruyonga against them. This was
the reason why Baker was made to wait for some time before
he could have audience with the king. After ascertaining
that he was not the leader of the hated Arabs, Baker was
given permission to cross the river and proceed to the capital.
He arrived at Kamurasi's court on 10 February 1864 and
asked permission to proceed to Lake Mwitanzige [Albert].

But Baker and his wife were suffering from fever which they had contracted during their journey. Kamurasi was very kind to them and took pity on them. He gave the king some gifts and Kamurasi repaid him by giving him seventeen cows and other things. The Bakers were moved to a house close to the palace.

In February Baker set out on his journey towards Lake Albert and the king supplied him with porters. He took the direction of the Kafo and camped at Agusi, Mbasa, Karace, Kiswihe, and Kigagaru before crossing the rivers Mpongo and Kafo. He crossed the Kafo at the Kakidi side near Biragwa village. While crossing this river, Mrs. Baker fell into the water and was nearly drowned. On top of this she was suffering from sunstroke and had to be carried unconscious for seven days. She regained consciousness when the party arrived at Kibyoka [in Bugoma]. On leaving Biragwa they camped at Kijamba, Kabango, Kibyoka, and Kijambia before reaching Pukanyi in Bugoma. On 14 March 1864 Baker first sighted Lake Mwitanzige and having explored it named it Lake Albert after the husband of Queen Victoria of England. Then he moved down to Buhuka, crossed the lake in a boat, passed through Bugungu, and arrived at Pajawo Falls before proceeding to Karume Falls. They remained here until 25 November 1865, waiting for porters. From here the Bakers headed northwards with Ibrahim and seven hundred porters who had been supplied by Kamurasi to carry their food and ivory. Ibrahim left thirty of his soldiers at Karume. Baker and Ibrahim continued their journey, following the route they had come by, and Baker eventually returned to Europe.[10]

Let it be understood that Samuel Baker was the first white man to set eyes on Lake Mwitanzige and the waterfalls at Pajawo just as [J. H.] Speke had been the first white man to set eyes on the Ripon Falls. It was also during their journey from Khartoum to Kitara that the explorers saw the terrible horrors caused by the slave traders and made the governments of Europe and Egypt aware of them.

Part IV

BABIITO KINGS OF KITARA (concluded): OMUKAMA CHWA II KABALEGA (1870-99)

Introduction

Kabalega succeeded his father Kyebambe IV Kamurasi and came to the throne while still a young man in his early twenties.

It is difficult to give all the facts about Kabalega's reign precisely because there are very many things to say. He is counted among the most powerful and bravest kings of Kitara. He compares well with the other hero kings of Kitara—Olimi I, Chwa I, Olimi III, Isansa, and Duhaga I. Kabalega was given the following praise names: "Ruhigwa, Kitule Kinobere abemi; Rukolimbo Nyantalibwa omugobe, Rwota Mahanga."

Although he is said to have put many people to death, Kabalega still remains one of the most respected and revered kings of Kitara. He was loved by his chiefs, his servants, as well as by the ordinary people of Kitara. Today, the people of Bunyoro recollect his name with pride and dignity. He brought no shame on his country but, on the contrary, restored its former power and prestige, which had declined considerably during the reign of his forefathers. This determination to restore his country's lost eminence was embarked upon with energy and purpose as soon as he was comfortably settled on the throne. And when in the end he was faced with insurmountable problems and difficulties, he exhibited this indefatigable spirit to the last. It must, however, be pointed out that he lacked good advisers who could have explained to him the new forces which had come to Africa [in the nineteenth century]. This should not justify the unfavorable things that many people have written about him. We shall deal with this later on.

CHAPTER 1

The Succession War

When Omukama Kyebambe IV Kamurasi died in 1869, all his brothers gathered to bury him and nominate his successor. Among those present were Princes Omudaya, Dwetakya, Kasami, and Princesses Nyakuhya and Rwigirwa [his sisters] as well as other Babiito. Significantly absent on this occasion was Prince Nyaika of Kigoye, brother of Kamurasi. Nevertheless, the rest decided to carry Kamurasi's body [from Kiryandongo] to Kitonya in Buhanika, where it was to be buried.

Meanwhile, Prince Nyaika, who had remained behind ostensibly to guard the palace and the capital, was planning to install Kabalega as king in obedience to Kamurasi's expressed wish. In this scheme he received Kabalega's full co-operation. But Kabalega was not liked by the chiefs and the Bahuma, who favored Prince Kabigumire Ruhwino of Kageye, Kabalega's elder brother. Indeed they made fun of Kabalega, saying: *"Kabalega alirega empango!* [Kabalega will sit idly and watch the throne being taken away from him]"; and *"Kabigumire nuwe aligumira empango* [Kabigumire is the rightful heir to the throne]."

But as Kamurasi's grave was being dug at Kitonya and other burial rites being performed, Nyaika sent the following secret message to Kabalega:

> Have you forgotten your father's wish? I was present when he expressed the wish that you should succeed him. You will lose the throne if you wait for them to finish the burial rites. Are there no other important men who are your friends and who can support you? Then come quickly and do not waste time.

When Kabalega received this message he rallied the support of some of his friends and that of the intimate friends of Nyaika. These were:

1. Nyakamatura s/o Nyakatura of the Bamoli clan, Saza Chief of Bugahya

2. Byarugonjo s/o Kanyonyi of the Bagonya clan
3. Bitega s/o Mambu of the Bakwonga clan
4. Kamara s/o Bamya
5. Kikomberwa s/o Nyarubona of the Bahinda clan
6. Babiiha s/o Kapimpina of the Basazima clan
7. Rugunje s/o Mpunde of the Balisa clan
8. Ruhirimya s/o Nyabatwa of the Bacunga clan
9. Kyamuhangire Ruhimbwa
10. Matebere s/o Ndyaki
11. Rusongoza s/o Byontabara
12. Kabagambe s/o Itera

He also got support from many others who were his companions. And because, unlike Kabigumire, he did not favor the Bahuma, Kabalega's popularity among the ordinary people—the *bairu*—was enormous. After conspiring with his friends, they stole away during the night and having crossed the river Nyabaleba, proceeded to Ngagi through Macunda, where they pitched their camp.

When Kabigumire went to pay his respects the following morning to his uncle, Omudaya, he remarked about Kabalega's absence and inquired from Kabigumire: "Where is your brother, Kabalega? Why, you usually come together to visit me. Is he indisposed?" And Kabigumire replied: "Sir, I did not visit his camp this morning. Nor have we exchanged messages yet. But in the evening I saw him together with Nyaika's messengers. Perhaps he wants a fight. I do not know." Omudaya was disturbed by this answer and immediately sent a servant to summon Kabalega to him. When the servant reached the place where Kabalega was staying, he found all the houses empty, everyone having gone away by night. Infuriated at this news, Omudaya said: "Oh, this child, Kabalega, has no feeling of shame. How can he do such a thing without telling us, his fathers?" Then he summoned all the Babiito, great chiefs and ministers, to a meeting at which they declared war on Kabalega. The army was mobilized and Omudaya gave orders that Kabalega should be captured and brought before him because he had forgotten his manners [*akahwa muno ensoni*—literally, lost good manners].

The leadership of this army was given to Prince Katabanda, son of Kigoye. He was to be assisted by Prince Biremesezo, son of Kikonge. Katabanda's army encountered that of

Kabalega at Kinoga, where a big battle was fought. The battle of Kinoga was a disaster for Kabigumire because the entire army led by Katabanda was wiped out. Not even the commanders escaped. Then a chief called Muhangi, son of Nyakairu, of the Basazima clan, formed his own army and moved against Kabalega. Muhangi's army met the same fate as that of Katabanda, and Muhangi himself was killed. This battle was fought in a market belonging to Mbwa, son of Bahemba. Then news reached Omudaya that Kabalega was difficult to beat and that he was marching towards Omudaya himself. On hearing this news, Prince Omudaya gathered his cows and fled with them. But he was intercepted at a hill called Musaijamukuru [near Hoima] by Kabalega's men and all his cattle captured. Omudaya and his men, however, escaped but Kabalega pursued him up to Mulina and stopped. And as Omudaya continued to flee carrying the dead body of Kamurasi, Kabalega's soldiers took the captured cows to Nyaika's home in Buruli.

Then Kabalega decided to raid the enemy's stronghold, between Hoima and Kikonda. His soldiers captured the cattle of Kacwera, Bumba, Kihuna, Buruko, and Busanga, and Kabalega took them. While these things were going on, Kabalega paid a visit to Rubanga, son of Kyagwire, to seek his aid because Rubanga was a great and well-known senior Mbandwa at that time. And at the same time he sent a message to Kabaka Mukabya [Muteesa I] of Buganda, requesting him to send an army to help him fight against Kabigumire and Prince Kamihanda Omudaya.

The succession war continued to rage for six months and Prince Nyaika, upset by the miseries bred by the war, lamented: "Oh, Bugahya is going to die! People have spent six months without cultivating their crops. How can they combat the famine and hunger that is sweeping everywhere?" (This concern may have caused Nyaika to change sides, for he moved down from Buruli into Bugahya, bringing with him an Arab slave trader called Sulemani [or Kirimani as Banyoro call him]). They camped at Kasingo and prepared to move against Kabalega. These Arab traders had been helping both Ruyonga and Kabigumire and using them for their own benefit.

Meanwhile Muteesa I had decided to send an army to help Kabalega. It was led by the Kangaho [official title of saza chief of Bulemezi] Nyika. That was in 1870. They en-

tered Kitara by way of Kyenkwanzi. Now hoping to get
Kabalega to fight without the assistance of Buganda, Nyaika
was looking for cattle to raid. By that time Kabigumire was
at Kitahuka. Kabalega pursued him to this place and inflicted
a heavy defeat on him at the battle of Buziba. Kabalega recovered his father's body here and took it to Kikangara, where
he left it and continued in pursuit of Kabigumire, who fled
to Kyegayuke.

At this juncture the chiefs and elders became fed up with
the succession war. They advised Kabalega to bury his
father's body, succeed to the throne, and so stop the fighting
and restore peace. Kabalega accepted their advice, buried his
father at Busibika Rukindo, and thus was crowned king as
Chwa II Kabalega. He built his capital at Kikangara, Kisagara.
Then he ordered the seizure of a young prince called Kabagungu, crowned him as king Olimi VI, and after nine days,
dragged him to Buziba, where he was killed and buried.[1]
Buziba is in the Mumyoka Gombolola of Buyaga. Kabagungu's mother belonged to the Bafumambogo clan.

In the meantime Kabigumire had taken refuge in Nkore
and Kabalega appeared secure on the throne. But then the
Arabs who had helped Kabalega during the succession war
demanded half of Kitara as a reward for their help. This gave
rise to a big quarrel between Kabalega and the Arabs. Kabalega turned his soldiers on them, killed some of them, and
drove the rest out of his country. And when Samuel Baker
arrived with Egyptian soldiers, the suggestion of dividing his
country was still rankling in Kabalega's mind.

More troubles, however, were still in store for him. Within
a short time Kabigumire invaded Kitara with an army given
to him by Omugabe Mutambuko of Nkore. This army was
led by Ireeta. The invaders were heavily defeated and
Kabigumire was forced once more to flee to Nkore. Ireeta
himself was captured and taken prisoner.[2]

While in Nkore Kabigumire made another effort to request
the Omugabe to raise another army for him. The Nkore king
refused to aid him any longer, wondering that a man who had
caused the death of many Banyankore should have the courage to ask him for more men. Kabigumire therefore left
Nkore and proceeded through Bwera, Kahanga, and Rugonjo
to his home in Kisuga. Here he was well received by his
people. But when Kabalega heard of his presence in Kisuga,
he set off with his army from Buruko in Bugangaizi and

marched through Kihaimi and Kikonda and camped at
Kikangara. Kabigumire, too, collected his own soldiers when
he learned of Kabalega's approach. The two armies clashed
in a big battle. Kabalega was defeated but he did not give
up the fight. He retreated into Kikube, where he collected a
stronger army and challenged Kabigumire once more. This
time Kabigumire was defeated and fled to Chope. Here he
reorganized his army and became formidable. Kabalega sent
Kisiga with an army to dislodge Kabigumire from his stronghold in Chope but Kisiga's army was defeated and the leader
himself slain. Another army sent by Kabalega under the
leadership of Rugongeza was also liquidated by Kabigumire.

At this juncture Prince Nyaika, despairing at the unending
war, went up to Kabalega and addressed him as follows:

> Many people have been destroyed as a result of this war.
> If the entire population is wiped out, what will you rule?
> If you do not want to kill your brother, then give him
> part of your kingdom so that he may also become king.
> However, if you still hate him, then give me a spear
> and I will go and kill him for you.

When Kabalega heard these words of his uncle, he was
stirred up to action. He handed Nyaika a spear and instructed
him to capture Kabigumire if possible but to kill him if need
be. Nyaika was also given command of a detachment of the
royal army. He was accompanied by some chiefs and
Nyakamatura was his deputy. When they reached Chope
they found Kabigumire with only a few men, for he had sent
the large part of his army to raid Bugungu. Even so, Kabigumire was successful at the first encounter and forced Nyaika
to request more help from Kabalega. When this reinforcement arrived another bloody battle was fought and Kabigumire's army was emphatically beaten. Kabigumire fought with
valor and did not surrender even when he discovered that he
was left with only one faithful servant, Jabara [Japari]. Eventually he was killed at Parangoli near Kwese. His servant,
Japari, was captured and brought before Kabalega, who
thanked him for fighting for his brother [Kabigumire] to the
end. He gave Japari the gun that had belonged to Kabigumire and made him a sectional commander in Rwabudongo's
army. He lived long and died at Mparo during the war with
Europeans.

The death of Kabigumire ended the succession war. From Kikube therefore Kabalega moved to Bulyasojo one year before Samuel Baker arrived at this place in 1872 with many Nubian soldiers.

CHAPTER 2

The Partition of Africa

When Stanley returned to Europe he wrote an account of his journey through Central Africa and helped to popularize the work of Livingstone. In this he pointed out the possibility of trade with East and Central Africa and exposed the need for more evangelical work. This gave an impetus to trading companies and religious orders. The former therefore came to Africa for commercial reasons and the latter came to spread the word of God among the heathen. For these reasons Africa was partitioned at the Conference of Berlin in 1885. The partitioning countries included such European countries as Belgium, Britain, France, Germany, and Portugal. The leading figure behind the conference was King Leopold II of the Belgians. These countries divided Africa among themselves for the main purpose of fighting the slave trade in these areas under their sphere of influence. And to this task they devoted a lot of their energy in the years to come.[1]

In order, therefore, to understand what happened during the reign of Kabalega, it is necessary to understand, first of all, developments which were taking place in other parts of Africa. Some of these events were known to Kabalega and Muteesa I of Buganda through the use of spies who operated far away in other parts of Africa. But a lot of information still remained unknown to them.

Egyptians, Mahdists, Nubians, and East Africa

In 1827 [1824] Egypt [under Mehemet Ali] conquered the Sudan and incorporated it as part of Egypt. Since then successive Egyptian governments began to cherish hopes of extending their tentacles further south and as far as Kitara and Buganda. It was the government of Khedive Ismail which sent Baker in 1872 to see the possibilities of annexing these areas to Egypt. Later the Egyptian government sent Gordon [who was the Governor of Khartoum—a town built by Mehemet Ali in 1824] into northern Kitara, where he built some forts. Long [1874] and Bellefonds [1875] were also sent on missions to Buganda by the same government. And Emin Pasha, who became governor of Rejaf [Gondokoro], followed afterwards.

The result of this Egyptian colonial and expansionist policy was the Madhist revolt in 1881. The Sudanese Muslims revolted against their Egyptian overlords and by 1885 had sacked the Sudanese capital of Khartoum; and Gordon himself was murdered by the Madhists. Emin Pasha, too, the governor of Rejaf was forced by the Madhists to retreat southwards into Wadelai and Pakwach, where he built stations. He had with him an army of about two thousand, made up of Egyptians, people of Arab-African parentage [the descendants of the African slaves who had been captured by the Arab slave traders], people from Rejaf country [who formed the majority of these soldiers], and Nubians.[2] In addition to these soldiers Emin Pasha had about 1,500 servants, women and children who, like their overlords, were Muslims. They were very cruel in their treatment of the inhabitants of the areas through which they passed. And this was particularly so when they were not under the strict surveillance of those Europeans who were not only against the slave trade but also against the ill treatment of Africans in general. For four years Emin Pasha was besieged by the Mahdists at Wadelai.

Early European Travelers and Slave Traders

It was during the reigns of [Kamurasi] and Kabalega that most of the great European explorers came to Africa. These included Livingstone, Speke, Stanley, and Baker. They discovered many parts of Africa which were still unknown to Europe. They discovered also that Africa possessed certain valuable products which would prove very beneficial to the external trade of their countries. In the course of their journeys through Africa, these Europeans obtained, too, firsthand information about the horrors caused by the slave traders. But they could not fight this evil trade on their own because it was carried on on an extensive scale, because the areas it covered were too large to control, and because the slave traders themselves were too strong and too numerous for them. The East African slave trade was carried on primarily by people from Turkey, Egypt, and other Arab countries, and they were assisted by some Africans themselves. Slaves were captured from Tanganyika [Tanzania]—especially from Tabora—Nyasa, the Congo, and Northern Uganda. Their main area of operation extended from the Sudan to Lango country. The nearest big trading stations to Kitara were those at Khartoum and Gondokoro [Rejaf]. They had about three thousand armed soldiers made up of Turks, Egyptians, Arabs, and Africans from areas near Khartoum and Gondokoro. Many of the Africans were captured slaves. From these bases they used to conduct regular raids inland. And their booty included cattle, women, and children, who were sold in the slave markets of Arabia, Turkey, and Egypt, usually in exchange for ivory. But many innocent people also lost their lives during the slave wars. In a word, these slave traders were very inhuman and used to force the inhabitants whose land was being devastated to feed the soldiers responsible for such actions.

The slave traders operating in Acholi and Lango established their stations at Fatiko [near Gulu], Faloro, and Debono [north of Gulu], Foweira and Pakwach and so forth. And they received the blessing and encouragement of the Khedive's regime in Egypt and the Sudan, which profited from this trade. And because of the horrors caused by these slavers, many Langi and Acholi moved their homes to Chope because it was only by the end of Kamurasi's reign that these slavers became a problem in Kitara.

Sir Samuel Baker, Gordon, and Emin Pasha did their best to suppress this trade, while the Belgians, Germans, and other Europeans also tried to do the same. Cardinal Lavigerie, for example, worked hard to arouse the conscience of European nations against this evil and inhuman trade. He toured many European capitals—among which were Brussels, Paris, Berlin, London, and Rome—and gave lectures on the evils of the slave trade. Consequently, a Slave Trade Conference [the sequel to the Berlin West African Conference, 1884–85] was held in Brussels in 1889 [1890], the purpose of which was to try and abolish the slave trade in the whole world and in

Africa particularly. The participating countries agreed on the establishment of an international army dedicated to the suppression of the trade. These soldiers were sent to the Congo in 1890, to Zanzibar in 1891, and then to Central Africa—Bukumbi and Zambezi—between 1892 and 1893.

We shall now say a few more words about those Europeans who passed through Kitara in the reign of Kabalega. There were a good number of them. This is understandable because, at this time, East Africa had become known to these explorers and because the nations of Europe wanted to partition it.

The first European to visit Kitara during Kabalega's reign was Sir Samuel Baker. That was in 1872. But because of the significance of his relations with Kabalega, we shall say no more about him at this stage but shall devote a whole section to him later on.

Suffice it to say, here and now, that when Baker was driven from Masindi he retreated to Northern Uganda, from where he returned to the Sudan. In 1874, he was succeeded by Gordon Pasha as Governor of Khartoum. Gordon continued the fight against the slave trade both in the Sudan and in Northern Uganda and, like Baker, worked to annex Kitara and Buganda to the Egyptian Empire.

In 1874, he sent Colonel Long [an American] on a mission to Kabaka Muteesa of Buganda for the purpose of establishing amicable relations between the two rulers. In the course of this mission, Long became the first white man to discover Lake Kyoga. On his way back to the Sudan he passed through Buruli [in Kitara]. But here he was attacked by Kabalega's forces because he had not obtained the king's permission before trespassing on his territory.

In 1875 Gordon sent a Frenchman called Linant de Bellefonds [Abdul Aziz Bey] with a few Egyptian soldiers to take presents to Kabaka Muteesa of Buganda. And meanwhile, Stanley had already arrived at Muteesa's court. When Stanley met the Frenchman he gave him a letter he had written to England in which he asked for missionaries to be sent to Buganda. Mr. Bellefonds was killed with his soldiers by the Sudanese on his way back to Khartoum. He managed, however, to preserve Stanley's letter by hiding it in one of his shoes. The letter was eventually discovered and sent to England.

In January 1876, Gordon Pasha himself arrived at Buruli

and built a fort at Mruli [Masindi Fort] and another one at Karakaba near the Nile. He left these forts in charge of his Egyptian commander, Nuehr Aga, with 160 soldiers. They were to proceed to Buganda with instructions to build another station at a suitable site near Lake Victoria. But Muteesa would not allow them to come to Buganda and build a station. Gordon therefore came back to Buruli in August and moved his soldiers to Pajao and Bugungu, where he built stations for the purpose of guarding the road from the Sudan to Lake Albert and to Buganda.

In 1876, Stanley, coming from Buganda, passed through the south of Kitara with the intention of reaching Lake Albert. He was marching with an army of more than a thousand soldiers made available to him by Muteesa. They passed through Bwera and reached Lake George. At this point, Kabalega would not let them proceed any farther because he hated the idea of having so many Baganda soldiers marching through his territory and laying it to waste. Kabalega therefore sent Stanley the following message: "If I let you pass, I will not allow you to go back." This message frightened the Baganda soldiers and they refused to go any farther with Stanley. Stanley consequently returned to Buddu [Bwera] and proceeded on to Karagwe.

Other Europeans were also sent over by Gordon to survey the land and lakes of Kitara. In 1876 Gessi Pasha [an Italian] rounded Lake Albert. After him came Sprout Bey, who traveled as far as Fatiko, Mruli, and Bugungu before going back to the Sudan due to illness. And Sprout Bey was followed by Mason Bey, who, like Gessi, surveyed Lake Albert.

Emin Pasha, 1877

One of the most prominent white men who visited Kitara in the time of Kabalega was Emin Pasha. He had also been sent over by Gordon to settle the disputes between Kabalega and Baker—disputes which had led to the battle of Masindi [1872] as we shall see.

Emin Pasha wrote of Kabalega thus:

> When I went to visit Omukama Chwa Kabalega, I found him dressed in a beautiful bark-cloth which covered all his body up to the chest. Another piece of bark-cloth was used as a sash. He had a beautiful head, shaven

with two marks as the custom of the Banyoro demanded. Four of his lower jaw-bone teeth had been removed as the custom also was. His upper teeth were slightly longer than the rest and very white. He had a beautiful necklace made of one big bead. He had very strong arms with two bangles around them. He had small clean hands— the smallness of the hands being accounted for because of his Kihuma [Hima] blood. I was satisfied with his ways and with all things around him. But one thing must be admitted: his face was frightening (by no means because of ugliness). He was well versed in the Arabic language.

All the time I stayed with him I never heard him say one bad word or exhibit any crude mannerisms except that of spitting on the floor now and then. But all the same, the floor was cleaned as soon as he had spat on it. Omukama Chwa was very glad to see visitors and talked and laughed freely with them. Unlike other kings, he was not capricious.

I am convinced that Kabalega had no habit of begging. On the contrary he was very generous and used to send me food every day. Every time I visited him, I found him to be a kind and understanding man. I came to realize his kindness mostly through the troubles caused by my soldiers. Though I had warned them not to do any harm to Kabalega and his people while in Bunyoro, these soldiers went on to plunder and kill many of the king's people. Their behaviour was due to bad leadership. They were led by foolish and evil commanders who were jealous of one another and so went on to do what I had forbidden them to do. When the king came to learn of this, he sent his man, Bitagurwa, to tell me that he was very angry with me. However, this did not destroy our friendship.

On 5 October, I visited the king and spent there a long time talking about what happened during Baker's stay in Bunyoro. I was surprised to hear information which was contrary to that which appeared in *Ismailia*.

There was a meeting on 15 October 1877 with the king and the work I had come to execute was well done and finished. I cannot cease to talk about my friendship with Kabalega—a friendship which was not destroyed

even by one bad word. I will always cherish the days
I spent with him.[3]

Emin Pasha came back to Kitara in 1879 and went to
Pawiri [Mutunda] and then to Fatiko [near Gulu], where
Gordon had built bases from where he continued to fight
against the slave trade. We shall now deal with Sir Samuel
Baker.

Kabalega and Baker: Baligota Isansa, Masindi, 1872

We have delayed our treatment of Baker for the reason
stated above. There is little doubt that the reasons which
caused the break in the friendship between Kabalega and
Baker should be of interest to many people. It is proposed in
this section to record a few facts which are undeniable.

For some time, two Arab slave traders, Sulemani and
Eddriss, had been operating in Bukidi country near Gulu.
They had many people working for them in this horrible
traffic in human beings. Even before Baker came to Kitara
these people had already acquired a rotten reputation for
which they were hated.

By 1871 Muleju [the bearded one], Sir Samuel Baker, had
arrived in Gondokoro [Rejaf] from Khartoum. Later he moved
to the borders of Kitara, where he established stations at
Fatiko and Foweira on behalf of the government of Egypt
for the expressed purpose of fighting the slave traders. Now,
when eventually these slave stations were closed, the hated
slave traders, Sulemani and Eddriss, with about sixty of their
soldiers, were absorbed into the Egyptian soldiers led by
Baker. The new recruits were regarded as irregulars, and
these were among the soldiers Baker led into Kitara. It was
the activities of these slave traders in Baker's army that caused
the first open breach between Kabalega and Baker.

When Baker reached Kitara on 5 April 1872, all his two
hundred porters deserted him because of the ill treatment
meted out to them by these slavers, now turned soldiers.
Baker therefore tried to find replacements by sending Abdul
Kader, a captain in his army, back to Payira to get other
porters. But his mission was unsuccessful because the Ganyi
[Acholi] people ran away on seeing Abdul Kader. The captain
therefore captured Kabalega's chiefs Katikara and Matosa,
as well as some others, tied them with ropes, and brought

them to Baker at Kisuna. But Ruhonko, son of Bukya, and
Saza Chief of Bugangaizi, eluded capture. The captured
chiefs were, however, released by Baker.

When Baker arrived in Kitara he had also about two hun-
dred soldiers with him. He was met by Kabalega's chiefs.
These are their names: Rukara s/o Itegeira, Kwanga s/o
Byamaka, Matosa, and Pitya.

On 25 April, Baker arrived at Masindi. The following day
he met the king, whose palace was situated where the tobacco factory exists today. And Baker and his soldiers built
their camps close to the palace in an area covering forty acres.
This is the area where the Uganda Railway Offices exist today. Baker explained to Kabalega that he was the representative of the king of Egypt. He also drew the king's attention to
the evils caused by the slave trade and slave traders. He
restored to the king the slaves he had managed to free from
Abboud, the Arab slave trader, while he [Baker] was on his
way to Kitara. At this time [1872] Kabalega was a young
king in his early twenties and was therefore inexperienced
and had in fact not yet completed the long-drawn ceremonies
connected with the kingship.

We find many errors in Baker's account of Kitara because
he was not well acquainted with the ways and customs of
the people. But through the reports of Kabalega's ambassador
in Egypt, a man called Kitwe Omuporopyo, the people of
Kitara had come to know the character of Baker very well.
Moreover, Kabalega used to send representatives to Egypt
and had therefore become well informed about Baker and his
intentions for coming to his country.

On 29 April 1872, Baker started erecting his government
headquarters in Masindi in apparent preparation to annex
Kitara to Egypt. He chose Chief Mbogo as his interpreter
because of his fluency in Arabic. And the people of Kitara
were hurt by Baker's presumption and impertinence. Moreover, they resented the fact that Baker appeared determined
to achieve his aims by force and not through treaties made
between him and Kabalega. Nor did he bother to seek the
advice of Kabalega and his chiefs, or to explain his action.

Eventually, on 14 May 1872, Baker publicly annexed Kitara
to Egypt. And for legalistic and propagandist purposes, he
conducted the whole thing ceremoniously and in style. Puzzled
by Baker's actions, Kabalega made him a present of twelve

goats to entertain his people. *Byamutago akugizire ata* [anyway, what could he have done at this stage]!

Meanwhile Baker had been carrying on an illegal trade in ivory and was known to be cheating his customers. Previously, the king had been the sole dealer in ivory because he did not want his subjects to be cheated by crafty foreigners. It was decreed therefore that everyone should sell his ivories to the king, who, in turn, sold them to the foreigners. In this way, Kabalega maintained a monopoly over the ivory trade and thus prevented his subjects from being cheated. But now Baker was buying and selling ivory without the king's consent. And, on his part, Baker resented Kabalega's monopoly of the ivory trade because he saw the king as a barrier which prevented him from cheating the people.

It must also be admitted that Baker praised the efficiency and effectiveness of Kabalega's system of government. One day, on 31 May 1872, four of Baker's soldiers had gone out to attend a dance when they heard the sound of drums coming furiously from the king's palace. They also noticed that people had gathered around the palace in no time. As soon as Baker heard this news he summoned his soldiers and ordered them to surround the palace. He then marched into the midst of the crowd, but Chiefs Ruhonko, Katikara, and Matosa assured him that nothing serious had happened, that everything was all right, and that he had no cause to be afraid. But Baker ignored them and made a grave mistake by ordering his six hundred men to sit down, an order which was obeyed. Now, this was a contemptuous thing to do in the customs of Kitara. And yet Kabalega sent him many presents as a sign of goodwill and assurance of peaceful relations. This occasion left Baker wondering at the amazing obedience displayed by the king's subjects. He was particularly impressed with the system of administration which would make it possible for thousands of people to assemble in no time on hearing the military drum [*Kaijuire*].

Another cause of the disruption in the good relations between Kabalega and Baker was the latter's action in forcing the chiefs to feed his soldiers every day. This is particularly important when it is remembered that these very soldiers were ill-treating the king's subjects. On 7 June Baker sent Abdul Kader and Mounsuru to the king to force him to send food to his soldiers. But there was no food available to send to them. Chief Matosa, however, gave them five pots of beer and promised to send millet afterwards. But Baker refused to accept the beer and sent the pots back to the chief. In the evening Matosa sent him seven pots of beer and two bundles of millet and promised to send more millet later on. Baker distributed the beer among his soldiers, who became sick after they had drunk it. We do not know what really happened. Perhaps the beer had been kept for too long and had gone bad as a result; or perhaps somebody had maliciously put poison in it, wishing thereby to bring misunderstanding between Baker and Kabalega. Baker gave his soldiers medicine to make them vomit; and he also treated in the same way Chief Mbogo, who had also drunk the beer.

On 8 June Baker seized Mbogo, his interpreter, and another chief, and tied them together. He dispatched a message to Matosa asking him to come and see for himself what his beer had done to his soldiers. Afterwards Baker marched into Matosa's house accompanied by a soldier. They arrived at the house at about 6 A.M., when Matosa's household were just getting out of bed. A quarrel ensued between the two parties, whereby one of Baker's soldiers—a Sudanese—was wounded with an *ekisasi* [a door frame!]. This incident gave Baker an opportunity to force a battle. He ordered that the trumpet of war be blown. A great battle resulted, during which Sergeant Mounsou was killed. But Baker succeeded in burning the king's palace to the ground.

Kabalega escaped to Kibwona. In the evening, a certain man called Katikara approached within three hundred yards of Baker's troops and shouted:

> Omukama Chwa II Kabalega is free of any blame. He has done no wrong. The beer in question was not sent by him but came from Matosa. However, Matosa has run away. But we shall do our best to capture him, and when we do so, we shall hand him over to you.

Baker did not appear to have been impressed by these words. He still kept Chief Mbogo prisoner and later executed him.

On 9 June Kabalega sent another message to Baker, assuring him of his innocence in connection with the beer incident and suggested that the guilt perhaps lay with Matosa. He also sent him presents to assuage his anger. But on 11 June Kabalega's subjects, fed up with the way they had been treated by Baker's soldiers, took the law into their own hands

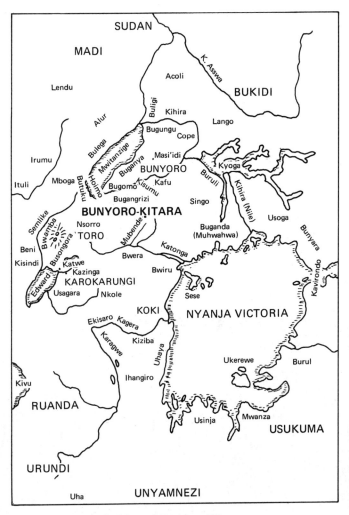

1. Map of Bunyoro-Kitara

2. Omukama Chwa II Kabalega

3. From *In Darkest Africa,* H. M. Stanley

4. Omukama Daudi Kyebambe Kasagama, M.B.E.

5. Mwanga II

6. Omukama Duhaga II Andrea Bisereko

7. Omukama Winyi IV

8. J. W. Nyakatura

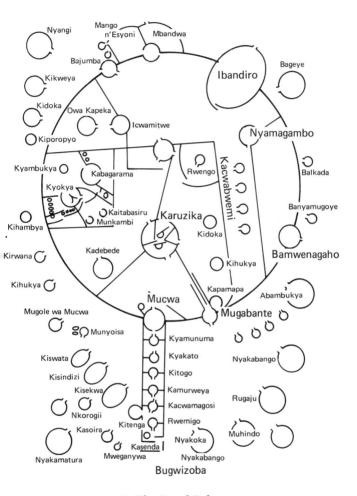

9. The Royal Palace

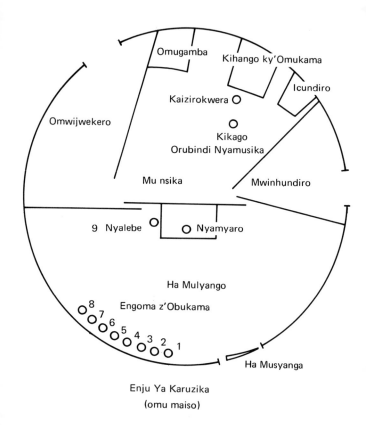

10. Battle Plan

11. Sir Captain H. H. Daudi Chwa, K.C.M.G.

12. Omukama Rukidi III George Kamurasi (Lieutenant)

13. Omugabe Kahaya II, Edward Sulemani, M.B.E.

14. Charles G. Rutahaba Gasiyonga II

and burnt down these soldiers' houses. This was done without
the knowledge of the king. But on 13 June fighting broke out
again and Kabalega was forced to retreat to Bulyango. And
Baker's soldiers burnt down the houses of the common people
who lived near the palace and around the Kihande hill area.
But Kabalega's soldiers regrouped and counterattacked on the
fourteenth. And this time Baker, hard pressed, gave up the
fighting and managed to retreat to Chope.

From here Baker crossed the Nile near Ruyonga's Island
and proceeded to Fatiko, where he built a military station
garrisoned by Egyptian soldiers before returning to the Sudan.
In the meantime, Kabalega's soldiers were waiting in readiness at Masindi to meet Baker's counterattack. But when
nothing happened after two days, some brave soldiers forced
their way into the enemy's camps but found all of them deserted. It was from this incident that the following proverb
was born: *"Ekya Muleju Baligota Isansa* [Those who want
to fight Baker will fight grass]."[4]

CHAPTER 3

Internal Developments

Wars of Tooro and Busongora

It was when Kabalega had his capital at Kibwona that he
killed off the rival Biito who had rebelled and wanted to seize
the throne from him. From Kibwona he moved his capital to
Bulyango, from where he sent an army to kill Butuku. He
lived in this place for three years. Then he moved his capital
to Mparo, from where he sent Matebere, son of Ndyaki, on a
raiding expedition into Bukonjo country. He brought back
many cattle. From Mparo also he attacked the Babiito—
Kabirere and Mukarusa—of Tooro and some other Babiito,
who were all captured, brought before Kabalega, and executed.

After some time had passed, another prince of Tooro called
Nyamuyonjo rebelled against Kabalega. Then Kabalega sent

Kikukuule to deal with him. Kikukuule suppressed the rebel prince and the whole of Tooro was restored to the dominion of Kitara. That was in 1876. The army sent against Nyamuyonjo was so big that on its march to Tooro the soldiers killed 5 elephants, 30 buffaloes, 2 lions, and 5 hyenas. The defeat of Nyamuyonjo saw the end of Tooro independence. Tooro had been in rebel hands for forty-six years, for it was about 1830, during the reign of Kyebambe III Nyamutukura, that Kaboyo established Tooro as an independent kingdom. But from 1876 to 14 August 1891, when Captain Lugard restored the kingdom of Tooro, that country remained part of Kitara.

After suppressing Tooro, Kabalega sent Ireeta to lead an expedition into Busongora—the war of Makoro. Busongora was also reconquered and restored to Kitara. Ireeta continued his advance and reconquered Bwamba and Mboga and annexed them all to Kitara. Kabalega lived in his new capital of Mparo for a long time and it was from here that he reconquered Tooro, Busongora, Bulega, Bukonjo, Bwamba, Bubira, and Mboga.

A Tree called Omukewo

After a short period the king gave orders that the *Omukewo* tree should be cut down and brought to him. This tree formed part of the royal custom and used to be brought to the king by a man called Katigo of the Bahinda clan. Before this tree was cut down it was customary that a sacrifice of a baby girl was offered to the lake by throwing the baby into it. Besides this sacrifice nine other people were killed at the spot where the tree was to be cut down. Therefore the night before this tree was to be cut down a message was sent to Kabalega saying: "We have cut down the Omukewo tree." Thereupon the king ordered his men to capture many people from his capital and from other parts of the country. He also dispatched Busansamura to another part of his kingdom called Nseka to capture a certain animal known as *Rujwiga mukama we bisoro* [Rujwiga, the king of animals]. From here we derived the proverb which says: "Whatever is called Rujwiga is feared by a lion." This animal is reputed to have many different marks on its body, which contains the hair of every animal. Its feet resembled those of a small child but it could kill any animal, including an elephant. But it is very difficult to see these Rujwiga because they live in caves; and if anyone by chance manages to see any of them, he should not tell anyone about it.

Now this animal, Rujwiga, was to be brought to Kabalega before the Omukewo tree. In the meantime the tree remained in the capital for nine months, during which period many people were killed. Tradition records that Kabalega was disgusted with the whole process because it caused the death of his people. "If it was not for my elders [ancestors] who carried out this custom," he was reported to have said, "this should not be done again." Thereupon he ordered that the tree be taken to Buruli to a man called Ndyabike. But here too many people were killed. It is very difficult to try to explain everything here because there is a lot of information connected with the Omukewo tree.

The Extent of Kitara

Now let us see the extent of the territory comprised in Kitara during the reign of Kabalega and before the British annexed some parts of it to neighboring countries. The information on which my account of the saza chiefs, their sazas, their clans, and their villages is based is the account given to me by the Saza Chief H. Karubanga, Kimbugwe, M.B.E.[1] It was in the saza of Bugahya that Kabalega built his capital at a place called Mparo near Hoima. From here the king controlled all the sazas from Lake Kyoga to the border of Busoga—a region called Bunyara [now Bugerere]—and as far as to beyond Lake Edward to the west.

Below are the saza chiefs, their clans and their villages:

1. *Bugahya County*—was ruled by Nyakamatura, son of Nyakatura, who built his headquarters at Kihaguzi on the hill called Kabyerya. He was of the Bamoli clan. His totem was *Engabi*. His saza or county stretched from Bugoma near Lake Albert to Kasokwa in Budongo. He was a native of Kihaguzi, Bugahya.

2. *Busindi County*—was ruled by Bikamba, son of Kabale. His capital was at Kibwona in Kibaiko village. He belonged to the Muranzi clan—[Ow'ekkobe in Buganda]. This county stretched from Kasokwa Ntoma to Nyabuzana and the river Kafo. He was born in Butengesa Rugonjo.

3. *Bugungu or Kicwante County*—was ruled by Mwanga, son

of Kagwa. His capital was at Kinyambeho in Bugungu. He
was of the Bachwa clan, and his totem was *Engabi*. This
county stretched from Lake Albert and Pajao to the hill called
Nyabuzana. He was a Mugungu [born in Bugungu].

4. *Chope County*—was ruled by Kihukya Katongole Rukidi.
It stretched from Lake Albert, Pajao on the river Nile, to
Nyabuzana and separated Chope from Kibanda, Kisongora.
His capital was at Panyadoli. He belonged to the Muchwa
clan and his totem was *Engabi*.

5. *Kibanda Chope County*—was ruled by Masura, son of
Materu. His capital was in the village called Koki. The county
stretched from the river Titi to Lake Pawiri [Victoria Nile]
on the border with Kihukya. He was of the Munyonza clan
and his totem was a bird. He came from Mwenge.

6. *Buruli County*—This county was taken by Buganda. It
was ruled by Kadyebe, son of Bantama, of the Mugonya clan
and his totem was a mushroom. The county was bordered by
the river Kafo, Lake Kyoga, and the river Kitoga and extended to the Bugerere border, near the county of Kangaho
[Bulemezi], in Buganda, and to the river Serwizi near the
Butengesa border. He was from Buruli.

7. *Bunyara or Bugerere County*—The saza chief was Mu-
tenga, son of Ikwambu. His headquarters were at Ibale, also
called Ntenjeru. The county stretched from the Nile to Busoga
and to the Buganda border. It also went as far as the Sekiboobo's saza of Kyagwe in Buganda and on to Lake Kyoga.
He was of the Babiito clan, a grandson of Omukama Olimi I.
He was born in Bunyara. His totem was the bushbuck.

8. *Rugonjo, Butengesa County*—was ruled by Mutengesa son
of Ololo. His capital was at Kicucu, Rugonjo. The county divided the river Rugogo and river Kafo and stretched as far
as Ssingo and Bulemezi in Buganda. It also stretched to Ki-
kule, Kikonda, near the river Mongo in Bugangaizi. He was a
Mubiito, a grandson of Omukama Winyi II. He came from
Rugonjo and his totem was the bushbuck.

9. *Bugangaizi County*—was ruled by Kikukuule, the son of
Runego. He had his capital at Kasaka, Bukumi, on the spot
where now stands the Catholic mission. He ruled from
Wesigire Kigoma to Nyabakazi on the Ssingo border and as
far as to Mubende hill where Nyakahumakati, King Ndahura's

wife who had guarded the capital [of Ndahura] lived. This *omugo* belonged to the Musazima clan. Her totem was *Entimba*. Bugangaizi County was also bounded by the river Muzizi, Nyakabimba, Kyaka, the river Nguse, Buyaga, and Kabale Kafo up to Bugahya. Kikukuule was of the Mwiruntu clan and was a native of Bugangaizi. His totem was the elephant.

10. *Buyaga County*—was ruled by Rusebe, son of Rukumba Rukirabanyoro a grandson of Omukama Kyebambe III Nyamutukura. His capital was at Nkeirwe, Pacwa. It stretched from the river Nguse and the river Muzizi to the south of Lake Albert.

11. *Nyakabimba County*—ruled by Mugema the son of Zigijja of the Babopi clan. His capital was at Bucubya. His job was to look after the king, guard the royal tombs of Kitara and to be head of the Babiito clan [Okwiri]. His county was bordered by Mubende, Kyaka, Mwenge, and Buyaga. He belonged to the Mubopi clan of the lion totem. He was also a native of Nyakabimba. This was a hereditary county from the time of Omukama Ndahura of the Bachwezi dynasty. It was Ndahura who gave it to Mugema's grandfather, Rubumbi, the man who had rescued him when he had been thrown into the river as a child.

12. *Kyaka County*—was ruled by Ntamara, the son of Nyakabwa. His capital was at Karwenyi. His area stretched from Bwiru Katonga to Nkore and Mwenge and Nyakabimba. He belonged to the Banyonza clan of the bird [*enyonyi*] totem. He was from Mwenge. He belonged to the same clan as the Queen Mother [official mother of the king].

13. *Mwenge County*—was ruled by Mugarra, son of Kabwijamu. His capital was at Bugaki in Mwenge. His boundaries were the river Muzizi, the river Semliki, Butuku, near Lake Albert, and Isigome near Kibale. Mugarra belonged to the Banyonza clan. He was a native of Mwenge and was also a clan relative of the Queen Mother.

14. *Tooro County*—was ruled by Ruburwa, son of Mirindi. His capital was at Kamengo in Tooro—a place called Kibimba. The county stretched as far as the river Semliki, Busongora, Bwamba, and Mwenge. Ruburwa was a native of Mwenge and belonged to the Banyonza clan, the Queen Mother's clan. He was given Tooro after it had been reconquered.

15. *Kitagweta [Kitagwenda] County*²—was ruled by Bulemu, son of Rwigi. His capital was at Kyanyamburara. It stretched from Nkore to Kyaka. He was of the Babiito clan, a grandson of Omukama Isansa. He was a native of Kitagwenda.

16. *Busongora Makara County*—situated on the north of the river Semliki, and the Congo, it was ruled by Kagambire, the son of Kajura Rujumba. His capital was at Kanamba. He belonged to the Balisa clan and was a native of Kibanda in Chope. His totem was a bird [*enyonyi*].

17. *Busongora Munuka County*—situated on the south, was ruled by Rukara, the son of Rwamagigi. His capital was at Katwe near the salt mines of the lake [Katwe] where King Kabalega's boats were stationed. They are still there today. Rukara was a native of Busindi [Masindi side] and belonged to the Baranzi clan of the *Kkobe* totem.

18. *Rwamba County*—was ruled by Rukara, the son of Itegeiraha. His capital was at Biranga. He belonged to the Bachwa clan of the bushbuck totem, and was a native of Kibanda in Chope. It was in his palace that Yosia W. Karukara was born in 1887.³

19. *Mboga County*—situated to the north of Tooro, near the Belgian Congo border, was ruled by Ireeta, the son of Byangombe. He belonged to the Basaigi clan. His capital was at Kayera in Butuku. He originally came from Nkore and had been captured during the time of Kabalega's wars against Kabigumire [his rival brother]. Ireeta was second in importance after Rwabudongo [among Kabalega's generals]. He was the general of the Ekirwana division of the Abarusura and the subsections of the army under his command were: the *Ekiporopyo, Ekikweya, Ekibangya,* and *Ekikube* and others. Ireeta was given the charge of guarding the Congo-Bulega border and Mboga. The defense of Mboga was divided between him and Rwabudongo so that each defended half of it. Ireeta was usually sent out to lead many wars because he was a very brave man. He was the man encountered by Kabaka Mwanga II when he fled from Buganda to Kitara. Ireeta had been sent to Biso by the king to meet Mwanga II. He died in 1906.

20. *Buzimba County*—was ruled by Nduru, son of Nyakairu. He was of the Balisa clan. His capital was at Kanyamburara. This county became part of Nkore from 1900.⁴

21. *Buhweju County*—was ruled by Ndibalema of the Balisa clan. It was taken by Nkore in 1900.[5] It used to be hereditary because it belonged to the people of the clan of the Queen Mother of Omukama Winyi Rubagiramasega.

All these counties belonged to Kitara and besides these were areas outside the kingdom which were her territories. These included Bulega [Congo], Ganyi [Acholi], Bukidi [Lango]. All these were part of Kitara and were ruled by Omukama Kabalega.[6]

Before we go on to talk about other things, let us explain how some of these sazas were lost from the time of Kabalega's capture and now.

1. Five counties—the first mentioned—that is, Bugahya, Busindi, Bugungu, Chope, and Buruli[7] were the only ones that Kitara retained. Bugahya was divided into two counties so that the number of the counties was raised to six. This was all that was left of the empire of Kitara [which now came to be known as Bunyoro, strictly speaking].

2. Six counties, namely, Buruli, Bugerere [Bunyara], Rugonjo, Bugangaizi, and Buyaga were given to Buganda in 1900.

3. Seven counties, namely, Nyakabimba, Kyaka, Mwenge, Tooro, Kitagweta [Kitagwenda], Busongora [proper], and Bwamba later became the kingdom of Tooro, which was restored by Captain Lugard on 14 August 1891, when he restored Daudi Kasagama Kyebambe as Omukama of Tooro. Omukama Kabalega was still alive at this time and still king—and was living at his capital of Kinogozi, Kabale.

4. Two counties, namely Busongora Makara, north of the river Semliki near the Congo, and Mboga were taken by the Belgian Congo [1908]. Besides these two, Bulega was also given to the Belgian Congo [1908].

5. Two counties, Buzimba and Buhweju, were restored to Nkore. That was how Kitara lost its territories and let us now go back to the reign of Omukama Kabalega.

The Colonies of Kitara

The king held councils in order to keep his power and the country intact and to settle disputes. He was ruler of all the clans in the country. Kitara was a very big country and had many territories which were populated with people.

Teso, Kahweri—There was a market here where the king's boats as well as other things were sold. Market dues were also collected and the proceeds came to Kitara. The chief market master was a man called Kamukokoma Katenyi. There were other lesser market masters in Teso. Katenyi belonged to the Bahinda clan. The profits accruing from these markets in Teso formed part of the Kitara state revenue. Teso had clan heads for whom Kabalega acted as an arbitrator in their quarrels and disputes. The people of Teso sent cattle and goats to Kitara in exchange for salt, iron hoes, and other things.

Busoga, Kamuli, and Budyope—These were territories or colonies of Kitara and were ruled by Prince Igabura, the grandson of Omukama Olimi I. When a prince was born, he would be taken to the Omukama's palace in Kitara, where he was brought up. When the ruler of the county [Busoga] died, the prince would leave the palace in Kitara to come over and succeed him. During the time of Kabalega, Prince Nyaika had been taken to Kabalega's palace, where he grew up. Nyaika was later expelled and Yosia Nadyope [Nadiope], the father of Kajumbura, was put in his place. Busoga was of great importance to Kitara because it had many markets— where the Bakitara could buy bark cloths, goats, and cows. The Basoga bought iron hoes, salt, and other things from Kitara. Kitara was also on friendly terms with Busoga and Kabalega was a judge over them when they had quarrels or disputes.

Lango—There were no chiefs in Lango society. But the Langi had heads of clans. Lango was ruled by Kabalega and they were greatly loved by him [his favorites] and they called him "Nyangatumu," that is to say, "the king of kings." The king would give them wives, salt, iron hoes, bangles, beads, and other things. Whenever war broke out, he would request their assistance to help in fighting against his enemies. These clan heads resided in Bukidi and whenever a dispute arose between them, they would come to the king for settlement. When the father of Ibrahim Olum [Orumu] killed the father of David Odore, for example, it was Kabalega who settled this dispute. The whole of Lango belonged to Kitara. There were amicable relations between Kitara and this territory.

Ganyi [now called Acholi]—Its major chief [Rwot], who resided at Kitgum, was called Owici [Awich]. There were

also other chiefs. Awich ruled over Chwa and Paira [Payira]
near the lake [Victoria Nile]. He was related to the kings of
Kitara. The regalia of chiefship—spears, the chair, and vessels
—all these were sent to him by the King of Kitara. When this
chief died, his successor was appointed by Kabalega and any
such successor must be related to the Babiito of Kitara.

*Madi, Atyaki, Palango, Ogwali, Paira, Muruya, Bokerumu
Oyere, Kori:* all these areas were situated south of the lake
[Victoria Nile]. Their chiefs were Orugwere, Opete, Koki,
and Lagonyi. All of these chiefs were installed by the King of
Kitara. Owici [Awich] and his elder brother once had a quarrel and Kabalega was the one who settled their dispute. He
found the elder brother guilty, punished him, and made Owici
chief.

Aruru [Alur—West Nile]—Here there was Oziri, a Mubiito,
who had his capital at Okuru. Oziri was the grandfather of
Jarawoli, who is now chief of this area. There were other
chiefs, Ole and Tukenda, who ruled north of Bugungu. Other
chiefs included Kakora, a Mubiito, Oketa, Huma, Mburukwa
Mulindwa, Kabale, Rutarurwa II, Mugera Bomera, and
Aliganyira. All these were installed by the king, who not only
settled their disputes but also furnished them with drums and
their stools of office [like the royal chair, but of less im-
portance].

Bukonjo, north of Bwamba—This region was ruled by a Mubiito, the grandson of Murro, himself also a Mubiito. His name
was Mudungu.

The Runyoro [Rukitara] Language—was something to be
proud of and was important in the areas from Bunyara
[Bugerere] to Kiziba and Rwanda. The Banyarwanda and
Banyankore used to speak the Runyoro language. It was also
spoken in certain areas in the Congo, the south of Lake Tanganyika, and the Lake Kivu region.

THE DIVISIONS OF THE NATIONAL ARMY
[ABARUSURA] AND THE PROVINCIAL OR
COUNTY ARMIES [OBWESENGEZE]

A national army was created by Omukama Kabalega. It
consisted of brave men whom he named Abarusura. This army

was divided into different divisions. These are their names and their leaders:

1. EKIDOKA—was under Kyamuhangire Ruhimbya, son of Majara.

2. EKIHUKYA—was under Rusongoza, son of Byontabara, and later on under Muhenda Ruhanika, son of Komubigo.

3. EKIPOROPYO—was led by Kajura of the Badoli clan. He was killed during the war with the Baganda, known as the Benga war.

4. EKIGWERA—was under Kabagambe, son of Itera. This was charged with the defense of the Busoga, Bukidi, and Buganda borders.

5. EKIKABYA—was under Rukara, son of Kabaseke.

6. EKIHAMBYA—was under Rwabudongo. He was also the Treasurer during Kabalega's reign. He is the father of Yonasani Wamara, the father of Akio Kamese.

7. EKIBANGYA—This was first under Katalikabu, son of Byamu, and when he was discharged from the army, his battalion was given to Rwansambya.

8. EKIRWANA—was under Saza Chief Ireeta, son of Byangombe. This was charged with the defense of the Congo border.

9. EKIBANJA—was under Saza Chief Kikukuule, son of Runego. It was charged with the defense of the border between Buganda and Bugangaizi. He had also his own county army.

10. EKIBALE—was under Saza Chief Nyakamatura, son of Nyakatura. This division was stationed in the heart of Bunyoro.

11. EKITALYA—was under Kasabe, son of Rujoimoza. It was charged with the defense of Mwenge.

12. EKIKWEYA—was first under Rwamukika but was taken away from him and given to Kiiza, son of Iteka, his chief.

13. EKIHANGURA—was led by Dona Kabejweka [the father of Martin Mukidi].

14. EKITIKYA—was first under Kibego, son of Mucokoco, and then given to Bikanga Kahuzi, son of Nyamugobwa.

15. EKISIGURA—was under Mucokoco, son of Ndinga. These last three [13–15] were subsections of Rwabudongo's *Ekihambya*. There were many other subsections of the first ten [1–10] *ebitongole* of the Abarusura, which were in fact the major divisions of this national army.

Battalions of the Provincial or County Armies (Obwesengeze)

There were other minor armies which belonged to the saza chiefs and the generals of the Abarusura. They were divided into the following battalions:

1. EKITANDA—belonged to Rwabudongo and was led by Tibakunirwa, a Muganda.

2. EKITASA—also belonged to Rwabudongo, and was led by Byendaimira, son of Nkumale.

3. EKIROHOZA—also belonged to Rwabudongo and was led by Mika Fataki, a Musoga.

4. EKIHINDA—also belonged to Rwabudongo, and was led by Sayi, a Nubian.

5. EKITALESA—belonged to Saza Chief Mugarra Ndunga, son of Kabwijamu of the Banyonza clan. There were many others besides these.[8]

The above were the divisions of the Abarusura who defended the kingdom of Kitara and its provinces—such as Bukidi, Ganyi, and Bulega—and suppressed any rebels who revolted against Kabalega. Now, the younger generation may wonder how Kitara lost its prestige, honor, and its extensive areas between 1891 and 1900. But do not forget our proverb which says: "Men are like eagles which fall and then rise again." This is to say that with your hard work, and perseverance, we would not fail to restore our kingdom to its past glory so that the future generation can also visualize its former greatness. Everyone should try to do his best and should not belittle the little things he does for his country, for, as our proverb says: "He who uses the only spear he has, is not a coward."

The Battle of the Kangaho, January 1886

From Mparo, Kabalega moved his capital to Bujumbura, where he remained for about a year. From Bujumbura he moved it once more to Bulera. And it was while he was in this place that an army from Buganda invaded Kitara. This army was led by the Kangaho Kibirango [Saza Chief of Bulemezi]. It arrived in Kitara in January 1886. When Kadoma heard of their advance, he sent a message to Kabalega which read: "The Baganda are advancing with a big army." Thereupon the king planned to wait for the enemy at his capital of Bulera. But his great chiefs advised him against the policy, pointing out the possibility of a Buganda victory, which would inevitably lead to the sacking and plundering of the capital. This, they argued, would be disastrous because it was against the custom of Kitara for the king's capital to be sacked and plundered by the enemy. Indeed, whenever a king moved his capital to another area, his subjects burned down the former palace to make sure that nothing was left behind. This was the practice in times of peace.

So Kabalega accepted their advice and decided to fight the enemy behind the forest of Rwengabi in Bugoma. From Wesigire on the border between Kitara and Buganda, the Ganda army marched for six days before they reached Bugoma. When the king got news that the enemy had reached Bugoma, he was filled with anger and excitement and ordered the war drum to be sounded. Whereupon his army leaders assembled with their men before him. He got hold of his shield and moved about his men uttering words of encouragement. In the evening he ordered his soldiers to go down on one knee in lines and he passed between these lines while conversing with his army leaders and chiefs. He employed this tactic to test the endurance of his army to see if it could match that of the enemy.

At cockcrow, the Ganda beat their military drums and their soldiers took up their positions. The Ganda first attacked the battalions of Saza Chiefs Nyakamatura, Mugema, and Nyakabwa of Kyaka, and were successful. Kabalega's battle strategy was as follows: the armies of the saza chiefs [*Obwesengeze*] were to hold the right and the left flanks while his Abarusura was to hold the center. The Abarusura were drawn up in twelve lines. Shots were exchanged from

both sides and it is said that these shots could be heard in
Mengo, the capital of Buganda. They produced sounds similar
to those of an earthquake. By 11 A.M. the Kitara army had
succeeded in capturing the drum of Kamuswaga, *Kikindo*.
The enemy was defeated and Pokino Tebukoza, a Muganda
chief and one of the army leaders, was wounded. The army
fled the field and the Abarusura pursued them to their camps
and plundered them. By midday there was a lull in the
fighting.

At this juncture, Ireeta and Rwabudongo—Abarusura generals—said to the king:

> Sir, order the vanquished enemy saza chiefs to fetch
> water for us. And you, sir, should give us a lot of meat
> so that we can spend the night here and polish off the
> Baganda in the morning. Now your soldiers are tired and
> fed up with hearing the booming of the guns.

While they were speaking the king was seated on an anthill, his eyes so red as to frighten anyone who looked at him.
And roaring like a lion, he said to his generals: "I don't want
to sleep while the enemy is still in my country. I want the
country to be mine alone. To possess this country the enemy
must kill me first." On hearing these brave words all his soldiers and generals sang his praise:

> Singa Rumenya mahanga, singa rwa Kanyange, Singa
> Rukolimbo Nyantalibwa mugobe, Kahangirize, Kabeho
> ebiro byona . . .
>
> [Honor to the conqueror of all countries, honor to the
> son of Kanyange, honor to you and may you live for
> ever]

He ordered the soldiers to regroup and advance towards
the enemy. And having passed one village, they spotted the
Kangaho marching towards them with many people, who
looked like reeds while their spears and shields looked like
mud walls. The enemy were not drawn in lines of battle but
were coming from all directions at the same time, only leaving
a space between them and the Kangaho, their commander.
On seeing what was going on, the Abarusura, too, abandoned
their own military formation and every *murusura* [soldier]
was ordered to get down on one knee up to the forest.
Kabalega ordered them not to shoot until the enemy had come

within reach, partly because he wanted to fire the first shot. He got hold of his gun, called *Bagwigairebata,* which could fire seventeen shots, and having fired first at the enemy, the battle started. Then the Ganda retreated and it appeared as if they were fleeing, the result being that the Kangaho's army was exposed to attack. Kabalega seized his opportunity and fired three shots at the Kangaho and killed him. But on seeing their leader dead, the Ganda attacked with more fury. Thereupon, Rwabudongo and Ireeta said to the king: "Sir, move away from the front because your people are dying." He moved away with his brothers and was escorted by Rwabudongo into the forest. The Abarusura was now left in the charge of Ireeta and fighting continued until the enemy fled. And as they fled they noticed that some of Kabalega's soldiers had captured the dead body of the Kangaho and a man called Olaka was dragging it by one leg. Whereupon the Ganda started shooting again and managed to rescue the body of their dead leader. This happened at about 6 P.M.

The battle of the Kangaho cost the lives of many people on both sides, although the Ganda suffered by far more losses. Those Ganda who survived the slaughter and returned home invented a song which went like this: "If anyone has not seen guns, let him go to Bulega." And the Bakitara also invented a song, which said: "The little bird which told me of it came from Buruli in the north and told me that Kangaho's body has been eaten by birds."

There were some other important Ganda commanders who were killed in Bunyoro, and these included Muguruma and Mmandwambi, who were killed by Nyamutukura, a commander who was the son of Isagara, and who had fought at Kiragura in Buruli; and Mujabi, who was killed by Kabigumire [while the latter fought with his younger brother, Kabalega, for the throne]. Mujabi died at Kisekura near Kitwara. But the Kangaho died with more honor than any of the others.

Kabalega Removes the Teeth of Some Baganda

When Omukama Kabalega was at his capital of Bwikya [near Hoima] there were among his pages three Baganda boys called Kasajja, Mukasa, and Mututa. One day these boys went to the king's store and lied to the guard at the door, whose name was Tibakunirwa, that they had been ordered by the king to collect certain things from the store. But these boys were thieves who wanted to steal these things and take them back to Buganda. These young scoundrels were admitted into the store and they took away seven rolls of cloth, four rounds of ammunition, etc. When Tibakunirwa discovered what the youths had done, he reported the matter to Rwabudongo who was the Treasurer of the country. Rwabudongo in turn passed on this information to the king, who summoned Bitagurwa and said to him: "My pages have stolen my things. Go after them and capture them. But do not kill or fight them even if they shoot at you. I want you to bring them back to me alive." Bitagurwa went after them, captured them, and brought them before the king, who demanded to know from them the reasons for their sudden departure. Thereupon Kasajja, the oldest of them, replied: "We were going back to our homes in Buganda." Then the king asked them: "Is Buganda better than Kitara?" And Kasajja replied: "No, my lord, Buganda is not better than Kitara." Kabalega forthwith ordered Kasajja's execution because he had dared to answer back the king. The other two were pardoned.

But this incident was to have wider repercussions. Kabalega, worried that foreigners were leaving the country, sought the advice of his counselors as to what should be done to discourage them from doing so. And they advised him: "Sir, pull out their teeth. You should make it a policy that from now on all foreigners who have come to this country for protection and those who have been captured should have their teeth pulled out." Thereupon Kabalega ordered the teeth of the two Baganda pages to be pulled out in front of him. "Now you have become Bakitara," he said to them, "even if you go to Nkore or Buganda." And on that day all the Baganda who resided in the capital had their teeth pulled out. Stones and even hoes were used in this teeth-pulling operation. It was at this time, too, that General Ireeta, who commanded the Ekirwana division of the Abarusura and Gutambaki, leader of the Ekiporopyo battalion, and many others had their teeth pulled out.

Thereafter Kabalega passed a decree that all his subjects should have their teeth pulled out, mainly because the Abarusura had developed the habit of not pulling out their teeth. In the past this was a matter of choice and not of compulsion and there was no law to enforce its practice. Indeed many people had their teeth pulled out in those days through

fear of being laughed at by the public, who were wont to say:
"Let us hang our traps on those who have the lower teeth,"
while others feared to have their lower lips pulled.[9]

The Chope Expedition

Since the reign of Kamurasi, Chope had been a disturbed
area. Kabalega's success against Kabigumire did not equally
achieve the pacification of Chope. Now Prince Komwiswa
had once more declared himself king of that region. Kabalega
therefore sent General Rwabudongo to lead an expedition
against Chope. Rwabudongo confronted the rebel prince at
Kisembe, and after some encounter, defeated him and brought
him before the king with all his belongings. The king did not
put him to death but rather imprisoned him at Kakindo
Bwanya. He was later moved to Kasimbi Buyaga, where he
was put in the charge of Rukinzo. He was moved once more,
to Mpigwa in Bulega, and remained there as prisoner until
the Europeans found him and set him free and later brought
him back to Bunyoro.[10] Komwiswa's young brother, Rujumba,
was sent to Mwenge by the king. Rujumba was the father
of Prince Kosia Labwoni, Saza Chief Kaigo [Bujenje].

Because the princes of Chope were always threatening to
rebel, Kabalega decreed that no Babiito [princes] should be
made saza chiefs in the regions of their origin. He therefore
appointed Katongole Rukidi saza chief of Kihukya [Chope]
and Masura, son of Materu, saza chief of Kibanda [Chope].

CHAPTER 4

Kabalega, Baganda, and Europeans, 1886–92

Casati [1886–88] and the Wakibi Expedition

With the emphatic success of the Mahdist rebellion following the fall of Khartoum in 1885, Emin Pasha found himself
and his men besieged at Wadelai. They were, for all intents
and purposes, prisoners. With Emin were two other Euro-

peans, Junker and Casati. In January 1886 Emin managed
to dispatch Junker to England with the aim in view of emphasizing to the British Government his perilous situation.
And because Emin was friendly with Kabalega, he instructed
Junker to pass through Kitara and proceed to Buganda. On
his way to this destination Junker passed through Kibiro
[northeast of Lake Albert].

Emin also managed to get out [Major] Casati and instructed
him to go to Kitara as well. He was to establish a base there
from where he would forward his letters to and from Buganda. At this time Kabalega was living at Bujwahya in the
gombolola of Kasingo. It was here that Casati met him. Casati
remained in Bujwahya until about June 1886.

It was indeed on 2 June that Casati was brought before
the king, who was glad to see him. At this meeting he explained to the king the purpose of his visit and his orders from
Emin Pasha. Emin had asked Kabalega to do the following
favors for him.

First, to grant him permission to send his letters to and
from Buganda through Kitara. Second, to oblige him by making peace with Mwanga, thus ending the hostilities between
the two monarchs. Casati had wanted to pay tribute to the
king, not knowing that the battle of the Kangaho had ended.
Third, to grant him the right to trade with the Arab traders
in Kitara and Buganda. Fourth, to allow his soldiers and arms
to pass through Kitara. Fifth, to ask the Omugabe Ntare of
Nkore on his behalf to allow him and his soldiers to pass
through Nkore if they could not pass through Buganda. And
sixth, to send a messenger to Wadelai.

Kabalega agreed to allow Emin's letters to pass to and
from Buganda but refused to allow his soldiers and their arms
to pass through Kitara. He would indeed have granted him
this request but he was apprehensive of the possible consequences of allowing numerous foreign soldiers armed with
guns to pass through his territory. He therefore insisted that
he would allow only a handful of soldiers to pass through
his territory at different times. This concession was acceptable
to Emin. In October 1886 Emin requested Kabalega's permission to build two military posts, at Tunguru and Mswa
[Muswa] in Bulega. The king accepted his request and ordered his chiefs in that area to help Emin's soldiers in this
task and supply them with food.

In January 1887 Kabalega, acting on Casati's advice, had

sent Mwanga presents as a peace offering, but by the following February news reached him that Mwanga was planning to attack him. Emin's messenger who carried letters and other things from Buganda to Wadelai was called Mohammed Biri. It was now rumored that this man was a spy and consequently Kabalega began to distrust Emin Pasha.

At the beginning of March the king left Bujwahya and moved his capital to Buhimba [about seven or eight miles from Hoima]. He also ordered the Arab traders to move their stations, finally forcing them to do so in April. It was while he was at Buhimba that the news of Mupina's [Emin Pasha's Anfina] death reached him.[1] He immediately sent the Saza Chief Katongole and later General Rwabudongo to pacify Mupina's stronghold within Chope. This was achieved with little fighting.

In May 1887 Kabalega asked Emin Pasha to remove Casati from Kitara. And by the end of May news reached the capital that the army of Buganda led by Wakibi had reached Bugangaizi. At the beginning of June Kabalega's army left Buhimba and, marching through Mparo, Nyamirima, Budongo, halted at Buruli. Meanwhile Casati, having visited the king at Mparo, retired to Bujwahya in Kasingo.

At the end of June the two armies clashed at Buhimba and Mparo. And on 3 July, Wakibi sent a delegation to Casati in Bujwahya who promised him that he would not only conclude an agreement with him but would also build a station at Kibiro if the Ganda army was successful. Casati was seen passing on a letter to the Ganda envoys to take to Buganda. After two days Kabalega's army counterattacked and forced the Ganda to retreat. The army followed up its success and fought three more engagements at the hill called Musaijamukuru, Muziranduru, and Nguse before the Ganda withdrew to Buganda. By the middle of July, the war had also ended in Bujwahya.

By this time, the king had moved near the Kafo River in Buhemba with the aim in view of intercepting the retreating Baganda army. Afterwards he went to Buruli, where he built his capital at Kiragura [now known as Nyakasongora]. He then sent for Casati, who merely asked permission to build an Egyptian garrison at Kibiro and to occupy the swampy area of Kitara. These requests were not granted, partly because of the large number of men Casati had with him. Moreover,

Kabalega had gained the impression that Casati was a spy acting in league with the Baganda against him. This belief was determined by the following reasons: first, because Casati had sent messengers to Buganda, Wadelai, and Bujwahya; second, because Casati had concluded arrangements with Wakibi affecting matters in his country following the expected Ganda victory; and, third, because Casati had not responded to his summons to move to his new capital.

Meanwhile Casati had written to Stanley and Emin Pasha that there was a wide-spread rumor in Buganda concerning the appearance of a large army from the Congo. The aim of this army was to link up with Emin Pasha by passing through Kitara into Buganda and laying to waste everything in its way. To emphasize the authenticity of this rumor Casati handed over to Kabalega the letters he was sending to Stanley and the others. And on 3 January 1888 a messenger sent from Mboga by General Ireeta [who was also chief of that province] arrived in Bujwahya, where he spent the night before proceeding to Kiragura. Here he brought to the king the news that a number of Europeans, some of them with soldiers dressed like those of Zanzibar, had passed through part of his province—Bulendu [now in the Congo]—on their way to Bulega. The leader of these soldiers was Stanley. Stanley's behavior [i.e., trespassing through the king's province] brought about a lot of ill feeling against Casati as well as against Stanley and his men wherever they passed.

Because of these developments, Kabalega felt that he had had enough. He immediately ordered Nyakamatura, Saza Chief of Bugahya, to "go and expel Casati from the country." He did not wish Casati killed primarily because the people of Kitara were still not convinced that these Europeans were not the Bachwezi of long ago who had come back to recover their throne. He did not therefore wish any of them to be killed in his country. He instructed Nyakamatura to ferry him across the lake in a boat and deposit him in Bulega, following the route they had taken the first time when going back.[2]

It also happened that on 3 January, too, Casati, Mohammed Biri, and their soldiers paid a visit to Nyakamatura. All of them were seized and taken to the saza headquarters, where they were imprisoned for a whole day. All their belongings including Casati's documents were taken away from them. But in the evening they were released and allowed to go back to their camps. Casati and his companions, however, escaped during the night, passing through Parajwoki, Kitana, and reached the hill of Kibiro the next day at noon. Here, to their surprise, they were welcomed by Nyakamatura's men, who were waiting to welcome them. Kagoro, since they were in his area, provided them with lodging. From here they were escorted to Bugungu on the Kihira [river Nile] and suffered greatly during their journey. But at Bugungu they were lucky to find Emin Pasha's boat and they were even luckier to be still alive thanks to the superstition of the king and his subjects.

When Casati reached Mahagi—where Emin Pasha was stationed at this time—a section of his soldiers, some Egyptians and some Sudanese, were planning to mutiny. This action was precipitated by the absolute deterioration in army discipline. Moreover, the African population of this area was fed up with the demands of these foreign soldiers, who forced them to supply them with food and to act as their porters. The result was that there was no love lost between Emin's soldiers and the local inhabitants and their patriotic feelings forced them to follow Kabalega, their king. In February some Bakitara [people of Kitara] were killed by these soldiers while some villages in Bulega were razed to the ground. In May Egyptian and Sudanese soldiers crossed over to Kibiro, Butyabwa [Butiaba], and Bugungu during the night and burnt down many villages and killed many people—including women and children. Kagoro escaped death by fleeing.[3]

Stanley (1888–89)

It was during this period that Stanley visited Kitara for the second time. His mission this time was the relief of the beleaguered Emin Pasha. His march took him through the Congo and he suffered greatly during this journey. And indeed as the message sent to Kabalega had stated, he reached Kasenyi, near Lake Albert, with his soldiers on 13 December 1887. He met Emin Pasha on 29 April 1888 and proceeded to the Ituri forest to collect the porters and soldiers he had left behind there. On 25 May he first set eyes on the Ruwenzori Mountains.

Earlier, on 10 April, Stanley, Emin Pasha,[4] and Casati had set out with their soldiers, who numbered more than a thousand, for Zanzibar. They passed through Bulega and Mboga, and having crossed the Semliki River, circled Mount Ruwenzori. Then they proceeded through Bwamba and Katwe, and having crossed the rivers Rwimi and Nsongi, passed through Bunyampaka. They crossed the river Kagera Kicwamba—also called Nsengezi—and reached Zanzibar through Karagwe.[5]

Kabalega and the Civil War in Buganda (1888–90)

Kabalega left Kiragura and built his headquarters at Kayera. It was here that he received the Baganda chiefs who had fled their country because of Mwanga II's persecution of the Christians and Moslems. They arrived at the king's palace towards the end of 1888. These fugitive Baganda chiefs included: Mark Kironde, who later became the *Kajubi*, Andrew Kiwanuka, who later became the *Omulamuzi* [Chief Judge] of Buganda, Samson Ddamulira, and Asa Nkangali Mukasa. Omukama Kabalega gave them a warm reception, made them his friends, and allowed them to stay with him. He was also friendly towards the Muslim converts and indeed allowed one of his men, Budarahamani, to build a mosque and gather around him those who wished to be converted to the religion of Islam. Within a short period the king received news that the Baganda Muslims and Christians had deposed Mwanga and installed Kiwewa as Kabaka. That was in September 1888.

When Kabalega left Kayera he built his capital at Kicwamba. While he was here messengers arrived with the news that the Muslims had executed a coup against the Christians, and deposed Kiwewa, and had installed Kalema on the throne of Buganda. That was in October 1888. Thereupon Kabalega dispatched Karubanga as an envoy to Buganda to pay his respects to the new king, Kalema. He also sent him presents consisting of four sticks of ivory, salt, and other things.

Then Kabalega turned his attention to Nkore. He sent Bikamba to lead an expedition against that kingdom. But having reached Butiti in Mwenge, Bikamba suddenly became ill. And this illness resulted in his being lame and he remained so until his death in Masindi at the hand of the Nubians. The consequence of this incident was that no serious engagements were fought against the Banyankore and Kabalega's Abarusura just captured a few cows from Nkore and returned home.

Meanwhile Karubanga, the envoy to Buganda, had returned with the news that the Christians had, in their turn, defeated the Muslims, and had deposed Kalema. This was in October 1889. [Kabalega's diplomacy having apparently been miscalculated], he lost his temper and decided to execute all Baganda living in the capital at that time. These Baganda had come with a Muganda called Kakumba. He was a very arrogant man. Kakumba was killed in the presence of Ireeta. But the king spared the lives of those who had fled from Mwanga's cruelty during his persecution of the members of the new religions. Their God [Ruhanga] protected them against Kabalega's wrath! Kakumba met his death in the town of Kabale situated near the small river valley of Kinogozi.

In 1889, Kabalega moved his capital once more, to Kabale Kinogozi. At this time, the deposed Kabaka, Kalema, who was at Kinakulya, sent him a message requesting his assistance because Mwanga's soldiers had deprived him of all his belongings. In response to this request Kabalega sent him many cows for meat and milk and bags of salt. Karubanga had also reported to the king that Kalema's chiefs had expressed a desire to buy Kitara cloth, millet, and chickens in exchange for wives and slaves. This mutual trading arrangement was entered into and there is reason to suppose that the people of Kitara increased in population as a result.

Meanwhile, Kabalega was planning to overthrow the Mwanga regime in Buganda. So after Kalema had spent about five months in Kinakulya, he sent against Buganda a force of three hundred gunmen, and innumerable hordes of spearmen under the leadership of Kabusagwa of the Batonezi clan. Kabusagwa challenged Mwanga's army at Vumba—where the Roman Catholic mission stands today—and a battle was fought. Many shots were fired on both sides and Apolo Kaggwa, the Katikiro [Prime Minister] of Buganda, was wounded in this battle. Nevertheless, Mwanga's army was victorious and Kalema fled the field. When he reached Wesigire on the Buganda-Kitara border—where now stands milestone 92 on the Kampala-Hoima Road—Kalema halted and, turning to his chiefs, said to them:

> Do not follow me into Kitara because you who had elevated me to the kingship have also betrayed me in battle by your cowardice in running away from the enemy. You fled the field and refused to accompany me back to Buganda. How can we all now go together to Kitara?

> Now that you have failed me, let me go alone to my
> father, Kabalega, who will give me a village to rule.

His Muslim supporters were hurt and angry on hearing these
words and therefore swore before him: "By Allah, we shall
conquer Mwanga and his infidels [abakafiri] a second time.
We do not mind if we all lose our lives in this venture." They
spent the night at the border at Wesigire. The next morning
they reorganized themselves in battle formation and marched
back towards Buganda. On the way they were challenged
by Mukwenda [Saza Chief] Wasswa, who was acting as general of the Baganda army in place of Apolo Kaggwa, the
Katikiro, who had been wounded at the battle of Vumba.
This confrontation took place at Kidada, where a serious battle was fought. Kalema's soldiers were victorious this time and
Mwanga's soldiers fled to Makonzi in Kagole's area. Kalema's
soldiers followed up their victory to Mengo, the capital of
the Kabaka of Buganda. Many people died during this war—
November 1889.

    After a short period had elapsed, Kalema sent a message
to Kabalega which said: "We have defeated the enemy. Send
me a chief who will escort me to Buganda to get my throne
back. I have no people available to escort me since they all
went to fight." Thereupon Kabalega selected General Rwabudongo, who belonged to the Bahambya clan, for this task.
Rwabudongo and his Abarusura arrived at Kalema's place at
Kinakulya with great pomp. Kikukuule was his second in
command. The whole country was practically drained of people because they had joined Rwabudongo's expedition in
their thousands. Among them were also many people from
Bukidi. Rwabudongo's followers were so many that it is difficult to give their number. It took them three days to reach
Kalema's camp. They spent the night in that vicinity and appeared before Kalema the following day. Kalema's military
drum—Wanga—was sounded and he addressed them thus:
"Let all the people and those from Bukidi [Abakidi] proceed
along with Kikukuule. I will march behind with Rwabudongo
and his Abarusura." The expeditionary force was arranged
in three rows with Kalema's men occupying the middle position. They carefully attempted to follow the route which
Kato Kimera had taken on his way from Kitara to Buganda,
where he declared himself independent of Kitara. This was
the reason why they passed through Bwinja.

When they reached Buganda they discovered that the victorious Muslims had completed a new palace for Kalema. Kalema once more ascended the throne of Buganda as Kabaka and was given a joyous reception by his supporters. After a short period Mwanga, having grouped his army, counterattacked Kalema and drove him and the occupying force out of the capital, which was then at Nansana. Indeed Mwanga's victorious soldiers chased them as far as Kitara. That was in February 1890.

When they reached Butanga, Kalema sent a message to Kabalega requesting his permission to build his headquarters at Kijungute. This messenger spent nine days at the king's palace before bringing back the following reply to Kalema: "Omukama Chwa II Kabalega has permitted you to build your palace in Kijungute. Kikukuule, Saza Chief of Bugangaizi, is nearby and will defend you." On 1 April 1890, however, ex-Kabaka Kalema died of smallpox at Kijungute. Mbogo, the brother of Muteesa, became the leader of the Muslims in Ssingo. Shortly afterwards Rwabudongo returned to Kitara. But Rwabudongo had spent so long in Buganda that people had composed the following song:

> It does not take very long
> For things to change
> Now that the military drum [Kaijuire]
> Had been sounded in Mengo.

If indeed the Baganda would accept the fact and count Kalema as one of their kings, they would logically have to admit the fact that Rwabudongo, a general from Kitara, was his Katikiro [Prime Minister].[6]

Captain Lugard, Nubians, and Kabalega

When Kabalega was still in Kinogozi he received information that Kabaka Mwanga had sent Apolo Kaggwa to fight against the Muslims who had come with Captain Lugard in May 1891. Thereupon the king sent his [eldest] son, Jasi, and Rwabudongo to confront the enemy at Kibijo in Bugangaizi. Fighting lasted for a whole night, but in the meantime the Ganda exiles who had fled to Kitara to escape Mwanga's persecution had stolen away and joined Mwanga's forces. Thus they rejoined their people once more and were happily received. Fighting broke out again in the morning. Many people died in this battle and they included Kabusangwa and Kibogo of the Bachwabigere and Babiito clans, respectively, and Kasumba of the Bacaki clan. Mwanga's forces were victorious and the army of Kitara returned home.

It was also about this time—June 1891—that Kabalega heard the news that Lugard had passed through Nkore in the company of Zachary Kizito Kisingiri. They had also with them Prince Kasagama, whom they wanted to crown King of Tooro. Kabalega was angered by the impudence of this white man—a mere European who was not a fellow African king like himself—in interfering in his internal affairs. Therefore he ordered Kiiza, son of Iteka, and Munyara, son of Nyakabito, as well as the saza chiefs of the areas around Tooro to deal with Lugard. But they soon found out that Lugard had made short work of Rukara, son of Rwamagigi, at Katwe and had expelled him. They also found that Lugard had built a fort at Katwe and had named it Fort George. They nevertheless challenged Lugard and in three engagements—at Mohokya, Nyamwamba, and Katoke near the Sebo River—the European was victorious merely because of his Maxim gun. Another encounter, however, took place at Butanuka with the same result. On this occasion Lugard captured Chief Irumba of the Bachwabigere clan, who afterwards managed to escape. This victory was so emphatic that the Abarusura fled from Tooro. Lugard therefore installed Prince Kyebambe Kasagama as Omukama of Tooro on 14 August 1891.

[Thus did Tooro once more become an independent kingdom.] It had always been part of Kitara up to 1830, when Kaboyo rebelled against his father and declared himself King of Tooro. A succession of Tooro princes ruled this kingdom until Kabalega reconquered and restored it to Kitara in 1876.

After Lugard had installed Kasagama on the throne of Tooro, he crossed the Semliki River into Butuku and, having followed the shores of the lake, reached Kasenyi at Rubale's palace on 7 September 1891.

As we saw earlier on, when Emin Pasha and Stanley had departed, they had left behind some Egyptian soldiers at Kasenyi, while others had remained behind in Mahagi, Muswa, Pakwach, and other areas further north. When Lugard reached Kasenyi he had an interview with the leader of these soldiers, an African called Selim Bey. Now, these soldiers, together with the other unemployed around the place, having no alternative employment, agreed to work for the British Government. Lugard therefore enlisted them into his army.

Among them were six hundred soldiers with guns and more than eight thousand women and slaves. He moved them to Tooro and stationed them at Ndugutu near river Mubuku, known also as Fort Edward, in Nyakabimba; and also in Fort Gerry, which later became Fort Portal; in Mwenge, at a place called Nsorro; and other places from Mwenge to the Buganda border—Forts Kahara in Rwanjali, Wavertree, Lorne, Nyako-rongo, and De Winton in Rwoko. The purpose of these forti-fications was to block the route to Nkore as well as the route used by Arab traders of Karagwe. Out of these soldiers was formed the first "Uganda Rifles" and it was only because of them that the Europeans managed to conquer all the parts of Uganda by 1897.

On his way back with the Nubian soldiers, Lugard passed through Bulega of Rukaihankondo, and having crossed over the Rukwi, he headed for the island of Bukokwa, where he remained for two days. He then set out for the shores of Rwentuha, from where he marched to the Ibale [area of stone]. It was here that Ireeta's Abarusura offered him battle. But Lugard defeated and scattered them. He then moved on to Nsorro in Mwenge, where he established a military base garrisoned by his Nubian soldiers. He himself continued his march to Buganda, passing through Kitagwenda, Nkore, Buzimba, where he built a fort and called it Fort Grant. He then proceeded through Ibanda, Kyarutango, and reached Kampala on 31 December 1891. At this time great swarms of locusts appeared everywhere [1891].[7]

Meanwhile, many rumors of evil forebodings were circulat-ing in the capital of Kinogozi. These rumors emanated from Chope as well as from those living around the lake. Some Bahuma men came to report to Kabalega that while they were sleeping they dreamt that they heard many shots and on waking up would find many of their cows dead. And when they cut the cows open they would find many bullets inside them. It was believed by some people that these cows had been struck down by a god. There also came some fishermen from the lake who told the king that there was a man in the lake who used to shout: "Build me a house on the shores at

Rwentuha." The king took these rumors seriously and ordered a house to be built on the shore of Rwentuha. When the house was ready, about five hundred gathered round it and brought with them a lot of milk. However, the cows continued to die and the king now ordered the rumormongers to be killed. But Kagoro, their leader, however, managed to escape to Bulega.

But this was not the end of the affair. After a short while, further rumors started coming in from Chope. It was reported to the king that in Bukidi was a tree which was heard to be speaking the following words: "Omukama Kabalega should leave the throne because I have come back to claim my throne." Kabalega apparently believed this story because he sent his servant Wasswa, son of Kakondo, with offerings to appease the tree. And yet another rumor reached the king concerning a man standing in the lake near Bugungu who was heard to say: "Kabalega, make room for me because I am coming back to my kingdom." Kabalega also sent offerings to this mysterious creature.

It must be pointed out, however, that these rumors had their foundations in the activities of the Nubian soldiers in Bulega and Pakwach. These soldiers had many guns and many rounds of ammunition and would go out to raid for food and cows, torturing the local population in many ways. The Banyoro and Bagungu [people of Bugungu] of these parts were subjected to the cruelty and barbarities of these soldiers for eight years—the Nubians having worked for four years with Emin Pasha in this area and for the next four years having remained on their own. This may account for the reason why the people of this region spread these rumors of evil omens.

While Kabalega was still in Kabale Kinogozi, he contracted smallpox but fortunately soon got well. It was after this event that he moved his capital to Mparo, where now his tomb exists. It was around January 1892 that he made this move. Having spent a short period at Mparo, he sent Nyakamatura and Masura to lead an expedition against the Nubian soldiers whom Lugard had stationed in Mwenge. They fought a severe battle with these Nubians at Kinoni, but the Abarusura lost the battle. Kabalega, however, persevered and sent another expedition under the leadership of Rwabudongo and Muhenda, son of Komubigo, against the Nubians stationed at Butiti, also in Mwenge. He also instructed Rwabudongo to

lead an expedition to Bulega with the intention of capturing
all the boats, thereby preventing the Europeans from crossing
the lake. But Ireeta had already engaged the Nubians in this
area and Kasaija, son of Kikukuule, succeeded in killing the
reputable leader of these Nubians, a man called Sekulaka.
His head was cut off and sent to Kabalega, who in turn sent
it to Rubanga, the son of Kyagwire.

The king was still at Mparo when Lugard challenged
Kikukuule, Saza Chief of Bugangaizi, on the hill called
Haburu. Kasaija, Kikukuule's son, a very brave man, was killed
in this battle and Lugard once more won the day.

Kabalega Sues for Peace

Kabalega sent messages of peace to Lugard on two occasions. The first message had been sent at the end of March
1891. He had requested a mutual agreement guaranteeing
peace. This was the period when Lugard was mobilizing his
army of Nubians and Zanzibaris in preparation for an attack
on the Muslims in Bugangaizi. Lugard rejected this offer of
peace and attacked the Muslims near the river Kanyagoro in
May 1891.

Now, a year later, Kabalega sent another message to
Lugard—March 1892—but once again he refused to sign any
peace pact. When news of this refusal of his peace offer
reached him, Kabalega became despondent but determined
to fight to the last to maintain the territorial integrity of his
kingdom. Shortly afterwards he received an envoy from
Lugard and Kabaka Mwanga. This envoy was a Muganda
chief called Isiah [Isaya] Mayanja and addressed Kabalega
thus, "Kabaka Mwanga II and the white man, Captain
Lugard, greet you." Then he produced the things he had
brought with him—a baggage of clothes, bark cloth, a stick,
a sack, a hoe, a gun, and said:

> Choose what you wish from among these things. But
> remember that if you choose the sack, hoe, or stick, then
> you would have chosen peace. But then understand that
> you will have to give me eighty pieces of ivory, six hun-
> dred hoes, and five hundred sacks of salt in return for
> peace.

Kabalega gave the envoy accommodation at Bikamba's house
in Butanjwa.

The next day the king summoned the following chiefs and generals: Nyakamatura, Ruburwa, Masura, Kasigwa, son of Byanjeru, Rwabudongo, Gutambaki, Ireeta, Nyangi, the mother of the king [who had been given a coronet as a sign of honor], and her mother, Nyamutahingurwa. They held a council and the king sought their advice. "What are we going to do?" he asked them. Then Nyangi replied:

> I am not trying to deprive you of your throne, but choose the sack, for it can be used for trade; or the hoe so that the people may plow the land with it. Moreover, as you are rich and have children, you will probably need more food. What good ever comes out of war? I have delivered my soul. The men can now speak.

Nyangi's peace proposal was supported by Rwabudongo, Nyakamatura, Ireeta, Gutambaki, and Kasigwa.[8] But Nyamutahingurwa, Nyangi's mother, Masura, and Ruburwa opposed the idea, and said:

> Impossible! Since when has any Omukama befriended Baganda? Do not let yourself be deceived by them. They have always been our enemies—a people only interested in raiding other countries. Do not allow them to fool you. A man is always ready for the worst. We are here to fight for you against Baganda. Please, do choose the gun.

Kabalega accepted the latter advice and chose to fight Lugard and the Baganda. But Ireeta and Rwabudongo did not hide their disappointment and anger at this decision.

The next day, Kabalega summoned his chiefs and his Abarusura to assemble before him. The Abarusura dressed themselves magnificently and arranged themselves in four rows. The king ordered Bikamba to go and fetch the envoy from Buganda. He arrived with the things he had been given by Lugard and Mwanga and arranged them before the king to see. Then with dignity, Kabalega addressed him:

> If Mwanga has sent these things for peace and friendship, why is he demanding eighty pieces of ivory, six hundred hoes, and five hundred sacks of salt? Did we ask for these things so as to be able to pay his ransom? [Mwanga, he reckoned, was a prisoner of the white man.] Even if he is a prisoner, why doesn't he send a message in his own name? Must he tie his message to the apron string of the white man?

He then chose the gun, and added: "I know Mwanga, my son, rebelled against me long ago, but we are ready if he wants war." He bade farewell to the envoy, gave him presents, and made a present of one piece of ivory to Mwanga with his compliments. He made it clear to envoy Isiah Mayanja that the present was not a fulfillment of Mwanga's demands but merely a friendly gesture. The envoy departed for Buganda.

Some two months elapsed and Mwanga sent another envoy, a man by the name of Tera Kigere Nakanyoro, who brought the following message:

> Do you still refuse Lugard's friendship? Do you think that you can withstand the power of the white man? Pay his price and I will send them to him.

Kabalega replied:

> If Mwanga wants to give presents to his temporary European visitor, why doesn't he make a present of what is his? And if one wants friendship, does one first make demands from one's neighbor as if this neighbor is paying for some wrong done? I, also, have had white men visit my kingdom, but I have never experienced anything like this. And won't I appear a coward if I send these things you ask of me?

He once more sent another piece of ivory to Mwanga with his compliments and fraternal greetings. He bade farewell to Tera K. Nakanyoro, Mwanga's envoy.

One month passed, and yet another envoy from Mwanga arrived. He was called Semu Kaggwa. He gave his message, which stated: "Do not choose to fight with the white man when he has offered you a hand of friendship." But Kabalega was adamant:

> These are Mwanga's ideas [he replied]. If the white man wants my friendship, does he need to pass through Mwanga? Can he not himself send a direct message to me? But I know the white man is not really friendly. He just wants to take my kingdom.[9]

It was about this time—1893—that General Nyakamatura, Saza Chief of Bugahya, died.

CHAPTER 5

Kabalega, Baganda, and Europeans, 1893–99

The Expedition of the Europeans against Kitara (1893–95)[1]

The departure of Lugard from Kampala in December 1891 did not signal the end of Buganda's troubles. On the contrary, these troubles multiplied with the intensification of the religious conflicts early in 1892. After Lugard had left Kampala he moved with Mbogo to suppress the Muslims in Ssingo. His aim was achieved in May 1892. In June 1892, he left for England, whither he had gone to examine how the British Government was going to take over the responsibilities of the British East African Company in Uganda. Sir Gerald Portal arrived in March 1893 as the British Government's envoy to Uganda, with the purpose of hoisting the British flag in Buganda. Before Sir Portal left for England he made some attempts to settle the religious conflicts in Buganda. He gave Buwekula to one religious group [the Catholics] and the other areas to the other groups [Protestants and Muslims?]. Portal, however, did not solve the religious question, for the friction continued between the three religious factions.

While in Buganda, Portal had also ordered the withdrawal of the Nubian soldiers garrisoning Tooro and their transference to Kampala and Entebbe. These soldiers were accused of torturing the local inhabitants, especially in the absence of their white commanders. Moreover, it was decided that they needed training in professional soldiering. But in June 1893, the Muslims in Buganda and the Nubian soldiers threatened to mutiny. But a quick action of the Europeans forestalled their move. Their guns were taken away from them and their leaders—Selim Bey and Mbogo—were exiled to Zanzibar.[2]

Now, how does the history of Kitara relate to the above developments? Well, in November 1893 Colonel Colvile had come to replace Major Macdonald, who had been left behind by Portal to manage events in Buganda. Within a short period he had worked out plans for attacking Kabalega and conquering Kitara. His policy was dictated by the following considerations: First, because Kabalega had attacked the British garrisons in Tooro as well as those on the Buganda border after the Nubians had been evacuated from these areas, Kabalega saw the withdrawal of these soldiers as a chance to reconquer Tooro and had used it. He sent Rwabudongo and Ireeta at once to lead an expedition against Kasagama. They clashed with Kasagama's forces at Rugonjo and were victorious. Kasagama fled to the mountains of Gambaragara. Second, Kabalega's reconquest of Tooro had important repercussions from the point of view of British imperialism. During the partition of Africa the borders of the Congo had not been secured to the British, who were very concerned that the French would occupy this area from the north and west. It was therefore necessary for British imperial aims to secure and guard this region. To do this the subjugation of Kitara was considered logical and essential. By attacking the Baganda in Bugangaizi and Tooro, Kabalega had led the British to believe that he was declaring war on Buganda. And third, Colvile considered the attack on Kabalega as a diversionary measure. His intention was to cool down the struggle between the three religious factions in Buganda [a move reminiscent of Napoleon III's intervention in South America in the mid-nineteenth century]. By taking thousands of Baganda to fight abroad and promising them part of the territorial spoils accruing therefrom he aimed at easing the tense political situation in Buganda.[3]

The Battle of Balihungiraha, December 1893

This battle took place during the dry season [ekyanda]. The Europeans declared war on Kitara on 4 December 1893 and Colvile left Buganda on the fifteenth. Thereupon Kabalega recalled Ireeta and Rwabudongo from Tooro because the intelligence division of the Abarusura had reported that Colvile was accompanied by a very large army of Baganda, Nubians, and Europeans. The Europeans included Major Macdonald, Major Owen, Captain Thruston, Lieutenant Arthur, Mr. Purkiss, Mr. Pilkington, who was a missionary, and many others. He had more than six hundred Nubian soldiers armed with guns, and about a million Baganda soldiers.[4] Simei [Semei] Lwakirenzi Kakungulu was the general of the Baganda divisions. They clashed with the Abarusura at the Kitara border on 25 December, and having brushed them aside marched for four days before they reached the Kafo River. They crossed the river by constructing a make-shift bridge, and marched to Butema [about seven miles from Hoima on the Kampala road]. Another two days' march brought them to Mparo, only to discover that Kabalega had burnt down his capital and had retreated to the Budongo forest. Colvile's forces reached Mparo on 1 January 1894 and from that day the war continued until 9 April 1899.

All those who have sympathetic hearts should realize the hardships which beset Kitara from that very day. The enemy pursued the king for ten days but failed to capture him. When Rwabudongo and Ireeta returned to Bugahya from Tooro they found the capital deserted and the king hiding in the forest of Biso. Colvile concentrated the Buganda divisions on Hoima and took the Nubians with him towards Lake Albert. They reached Kitana [now seventeen miles from Hoima on the Butiaba road] on 17 January and Kibiro on the 18th. Major Owen and Captain Thruston proceeded with two hundred Nubian soldiers to Bugungu. Their mission was to march to Wadelai and attempt to recruit the soldiers who had been left there by Emin Pasha. But, failing to cross the lake, they nevertheless managed to reach the station built by Gordon and Emin Pasha which was situated nine miles from the lake, but found this station destroyed. They marched back to Kibiro. Another attempt was made to cross over to Wadelai. This time Owen and Purkiss took ten Nubian soldiers with them and managed to effect a crossing in an iron boat [to distinguish it from the boat made of wood], which had been carried in pieces all the way to Kibiro. They reached Wadelai and hoisted the Union Jack there on 4 February 1894, leav-ing some soldiers to guard it. When they returned to Kibiro, they discovered that Colvile and others had left the place after building forts in Kibiro and Kitara garrisoned by Nubian soldiers. Reaching Hoima at the beginning of Feb-ruary, Colvile built another fort at Katasiha near the river Wambabya. Other forts garrisoned by Nubians were erected at Baranywa and Kafo Mugubi.

Throughout these developments Kabalega was still in the area around Budongo. Finally, however, he was challenged by an army of Baganda and Nubians. This encounter is called the battle of *Ekya Balihungiraha* [where could the people es-cape to?]. It was a great battle, after which Kabalega moved to Kihaguzi, where he built his capital. He spent about a

month in this place when a certain man arrived with the
news that the enemy were marching towards Kihaguzi and
had reached Biso, although, in fact, they had reached Kitoro.
Thereupon the king hurried back to Kigarra. The enemy in
question was the Baganda army led by Kakungulu, who had
left Mparo on 28 January and marched for three days before
reaching Kihaguzi. A big battle was fought the next day with
Kabalega leading his Abarusura in person. The Baganda won
the day and captured many goats and cows.

After fifteen days Kakungulu sent the following letter to
Kabalega: "Send someone to fetch the things we captured
from your kingdom." To which the king replied through the
messenger: "Go and tell Kakungulu that I do not wish to have
those things returned to me. Tell him to take them to his
king, Mwanga, whose thirst has never been quenched."

Colvile returned to Buganda at the end of February to
organize a new and stronger army with which to attack
Kabalega. But before he had reached the Kafo, he heard
that the Abarusura had engaged the Baganda at Mparo. So
he marched back to Mparo and fought a battle which lasted a
whole day until dusk. The entire Buganda army was forced
to flee from this battle, and asked Captain Thruston to come
to their aid, with his Nubians. But the next day they discovered to their surprise that the Abarusura had retired to
their original positions and did not follow up their advantage.

At the beginning of March a serious smallpox epidemic
broke out and the Buganda army, because of the soldiers having contracted this disease, was recalled home. They did not
all return to their country, for many of them were to die on
the roadside because there was no one to care for them. Captain Thruston remained in Hoima with his six hundred Nubian
and Zanzibari soldiers armed with guns. He had another sixty
soldiers as auxiliaries. Major Owen was given the command
of Tooro.[5]

Kabalega Orders the Saza Chiefs to Return to Their Areas

The chiefs delegated Kasigwa to go to the king and explain
to him the state of affairs. By this time he had moved to
Kinyara. On receiving this information he ordered the chiefs
to return to their respective areas. Kikukuule went back to
Bugangaizi, Bikamba to Masindi, Rwabudongo [he was not a
saza chief] to Muziranduru [his own village near Masindi on

the Kampala road], and so on. Kabalega and his children remained in Kinyara. And another saza chief of a neighboring county, called Masura, son of Materu, remained with him.

On their way to their various homes, these chiefs found some women who had been captured by the enemy at Kisagura, which was ruled by Kaheru, son of Gararukire. They were surprised to discover that the Baganda had actually spared these women. They concluded, however, that the Europeans had taken over the country and had deliberately released these women so that when their husbands saw them they would be extremely happy and would therefore be disposed to accept white rule. The truth, however, is that slavery had already been abolished in Buganda by the Lugard-Mwanga agreement of 26 December 1890.

On their way back to Kitara some of Rwabudongo's men attacked the British fort at Hoima. This led to the Europeans' counteroffensive against Rwabudongo which was fought at Wairime. The Europeans were victorious and Rwabudongo narrowly eluded capture because he had remained behind after his men had deserted him. The Europeans were supported by Wamara and some Banyoro. Wamara was a Mugungu [a native of Bugungu near Lake Albert] and belonged to the Bachwa clan. He had been exiled by King Kamurasi and had fled to Emin Pasha at Pakwach. He later teamed up with the Nubian soldiers and moved with them to Kitara under Captain Lugard, driven perhaps by the desire to exact revenge from Kabalega. He was an officer in this army and did everything possible to capture Rwabudongo, but failed. Ireeta also eluded capture.

When Kikukuule returned to Bugangaizi he discovered that the Baganda were now in occupation of his country and that Father P. Achte had started building a mission [Roman Catholic] at Bukumi on 2 April 1894.

Mahagi Nubian Soldiers Are Brought to Buganda

At this time there were about three Europeans—Captain Thruston, Moffat, and Forster—stationed in Hoima.

At the beginning of May, Captain Thruston went to Mahagi in a bid to persuade the remnants of Emin Pasha's Nubian soldiers left there to come to Buganda. His mission was successful and it took many days before they arrived in Buganda. They numbered some 400 soldiers and about 10,000 servants

and slaves. Their march took them to Kihira, Pakwach, and
Bugungu, where they were carried over in a boat. It was
discovered at this place, however, that about 5,000 had deserted and gone back to Acholi and that others had died.
The rest continued their march to Hoima, where they spent
several nights near Mugabi Station. They then continued their
march, taking the Kibingo-Ngogoma route because food was
plentiful in this area. Nevertheless, the desertion continued
and only 3,000 soldiers reached Kampala. These 3,000 soldiers and 1,000 young men and servants were drafted into
the army. The rest were women and slaves [from Lendu, Alur,
and Makraka]. That is how the people we now know as
Nubians came to [B]uganda.

The Battles of Musaija Mukuru Hill, Wambabya River, and Bakumira Hill, August 1894

Kabalega's chiefs were engaged in regular confrontations
with the European forces which passed through Mugabi or
Kibingo-Ngogoma on their way to and from Buganda. Kabalega's soldiers usually camped on the hill of Musaija
Mukuru,[6] from where they descended to mount sporadic attacks on the passing enemy. At the end of May 1894, Captain
Thruston decided to dislodge them. He left Hoima early one
morning at the head of his Nubian soldiers and the soldiers
commanded by Wamara. By the afternoon they had reached
Musaija Mukuru hill. A battle was fought and Thruston was
victorious. Byabachwezi managed to escape but one of Kabalega's sons fell in this battle.

At this time Kabalega was still at Kinyara. While there,
news reached him that Mwanga of Buganda had sent Yona
Wasswa, Mukwenda, to capture his ivory. Mwanga believed
that Kabalega possessed a lot of ivory which he had hidden
in Nyamugya Island. Consequently, Kabalega retreated from
Kinyara to Kanyamaizi. It was here that he executed all his
Baganda prisoners, who numbered more than eighty. He decided to execute them because he regarded them as spies and
no longer trusted them. But he personally pardoned one of
them, a man called Kanagguluba.

The Baganda soldiers in search of the king's ivory were led
by a European called Captain Gibb. Kabalega defeated them
and they retreated to Buganda empty-handed.

By August the king had moved to Rwempindu. From here he ordered Rwabudongo and Ireeta to attack the European station at Hoima. They camped near Mparo and spent the night there. The Europeans learnt of their advance and on the morning of 27 August, some soldiers were sent to ascertain their exact position. They discovered that the Abarusura had set out for battle and brought this intelligence back to their commanders, who also decided to offer battle. Fighting continued from sunrise to about 1 P.M. The first engagement was in Hoima town near the place where the ginnery exists today. The Nubian soldiers were drawn up on one side of the river Wambabya, while Kabalega's forces were drawn up on the other side of it, those armed with guns spearheading the attack, followed by the spearmen. They were led by Rwabudongo and Ireeta. Jasi, the king's eldest son, stayed back in Rwempindu with his father. Rwabudongo and Ireeta stood in the middle of their soldiers together with those holding aloft the flag of Kitara. They paced from one end to the other issuing instructions. Sometimes they were carried high by their soldiers so as to make it possible for them to see how the battle was progressing as well as to ascertain their numbers [probably to make sure that there were no desertions] and to encourage their men. Simultaneously, another battle was raging at Bakumira hill. This battle was fought mainly with spears on the Kitara side.

In the heat of the Wambabya battle some Nubians secretly crossed the river, while others remained in their positions, firing away. The aim of this tactical move was to surround Kabalega's soldiers and then to attack them from all sides. This strategy paid off, because they caused a split among the enemy's rank, who now began to retreat towards the Bakumira hillside. They continued, however, to put up some resistance, but by the afternoon it was all over. The Europeans had won a decisive victory. Rwabudongo's and Ireeta's standards were captured on that day, and Kiiza, whose duty it was to announce the declaration of war, lost his life on the same day. He was captured after he had been wounded, and executed along with other wounded captives despite the order issued by the white men that the lives of wounded soldiers should be spared. Excluding the wounded, more than seventy Abarusura fell on that day.

This disaster was caused partly by the treachery of a Sudanese hireling of Kabalega. This man had defected to the enemy's side during the battles of Wambabya and Bakumira and revealed the military secrets of Rwabudongo and Ireeta to their opponents. We shall see this man again leading the Europeans to attack Kabalega at Rwempindu.

After this battle the Abarusura retreated to Buraru, but within a few days the white men challenged them there. They clashed at the battle of Kinogozi, situated in a small river valley. The Abarusura killed Busungu and defeated the Europeans. Afterwards Rwabudongo retired to his village of Muziranduru.

After this battle the commander of the European forces proceeded to see Lake Albert and Mahagi. Kabalega decided at this time to send an envoy called Katama with about eighteen pieces of ivory as a peace offering to the European. But Katama was too late, for the European had already left for another destination, perhaps towards Rwempindu in his bid to capture Kabalega.

Rwempindu (11 November 1894)

On 8 November Captain Thruston left Hoima and proceeded to attack the king at Rwempindu. His forces consisted of some 250 Nubians, a number of Wamara's men, and some Baganda Muslims. They left Hoima secretly and after three days' march, crossed the river Titi near Rwempindu. This crossing was executed at night and they also managed to capture those who had been sent to inform Kabalega of their advance. Three of these were shot on the spot, while one had a rope tied round his neck and was forced to lead them to Kabalega's camp. They reached there at around three o'clock in the morning and the Sudanese hireling who had earlier betrayed the king's military secrets to the enemy was too petrified to lead them into Kabalega's apartment. At this point, Kabalega's man who had been captured tried to warn his master by shouting but was prevented from doing so by the rope being pulled tighter around his neck. In the meantime the enemy were crawling on the ground in an attempt to capture the king unawares. But he was saved by the cry of a donkey which set the dogs barking. One of Kabalega's guards shot point blank into the air and thereupon everybody was awakened. The soldiers grabbed their guns and ordered their wives to run away first. After some brief skirmishing with the enemy they managed to make good their escape, largely because it was very dark, which made it difficult for them to be detected. But Kabalega himself narrowly escaped capture and death. The enemy burnt down his camp, which contained a lot of his property. His gunpowder, bullets, and regalia were destroyed. The *Kajumba* drum together with two royal spears and the throne were captured. These were sent to Colonel Colvile, who took the *Kajumba* back to England.

Kabalega's guards did not put up an effective resistance, because they had been surprised. No one, except the person who had refused to lead the enemy to Kabalega, lost his life in this encounter. But the enemy captured a lot of cattle and ivory which belonged to the king. The Rwempindu incident occurred on 11 November 1894.

Around December Kabalega once more sued for peace. The white man agreed to halt the fighting for some time but decided to postpone the peace negotiations to a later date. Unfortunately he left his command before anything could be done.[7]

Developments in Bugangaizi, 1894–95

Meanwhile some important developments were taking place in Bugangaizi. By April 1894, Kikukuule had gone back to Bugangaizi and discovered that Buwekula had already been annexed by the Europeans to Buganda on 7 April. He also found an army of Baganda threatening to enter Bugangaizi. By the beginning of April, too, Father P. Achte had started building a Roman Catholic mission at Bukumi. On his way through Buwekula and Buddu he had heard that Bugangaizi and Buyaga had been given to Baganda Catholics while Bulemezi, in the south, Ssingo, and Bugerere had been given to the Protestant faction. And in order to defend their counties, the Baganda Catholics had moved to Kakumiro. To stop the spilling of blood, however, Father Achte decided to befriend Kikukuule and to teach him.

But in October the Baganda insisted that Kikukuule's children and those of the other chiefs of Kabalega in this county should proceed to Mengo to pay their allegiance to the Kabaka, thereby recognizing his paramountcy. They refused to go to Mengo and fighting nearly broke out. Later on the Baganda forced Kikukuule to allow them to extend their rule over Buyaga. Consequently he decided to leave Bugangaizi

and settled in the area of Buhemba. This was in January 1895.
War broke out in Bugangaizi from that date and lasted until
1899. The missionaries erected a church made of brick walls,
within which they also hoped to defend themselves against
attack. The first of these churches was completed at Bukumi
in April 1895, and the second at Bujumi in 1896.

At this time the Baganda Protestants, led by Apolo Kaggwa,
the Katikiro, were fighting among themselves for the areas
allotted to them. It will be remembered that the Catholics
were given Buwekula, Bugangaizi, and Buyaga, while the
Protestants received Bugerere, Buruli, and Rugonjo. Now, to
sort out their differences they divided Rugonjo into two counties—Bulemezi and Ssingo.

The Expedition against Kabalega in Bukidi

When Kabalega escaped from Rwempindu he retreated
northwards to Kitaho, where he built a camp. But the Europeans pursued him to this place and attacked him. A great
battle was fought, during which a Captain Daming lost his
life. After this battle Captain Thruston built a fort at Masindi
Bulyasojo, intended to block the king's return to his country.
He placed Nubian soldiers in charge of this fortification and
they made it their base of operations against Kabalega.

After some time the king ordered his Saza Chief Byabachwezi to return to his saza of Bugahya. He was instructed to
comfort the people and to assure them that there was nothing
to worry about. In July 1895 Byabachwezi performed an important service when he brought the Europeans and some
of his people together and managed to get an assurance from
the former that no more parts of his county should be given
to the Baganda who were the friends of these Europeans.
Byabachwezi became converted to the Protestant faith and
was baptized Paulo [Paul]. He had many children of both
sexes and, as we shall see presently, many of his sons became
saza chiefs during the reign of King Duhaga II.

By this time Kabalega had retreated to Rukungu. Captain
Ternan and Apolo Kaggwa pursued him to this place. On
hearing of their approach the king had dug trenches, from
where he prepared to give battle. There were also some soldiers drawn up on the other side of the lake. The enemy built
emizinga [stockades], from where they could fire across the
lake. Kabalega was defeated and the enemy captured many

cows. Among those also captured in this battle were Nyamutahingurwa, the king's mother; Prince Karukara and Princess Victoria Mukabagabwa; Rubuga, the Kalyota [official sister of the king]; the future King Kitahimbwa I; and the future King Duhaga II. Having forced the king to flee from Rukungu, Apolo Kaggwa collected his booty, which he took back to Buganda while the Europeans returned to Masindi.[8] It became apparent that the Nubians were victorious in any engagement they fought against Kabalega.

After Rwabudongo had settled down in Muziranduru for some time, he became restless and decided to move towards Tooro. By this time the Europeans had established eight forts in Kitara—Hoima, Kitana, Kibiro, Mahagi, Pajao in Bugungu, Pawiri in Mutunda, Buruli Kikaito near Masindi Port, and the main garrison, which was at Masindi.

Captain Thruston came back to Kitara again in May 1897. He found there Mr. Dugmore, Dr. Ansorge, and a man called Moses. It was Thruston who suggested that Prince Karukara should be enthroned. By August, however, he had returned to Buganda.

The Nubian Mutiny and the Mwanga Revolt

In order to understand fully what happened during the following years as well as the wars of Kabalega, it may be necessary to explain briefly the Nubian mutiny and the rising of Mwanga. These two—the Nubians and the Mwanga factions—later merged into one group.

In July 1897 Mwanga revolted and fled to Buddu. He was followed by the Muslims, pagans, and a few friends. He was given assistance by the kings of Kooki and Nkore. The Arabs who had settled near the Kagera River also supplied him with soldiers. Mwanga was defeated by Captain Turnan Kabwoko in the month of August. He fled to Mwanza, where he was captured by the Germans. He, however, managed to escape from them and returned once more to Buddu in December. He burnt down the mission at Kooki as well as many villages, and moved near Bikira. Here he was challenged by Major Macdonald, who defeated him at Lusalira. Macdonald was commanding a few Nubians, some Baganda, and a few Indians. He had marched from Luba near Jinja, where the Nubian soldiers had mutinied. It was indeed at Luba that the Indians were first heard of and first fought in Uganda.

The Nubian mutiny had occurred in September 1897[9] because they were ordered into Kenya.[10] They slowly returned to Jinja and captured the garrison at Luba. They numbered about 500 and were all armed with guns. They barricaded themselves in the garrison and killed three Europeans they had taken hostage, including Captain Thruston. Two others died during the fighting.[11] The mutineers were fighting against a handful of Europeans, Indians, 350 Swahili soldiers who belonged to the East African Rifles, about 2,000 Baganda, and about 500 Basoga soldiers. After this battle, the Nubians left the garrison with their wives in January 1898 and, passing through Kabagambi, headed towards Lake Kyoga. They were challenged by Kakungulu's forces at Mbale but were victorious. The Europeans made a forced march to Bugerere in an attempt to prevent them from reaching Buruli at Masindi Port because they feared that these Nubians might join hands with Kabalega's forces. The Europeans had about 150 Indians, about 200 Swahili soldiers of the East African Rifles, and some Baganda. The mutineers were ejected from their garrison at Kabagambi by the Indian and Swahili contingents. During this encounter—23 February—a white man, Mr. Maloney, was killed. At this time, the Katikiro of Buganda, Apolo Kaggwa, was at Bugerere with some Baganda soldiers and Mr. Blakledge. His assignment was to guard the routes to Kampala. The mutineers fled to Bukidi and the Europeans proceeded to Buruli and Masindi. Here they tried to persuade those Nubian soldiers garrisoning Masindi and Buruli not to follow the example of those at Jinja. Determined to take no chances, however, they moved about 350 of them to Buganda. They were replaced by Indians, while the Nubian garrison at Pajao was closed. Another one, however, was opened at Nyakasongora.

It was during these months that the Nubians at Masindi killed Bikamba, the saza chief of that county, as a result of the troubles which had developed between some Nubians and some chiefs. They also nearly killed the white man Dr. Ansorge (*vide* Ansorge, *Under the African Sun*, pp. 155–66 —Author). Meanwhile the Nubians in Hoima had summoned Byabachwezi to appear before them but, suspecting foul play, he fled to Buganda near the Kafo. They burnt down his saza headquarters and seized his wives. They were in fact at the point of proclaiming their mutiny when the European in charge of Hoima cleverly managed their transfer to Buganda.

Throughout this period Ireeta was still at large and would appear now and then to lay ambushes near Masindi. His Abarusura were encamped at Kicumbanyobo near Kitoro on a hill in the middle of the Budongo and Pajao [Murchison Falls] forests. Jasi, Kabalega's son, also came down to fight in the area from Atura to Masindi Port in Buruli County near the Kafo River.

Mwanga Attacks the Missions at Bukumi and Joins Hands with Kabalega

Let us return once more to Bugangaizi. It was by no means quiet at this time. After the defeat of Mwanga at Lusalira and later at Katonga on 2 March 1898, he had retreated to Nkore, apparently to organize another force. At the same time he had sent some 800 Baganda Muslims and Nubians who had been fighting on his side to pass through Bugangaizi and join hands with the Nubian soldiers stationed near Lake Kyoga as well as with the forces of Kabalega (*vide* H. Austin, *With Macdonald in Uganda*. London, 1903, p. 110—Author).

Now, on their way through Bukumi they made an attempt to capture the Bukumi mission. On 1 March the inhabitants of Bukumi Parish noticed the villages of Buwekula County being burnt down; and on 2 March ten more villages near Bukumi were burnt. The attempt to burn down and capture the Bukumi mission placed those inside it in very grave danger. They were about 1,000 people in all—women, children, the sick, the wounded, and even soldiers—and they were besieged inside the mission. On 11 March another army of Muslims and pagans arrived to reinforce the besiegers. But despite this reinforcement, the besieged forces broke through and defeated their opponents. Another battle was fought on 13 March, when Captain Sitwell arrived with sixty soldiers and a Maxim gun; and during the night, more Europeans arrived with 150 Indians. On seeing such large reinforcements, Mwanga's army decided to retreat, and burnt everything on their way. They also captured women and children. They divided themselves into two sections, the one heading for Buruli, and the other towards Iguramu near Hoima.

In the meantime Mwanga himself was moving towards Kitara. He traveled through Buwekula, Kahanga, Buziba, and reached Iguramu. And at Ikoba near Kirimbi, he met Kabalega's delegate, Prince Hermenegildo Karubanga. They

passed through Bugambe near Hoima, Nyamirima, Kason-
goire, Biso, and reached Ireeta's home at Kicumbanyobo.
Mwanga waited here while Karubanga went to announce
his arrival to the king, who was now at Pamwa near Jaber.
Mwanga then crossed Pajao and arrived at Kabalega's camp
at the end of March. Two Nubians fought a duel that day
until evening.

In April the Europeans sent 150 Indian, Somali, and Swahili
soldiers to guard Masindi and Buruli. Colonel Martyr defeated
the Nubians in Buruli near the Kafo River and captured their
garrison. The Nubians merely retreated and built another garrison only some five miles away. But another of their contingents was defeated near Atura.

By now the Europeans and the Baganda had decided to
establish Prince Karukara on the throne of Kitara as an effective way of eroding the people's loyalty to Kabalega, and
thereby keep him out of the country. The coronation of Prince
Karukara took place on 3 April 1898. At this time Rwabudongo returned from Tooro and a struggle for the Katikiroship
started between him and his colleague Byabachwezi.

After Kabalega had been chased away from Rukungu by
the European forces, he retreated to Rukunyu in Bukidi,
where he fought two battles with these Europeans and defeated them on each occasion. From Rukunyu he moved to
Kamudindi, where he was attacked once more by the Europeans and was this time defeated by them. Bikanga Kahuzo
Maguru Nsamo, son of Nyamagabwa, the king's brave man
and chief, died in this battle. Kabalega then retreated to
Hekedi, where he spent two days, and then headed towards
Acholi in Mwahura's area. From here he moved to Domoro
and, while here, sent messages to Ruburwa Munyara, son of
Nyakabito, and Muhenda, son of Komubigo, ordering them
to go to the Catholic areas to summon the Catholics to his aid.
He dispatched six hundred guns to them and the Catholics
agreed to come and help him. On their way back to Kitara,
the Abarusura managed to block the way and fought with
them for four days. Many lives were lost during this battle
and indeed only forty armed men managed to return. But
for them it was a narrow escape because of the shortage of
food. On their way they depended for food on wild fruits
and other wild things. When Kabalega heard of the disaster
that had befallen his men, he moved to Kigali's place. It was
here that the Nubians from Butaleba found him. These Nu-

bians joined him and his forces grew once more in strength. And when the Europeans attacked him again, he defeated them.

Kabalega then moved to Muruya's area. This was where Mwanga II, King of Buganda, found him. At first, Kabalega had been filled with anger and had said to Mwanga: "Now, why have you come this way?" But his elders and advisers prayed him not to be too harsh on Mwanga. "Be kind to your son, who is also in trouble," they said. Thereupon he decided to leave Mwanga in peace. Meanwhile, seeing the two kings at one place, the elders were filled with a great sense of history, and after serious discussions among themselves, said to the two monarchs:

> You are once more united, Isingoma and Kato. You are now on the way through which your ancestors [Babiito] had passed on their way to rule Kitara. But you two are not going to be victorious in this war. Nor are you going to be killed in battle. But you are both going to be captured on the same day.

The two kings separated after this address and camped separately. They only exchanged ideas through messengers. But Kabalega's children used to visit Mwanga very often because he loved them.

When the two monarchs left Muruya's area, they went back to Rukunyu. Here they were attacked by the Europeans, whom they fought and defeated. But some of Kabalega's children fell on that day. After this battle, Kabalega and Mwanga also fought another engagement with the Europeans, at Rwesaza in Buruli, and for the second time beat them. They then moved to Kyokwara, where once more they defeated another European force sent against them. After this battle they moved to Kisojo in Buruli, where they spent two days. At Kisojo Kabalega ordered Kabejweka, the commander of the Ekihangura battalion of the Abarusura, to march back to Kitara and challenge the Europeans there. Kabejweka was the father of Martin Mukidi and Isidore Kwebika. When Kabejweka reached Masindi, he decided at first to leave the Europeans alone and proceeded to attack the Baganda at Bukumi. But he was defeated by the Baganda.[12]

Kabalega and Mwanga Are Captured, 9 April 1899

Meanwhile the two kings had retreated to Dwara's area in
Bukidi. From here they moved to Ireeta's area and afterwards
to Mikyora. It was at Mikyora that Kabalega started to suffer
from an eye disease. But all the same, fighting went on
every day without any stop. Then there came an army of
Baganda and Europeans led by Colonel Evatt, and Kaggwa,
Semei Kakungulu, and Andrea Luwandaga Kimbugwe. They
attacked Kabalega and Mwanga and first managed to capture
some cattle and goats. The kings retreated from their hiding
place after two days. On the third day, 9 April 1899, a morning mist covered the river valley and visibility was difficult.
It was on this very day that the two kings, Chwa II Kabalega
of Kitara and Mwanga II of Buganda, were captured by the
Europeans. Kabalega was captured still fighting like the brave
man that he was. He was captured only after he had been
wounded. He was shot in the arm and another shot broke off
his thumb from another hand. As a result his gun dropped
from his hands and in this way he was captured by the enemy.

By this time Kabalega had already given away the
ekikwekweto. This was fortunate, because by so doing he
managed to save the lives of some of his elder children who
possessed guns. Jasi, his brave son, who fought with his father
in this battle, was shot in the back—the back being fractured
as a result; while another son, George Nyakana, was shot in
the thigh. These two princes were captured also with their
father. Captured also were two of the king's wives—Sarah
Nyinabarongo [the mother of twins] and Malyamu [Mary]
Kasemeire.

On the way to Kisalizi in Buruli Jasi died! That was on
3 May 1899. Omukama Kabalega had no more wish to live
and had in fact refused to allow his wounded arm to be
operated upon by the Europeans until he was persuaded by
his son, George Nyakana, to consent to an operation. Some
people claim that Kabalega killed many Europeans during
this battle. This is not true. The seven Europeans who died
in this battle were killed by the remnants of the Nubian mutineers, who had now joined hands with Kabalega. But it is
true that he killed some few Indians and Somalis, who were
light-skinned and were therefore referred to as "Europeans"
by the people of Kitara.[13]

We saw that our country used to be very big in size but that many parts of it were annexed to our neighbors by the Europeans. Now the capture of Kabalega was a further blow to the people of Kitara. He was taken with Mwanga to Kismayu in Jubaland. Afterwards they were exiled to the Seychelles [Sesere]. Mwanga died in exile on 8 May 1903 but Kabalega lived there for twenty-four years, after which he was freed by a European administration which was sympathetic to him because of his old age. He was allowed to return to his people and spend the remaining days of his life with them.

Unfortunately he never saw his country again. He died on the night of 6 April 1923 at Jinja in Busoga while he was on his homeward journey. But his body was brought home and buried at Mparo—his old capital, from where he had set out to conquer all countries. He was buried on 26 April 1923 in the gombolola of Sabawali, in Buhaguzi County. His mother was the lady Kanyange Nyamutahingurwa of the Banyonza clan.

The Children of Chwa II Kabalega

Omukama Chwa II Yohana [John] Kabalega[14] had very many children. Their exact number is not known but below are the names of those who are remembered:

PRINCES

Yosia Karukara—who became king as Kitahimbwa I.
Andrea Bisereko, M.B.E.—became king as Duhaga II.
Tito Gafabusa, C.B.E.—became king as Winyi IV.

Musa Nyakabwa I	Yobo Rwanyabuzana
Leo Nyakabwa II	Arseni Kakalema
Yozefu Rwedeba	Alberto Mucokoco
Marko Kairumba	Ezekeri Murusura
George Nyakana I	Blasio Balyakwonka
Zekereya Kasohera	Petro Nyakana II
Zabuloni Kamugasa	Kezekia Rwakiswaza
Edwardi Isingoma I	Ernestie Katyetye
Muhamadi Mukababanja	Isaka Muntukwonka
Aramanzane Mwirumubi	Swithen Kaijamurubi
Kosima Kabeba	Nikola Kakyomya
Eria Kamugasa	Nyakana III Basambagwire
Yobo Karakaba	Jasi I

Mikael Jasi II	Rwomwiju
Isingoma II	Kabanda
Nyakaisiki	Y. Kakyomya
Kato I	Karagura
Kairagura	Kabahembya
Muporopyo	Kabandi
Kanyonyi	Mukurehya
Kabakuba	Kisagama
Kabututuru	Kato II
Rwahwire	Nyakakaikuru
Manyindo	Mucope
Muhomboza	Kabuzi
Mutikya	Kabusoga
Kanyabuzana	Isingoma III
Kafukera	Musoke
Arajabu Kababebya	Kabugahya
Mujwara	Kakahya
Wakame	Kawamara
Kagumali	Kakibi
Kafuzi	Kato KIII
Kityokityo	Katwire
Byambwene	Mulesa
Maturo	L. Mphohote
Majegeju	P. Katamutole
Kabafumu	Nyakana IV
Kiribubi	

PRINCESSES

Victoria Mukabagabwa—she was the Rubuga [Official Queen-Sister of the King, who had an official position and/or seat on the King's Council] of Kitahimbwa I.

Jerulina Kaikara—she was the Rubuga of Duhaga II.

Ruiza Mukabahaguzi—she was the official sister [Batebe] of Winyi IV.

Yudesi Mukabakuba	Zeresi Mukabatalya
Yudesi Kyonzira	Sara Mukabahemba
Yudesi Mukabaliza	Lakeri Mukababagya
Lea Dunyara	Losira Mukabatasingwa
Yunia Mukabaganja	Serina Mukabadoka
Sara Nyamayarwo	Eseri Kahinju
Eseri Kamugoza	Feresi Mukabanyara
Mariza Kahemwenkya	Martina Katengo

Rozalia Mukabajumba
Zanabu Mukabacanda
Saniya Nyakato I
Fatuma Nyakato II
Asa Nyangoma I
Tezira Mukabasindi
Zanabu Kaniongorro
Zihura Kwebiha
Sofia Mukabahukya
Eva Mukabakonda
Agiri Mukabakwonga
Labeka Kukabacwamba
Anastazia Mukabacope
Maliza Kasomi
Seforoza Mukababale
Amina Nyangoma
Eseza Mukabasindizi
Kigali
Mukabayamba
Mukababanja
Kasaya
Warwo
Mukabasuli
Kababamya
Kayoyo
Kavogoro

Mukabafumu
Kabatwanga
Kabaramagi
Baitwoha
Nygonzinsa
Mukabajwera
Kabajangi
Kabokya
Kabahesi
Kafukera
Kasakya
Kabalisa
Kabajweka
Kahengere
Kababyasi
Kabakuba
Kabokya
Rwomwiju
Kabasuli
Kabanyara
Kabarogo
Kabahinya
Kabahwiju
Kabaganja II
Mukabagwera

As I said earlier it is extremely difficult to give the number of all Kabalega's children. The names listed above are those which could be easily remembered. Many died during the wars with the Europeans and therefore a good deal of their names have been lost to us. Kabalega ranks third among the kings of Kitara who had the greatest number of children. The others were Oyo I Nyimba Kabambaiguru and Duhaga I Chwa Mujwiga.

CHAPTER 6

Later Babiito

OMUKAMA YOSIA KITAHIMBWA I KARUKARA, 1898–1902

King Kitahimbwa was born in Biranga Bigando at the saza headquarters of Rukara W'Itegiraha in 1887. He was captured during Kabalega's wars with the Europeans. He was taken to Buganda together with Lady Nyamutahingurwa, Kabalega's mother. Because Kitahimbwa reigned for only a few years he is not really counted among the kings of Kitara. He was king, nevertheless, because he was addressed by the royal title of Okali and wore the royal sandals. He was made king on 3 April 1898 by the British and meanwhile was filling the place of his father, who was fighting with these Europeans while a fugitive in Lango.[1] He was placed on the throne because the Baganda were threatening peace and were also preparing to move into effective occupation of those parts of Kitara alienated to them by Colonel Evatt.[2]

We shall not dwell for too long on this king because he spent only five years on the throne and he was in any case deposed by the British. The most memorable events of his reign were these: In 1898, the C.M.S. missionaries arrived in the kingdom led by the Reverend Fisher. In 1901 came the Catholics led by P. Grange. There was also a terrible famine during his reign. This occurred in 1898 and was known as *Kyomudaki* [meaning, of the Germans] or *Igora*. It lasted for three years.

Kitahimbwa was the first Omukama to rule Kitara in its diminished form. He was also the first Christian king. During his reign the kingdom was divided into ten counties:

Kaigo—ruled by Jemusi [James] Miti, a Muganda (Bujenje)
Mukwenda—ruled by Paulo Byabacwezi (Bugahya)
Sekiboobo—ruled by Mika Fataki, a Musoga (Chope)
Kangaho—ruled by Kirube Antoni, a Muganda (Chope)
Kitunzi—ruled by Katalikawe (Masindi)
Kimbugwe—ruled by Basigara (Buruli)
Katambara—ruled by Daudi Mbabi (Buruli)
Mugema—ruled by Komwiswa (Cope)

Pokino—ruled by Sirasi Tibansamba (Bugungu)
Kasuju—ruled by Mikaili Buligwanga (Bulega)

Unfortunately this king was ill advised by his counsellors, who influenced him to think in different ways and in fact cheated him because he was very young. They could have helped him by their counsel but failed to do any such thing.

In 1902 he was deposed by the government [central] and was taken to Bugangaizi—now in the area of the lost counties —and given *mailo* [freehold] land.[3] He is still alive. His mother was the lady Nzahe of the Bayaga clan.

OMUKAMA DUHAGA II ANDREA BISEREKO, M.B.E., 1902–24

Duhaga was addressed by the name of "Rubaza n'ekaramu Kalera bikya." He succeeded his younger brother, Kitahimbwa I, to the throne of Bunyoro[4] on 17 September 1902. In the past he would have been named Kyebambe [usurper] because Kitahimbwa was still alive; but because he was a weak, small man, he was given the name of Duhaga II after his great and illustrious great-grandfather, Duhaga I, thus signifying that he would kuhaga [expand in size] on the throne.[5] He is counted among the very brave kings of Kitara because of his determination to abide by his decision.[6]

The most important events during his reign were, first, the Nyangire revolt. In 1907 Saza Chief James Miti, a Muganda, planned secretly with some of his fellow Baganda who lived in Bunyoro to fill vacant sazaships with Baganda. This caused very bad feelings among the people of Bunyoro. There started a cold war—a war not involving the use of guns, spears, or sticks, but a war of words which came to be known as "Nyangire [I have refused]." This war was spearheaded by Leo Kaboha, Saza Chief of Buruli, and the gombolola chiefs Daudi Bitatule, Ibrahim Talyeba, Zabuloni Tibesigwa, Asimani Murohoza; three princes, Zekereya Kasohera, Eria Kamugasa, and Rujumba Ruyonga,[7] son of Kalimira, Enkoto ya Pawiri; and many others. About fifty-five participants in this cold war were deported to Buganda, while twelve others were banished to Kitui in Kenya for three years. After this revolt the government [central] made the king the sole ruler of the country. Saza Chief Paulo Byabachwezi was made to pay 7,500 rupees to the king. He also gave his *obwesengeze*[8] [villages under his control] to the king.[9]

Other events included a famine called Kiromere. It broke out in 1907 and continued into 1908. In 1909 sleeping sickness descended on the regions of Lake Albert and carried off the Saza Chief [Pokino] of Bugungu. Consequently the Bagungu were forced to move into Bugahya. Paulo Byabachwezi, who had been saza chief during the reign of many kings, died in 1912.[10] Because he had collaborated with the Europeans, the government allowed his children to inherit his saza of Bugahya.[11] It was divided into two counties[12] —Bugahya, which was given to his heir, Zakayo Jawe, and Buhaguzi, which was given to his second son, Andrea Buterre, who also became saza chief of another area, the Sekiboobo of Chope. After Byabachwezi's death, the government assumed responsibility for his other son, Petro Rwakaikara, who later became saza chief of Chope [Kangaho] and of Bugungu [Pokino]. He retired in 1940. Paulo Byabachwezi had the good fortune of having many children. He had married a princess by whom he got a son called Leubeni Komurubuga, who died in May 1947. Komurubuga's children are also heirs of their grandfather's property. They are still young and are at a boarding school at Budo in Buganda.

In 1913 the king's capital was moved from Hoima to Masindi because of the construction of ports at Masindi Port and Butiaba, in Masindi. His palace was at Kihande.

In 1914 the First World War broke out. It was caused by the Germans. The king summoned his army and put it under the charge of Prince Kosima Kabeba. It was, however, commanded by a government officer, Captain Place. The king's men fought well and proved their worth. After the war the king was awarded the M.B.E. in 1918.

In 1914, too, a serious famine nicknamed, "Zimya etara" [meaning, switch off the light—because husbands would prefer to eat in the dark so that they could not see their family starving] broke out.

In 1917, Petro Bikunya, now saza chief of Bugahya, was appointed Katikiro [Prime Minister] by the king. He was to do everything in the country in the king's name. In 1918 another famine broke out, the famine of *Kabakuli* [bowls]. The government helped a great deal by bringing food from other countries. There were three major famines during Duhaga II's reign—Kikomere in 1908; Zimya etara, 1914; and Kabakuli, 1918. And some Banyoro prophets have predicted another serious famine in the future to be known as the famine of Kalyeitaka. It would be a very serious one and would cause the death of many people.

In 1923 the government released Omukama Chwa II Kabalega from detention and allowed him to go back to his country. Omukama Duhaga II sent emissaries to meet him at Mombasa. They were Prince Tito Gafabusa and Yakobo Byomere Kaijongoro. They accompanied him as far as Jinja and returned to Bunyoro. Then Duhaga sent Princesses Ruth I. O., the king's daughter, and Jerulina K. Kalyota [the king's official sister] to meet him. Later on he proceeded to Jinja himself but Kabalega died while he was still on his way.

After Kabalega's death another coronation ceremony was held to install Duhaga as the real king and heir to his father. But he died soon afterwards, on 30 March 1924. Delegates from many countries attended his funeral. They included Prince Yusufu Sunna, Sir Apolo Kaggwa, Jacob Musajalumbwa [from Buganda]; Nasanairi Mayanja, the Katikiro of Tooro; and Yekoniya L., who was sent by the President of Busoga. Duhaga II had a very honorable funeral. His tomb is at Kinogozi. His mother was the lady Ruyonga of the Basiita clan. Duhaga II had three daughters and no male heir. And here are their names:

1. Ruth I. Oliver Bisereko
2. Alexandria Komukyeya Bisereko
3. Nora Bulituli

During the reign of Duhaga II, some Sazas of Bunyoro were amalgamated because of changes in population patterns, and were reduced to six as a result:

1. Bujenje—ruled by James Miti (Kaigo), a Muganda.
2. Bugahya—ruled by Zakayo Jawe (Mukwenda) of the Bamoli clan.
3. Buhaguzi—ruled by Daudi Katongole (Pokino) of the Basaigi clan.
4. Buruli—ruled by Tomasi Mbeta (Kimbugwe) of the Babwoya clan.
5. Kihukya—ruled by Andrea Buterre (Sekiboobo) of the Bamoli clan.
6. Kibanda—ruled by Prince Hermenegildo Karubanga of the Babiito clan.

Omukama Duhaga II spent a long time on the throne and should be remembered for his good and efficient rule.[13]

OMUKAMA WINYI IV TITO GAFABUSA, C.B.E., 1924–

Omukama Winyi succeeded his elder brother, Andrea B. Duhaga II, on 12 April 1924. He is addressed as "Rubaza n'enkuba, Ngambonyingi." He is addressed as "Rubaza n'enkuba [the one who speaks with thunder]" because he traveled in an airplane made by white men from Masindi to Hoima in October 1923. He spent a long time in the clouds and that is why he is honored with the title of "the one who speaks with thunder." He is honored with the title of "Ngambonyingi [many languages]" because he can speak English, Swahili, and the language of the people of the islands of Seychelles, and with that of "Rubaza n'ekaramu [one who speaks with a pen]" because he can write. And he is also given the honorable title of "Muzahuranganda [the one who brings back home all the clans from foreign countries]" because he was the first king to visit other kingdoms and countries purely for friendly or business reasons and not, as of old, for the sake of waging war. His intentions were to get to know his fellow kings, to cause them to come together and love one another, and to break with the tradition which prohibited kings from visiting one another. Winyi IV is counted as a king of peace because no wars have broken out during his reign. His mother is the lady Elizabeth Kasemira of the Mweri clan.

Now, it is necessary to record the important events since he became king. In 1925 the Hoima–Masindi road was built and was called Karungi or Kawinyi [literally, of Winyi]. Masindi was the capital of Bunyoro at the time of his accession to the throne. But it was Winyi IV who moved it back to Hoima. The cotton crop was also introduced into Bunyoro during his reign and Banyoro were encouraged to grow it as a cash crop. A ginnery was also built to process the cotton. Tobacco was introduced by the white men in 1927,[14] and Banyoro were also encouraged to grow it. These two crops became very important in the Bunyoro economy and our thanks must go to the Uganda Colonial Government for their efforts to develop our country. In 1928 an outbreak of *nsotoka* [cattle disease] killed off many cattle. But the advent of two

European veterinary doctors prevented the breed from being decimated.

In 1928, too, Bunyoro was honored with the visit of some very important white men led by Sir Hilton Young. The aim of their visit was to make investigations relating to the feasibility of creating an East African Federation of Kenya, Tanganyika, and Uganda. They were welcomed in the Bunyoro Rukurato [local Parliament] on 17 January 1928. And on 13 March of the same year Omukama Winyi IV got his first son and named him John David Rukidi.

In 1931, a conference to deal with the issue of an East African Federation sat in London and the Omukama sent a delegate to explain the obstacles in the way of such a federation. The envoy was Prince Kosia K. Labwoni, Saza Chief of Bujenje [Kaigo]. Prince Labwoni left Hoima on 30 March 1931 and reached London on 26 April. He remained in London until 14 May and arrived back in Hoima on 8 June 1931.

Land and Land Taxes

A commission to inquire into the system of land tenure in Bunyoro was set up in 1931 by the Colonial Government. It met on 28 August 1931, first at Masindi town in the Provincial Commissioner's office, and then moved to Hoima on 1 September and sat at the District Commissioner's office. They reported back to the Colonial Secretary in London, recommending the reorganization of the land system in Bunyoro. This involved the abolition of the individual ownership of enormous areas of cultivated and uncultivated land, as well as the abolition of chiefly *obwesengeze* [fiefdoms]. These disappeared completely by 31 December 1932. The central government declared the common ownership of land in Bunyoro. The possession of land would be allowed to anyone who could make the best use of it. Everyone was entitled to land ownership and the only thing he had to do was to procure a certificate of occupancy from the government which recognized the ownership of his plot. Bunyoro land became public property in this way. In future this land system would not fail to create happiness among the people, who would gradually come to realize its benefits. In short, it abolished the old system of *mailo* land, which was resented by the common man and which has created untold sufferings for the poor in other parts of Uganda because of the exacting demands of the system.[15]

In 1933, there started the system of the "New Bunyoro" when all the money accruing from land taxes was put in the national exchequer and used for the public good. For the first time, all the chiefs and public servants from the Omukama himself to the Katikiro, saza chiefs, gombolola chiefs, bakungu and muluka chiefs—all these were paid salaries. From that date, too, long and faithful servants of the government became entitled to life pensions.

The Omukama Visits Other Areas

In 1933, Winyi IV began his visits to other areas. He set off in May 1933 and visited Buganda, Ankole, Kigezi, and Tooro. On 2 May he visited the Roman Catholic missions in Buganda. He also visited Buddu, which was at that time ruled by Rauli Kiwanuka. On 3 May he paid a visit to George Sefasi Kabumbuli Kamuswaga, Saza Chief of Kooki. Kooki used to be an independent kingdom in the past. Its independence ended on 14 November 1896, when this kingdom was made into a county of Buganda. George Sefasi Kabumbuli Kamuswaga is a true Mubiito of the direct line of Omukama Olimi III Isansa.

The Omukama also visited Mbarara, the capital of the Omugabe of Ankole, on 4 May. On 5 May he was welcomed into the palace of Sulemani Edward Kahaya, M.B.E., Omugabe of Ankole. The two monarchs sat in the royal chairs and conversed like ordinary men. They also inspected the regalia of Ankole and Winyi was able to see the main royal drum of Ankole called *Bagendanwa*, which was cut off from that of his great-grandfather Duhaga I, who had led an expedition into Ankole around 1770. These were important events in the history of Uganda, for Sir Tito Winyi IV was the first king to visit other kings.

On 8 May, he visited Kigezi in the Southwest of Uganda and the areas which had once been conquered by his great-grandfather Chwa Mali I. This was also a great event in the history of the country. On 12 May he crossed Lake George and in the lake he saw one of Kabalega's boats which were used to cross his men when they went on expeditions into Ankole and Rwanda. The king went as far as Lake Katwe, from where salt is collected. He climbed onto the top of a

hill called Katwe and saw the Ituri forest in the Congo and
caught a glimpse of his father's [Kabalega's] extensive
kingdom.

He then visited the capital of Tooro. He did not enter the
palace because the Omukama of Tooro, George Rukidi, was
out of his capital on a visit to his county of Kyaka.

On 15 May he went to Mubende before returning to his
kingdom. When in Mubende he climbed up to the top of
Mubende Hill and tried to draw a picture of the old capital
of Ndahura, the first of the Bachwezi kings. Standing on
Mubende Hill one can see all the four kingdoms of Uganda.
Mubende Hill is situated in the heart of the four kingdoms
because nearby, on Mubende Road, there is a milestone
which reads 104 miles to Hoima, Fort Portal, and Kampala.
It would also be 104 miles if a road was built from Mubende
to Mbarara.

The Bunyoro Agreement, 1933

The most important event during the reign of Omukama
Winyi IV so far, and which should be remembered at all
times, was the Bunyoro Agreement signed by the central
government and the Bunyoro Kingdom Government. It was
signed on 23 October 1933 and by it the Colonial Government
contracted to defend Bunyoro at all times.[16]

Another big event in this period was the visit of Sir Philip
Gunliffe-Lister G.B.E., P.C., M.C., M.P., the British Colonial
Secretary, to Bunyoro. He came by airplane and arrived in
Hoima on 12 January 1934. He visited the Bunyoro Rukurato
in the afternoon of the same day at about 3 P.M. On this day
the good honorable Sir Bernard Henry Bourdillon, Governor
of Uganda, conferred on Rukirabasaija Agutamba [one who is
above all men] T. G. Winyi IV, the Omukama of Bunyoro,
the honor of the Commander of the British Empire [C.B.E.]
awarded to him by the king of Britain. The king also awarded
our good District Commissioner of Bunyoro, Mr. E. D. Tongue,
who was responsible for the Bunyoro Agreement as well as
the new good system of land tenure and salaries for government officials, the honor of the O.B.E.

On 2 May 1934 the Omukama received a letter from King
George V of England. This letter bore the signature of the
illustrious prince: H.R.H. the Prince of Wales, and conferred

on Winyi IV the "Companion of Honour," thereby making
him a member of the British Royal Guard.

World War II

On 3 September 1939 a war broke out in Europe because
of the German invasion of Poland. During this war Britain
combined with the U.S.A. and other countries to fight against
the Germans and the Japanese. Their aim was to stop a world
conflagration.

The Omukama of Bunyoro allowed many of his subjects
to enlist in the fight for peace. They fought in Kenya, Abyssinia, Somaliland, Egypt, Palestine, Ceylon and Burma [in
Asia], Madagascar, and other areas.

R.A.,[17] the Omukama of Bunyoro, sent a delegate to visit
the soldiers who were fighting abroad. The delegate visited
Nairobi, Yata, Nanyiki, Mombasa, and Moshi [all in East
Africa]. The name of this delegate is John W. Nyakatura,
Saza Chief of Chope [Sekiboobo]. Nyakatura left Bunyoro
in December 1943 and returned in January 1944. He is the
author of this book.

In May 1944 R.A., the Omukama, T. G. Winyi IV, C.B.E.,
decided to inspect the soldiers in East Africa. He was accompanied by J. W. Nyakatura, Saza Chief, and his Secretary,
Polycarpo Kwebiiha. He visited many military stations where
Ugandan, and other African, soldiers were stationed. He returned to Bunyoro in June 1944.

World War II ended on 8 May 1945 in Europe, while it
lasted until 15 August in Asia. Already on 4 September 1942,
some Polish refugees who had been captured during the war,
had arrived in Bunyoro. The Omukama and his government
housed them at Nyabyeya in the saza of Bujenje.

These Poles numbered more than four thousand. They have
remained in Bunyoro up to this day. The aforesaid are the
most important events which took place during the reign of
Omukama Winyi IV. May he reign for long on the throne
of Bunyoro and may God give him peace and good fortune
so that he may restore the kingdom's former glory which
has been destroyed.

Part V
KITARA MONARCHY

CHAPTER 1

The Regalia of Kitara, The Government, and Miscellaneous

The Crowns [*Amakondo*]

There was a kind of distinction bestowed by the king upon his subjects who had rendered service of outstanding merit to the kingdom or those who had gained his favor. This kind of honor was known as *Ekondo*, or crown. I am going to give the names of some of the wearers of these *kondos*. The wearers of these crowns, or *kondos*, were known as *Abajwarakondo*, or crown-wearers. I am also going to give you the list of the important crowns.

The people on whom this honor had been bestowed had to observe some restrictions with regard to food. They did not eat potatoes, beans, and other vegetables, because such foods were regarded as low. They kept these food restrictions until death. If they did anything unbecoming, their heads were cut off with an ax known as *Karamaire*.

The Crowns of the Babiito

1. The two most important crowns are known as *Rwabusungu* and *Kasunsunkwanzi*.
2. Omukama Rukidi's crown is known as *Nyakwehuta*, named after one of the royal musicians who was of the Muyaga clan.
3. Bamuroga, the Chief Minister of the Palace, also had a crown.
4. Nyakoka, the Royal Diviner, also had a crown.
5. Kasaru, the interpreter of the Omukama Rukidi, who did not know the language of Kitara, also had a crown.

6. Kadongolima of the Bakwonga clan, a rebel who defied the king by greeting him with her back turned towards him, also had a crown. She was the mother of Rukidi. Kadongolima's crown was made of chicken feathers and covered with bead work.

7. Rupiri Kisenge, who came from Bugahya, and was courteous to a fault, was rewarded with a crown. He was the person who had a spear known as *Kabazi* stuck in the roof of his house. Rupiri Kisenge's house floor was covered with grass and a piece of ivory at the door. He was a Mubiito of the Bacaki subsection. He was the brother of Rukidi and had the same mother as he. He came to Kitara together with his brother Rukidi.

8. Kasoira Kamulimba also had a kondo. He used to smoke his pipe in the sitting room of *Karuzika,* the main house in the palace. He was the Royal Diviner of the Bachwezi and had been left behind by them so that he could carry on his work under the Babiito dynasty. Kasoira's pipe was lit by Bamuroga, the Chief of the Palace. He was very much loved by Rukidi, who gave him his pipe which he had brought with him from Bukidi.

9. Zigija Mugema had a kondo. He was of the Bapopi clan. His kondo was the most important of all the kondos belonging to chiefs. Whenever foreigners came to see the king, Mugema was made to wear his kondo and was the one who welcomed important foreign visitors on behalf of the king. If the king did not wish to meet those foreigners at all, they invariably left the country convinced that they had met the real king, whereas in fact they had only met the Mugema.

10. Kanagwa's kondo: Kanagwa was the chief of *Karamaire* house. He was of the Bachwa clan.

11. Kyakora kya Ibanda's kondo: Kyakora kya Ibanda was the mother of Omukama Duhaga I and was of the Basaigi clan.

12. Mutwanga's kondo: Mutwanga was the mother of Omukama Kyebambe I and was of the Bazikya clan.

13. Olimi's kondo: Olimi was the mother of Omukama Isansa Olimi III.

14. Nyakabango ka Rugwa's kondo: Nyakabango ka Rugwa was of the Bakurungo clan and was the washer of the king's dish known as *Kayanja.*

15. Isingoma lya Kabu's kondo: Isingoma lya Kabu was of

the Batonezi clan. He was the executioner of the *Bajwarakondo* [crown-wearers], chiefs, and Babiito if they did anything wrong. Isingoma lya Kabu's house was near *Mugabante* on the left side where the sun rises.

16. Oraro's kondo: Oraro was the first Mubiito to wear a kondo.

17. Kasunsunkwanzi kondo: this kondo was for the Tooro region. It was seized by Kaboyo [in the nineteenth century]. Kasunsunkwanzi crown was originally a royal crown belonging to Rukidi.

18. Omuhaguzi Rujunde's kondo: [no information supplied].

19. Kisaka's kondo: [no information supplied].

20. Mupacwa Rukumba rwa Majamba's kondo: Mupacwa Rukumba rwa Majamba was the grandfather of H. Karubanga, M.B.E., Saza Chief Kimbugwe.

Crowns Given by the King

21. Rusongoza's kondo: Rusongoza was the son of Byontabara. This kondo did not originally belong to him but belonged to a king's mother [the particular king not mentioned], the lady Nsera Nyabyoma, who lived at Kitemba. Rusongoza had taken sides with Kabalega during his rivalry with his brother for the kingship.

22. Nyakamatura's kondo: Nyakamatura was of the Bamoli clan. This kondo had once belonged to Jawe, the mother of King Kyebambe III Nyamutukura, who belonged to the Bachwa clan. It was given to Nyakamatura by Kabalega because he had won the king's favor. Nyakamatura had sided with him in his schemes to become king.

23. Bapuya's kondo belonged to Kyamuhangire of the Badoka clan, who joined Kabalega during his fight for the throne.

24. Katongole ka Kikatu's kondo: Katongole ka Kikatu was the Chief of the *Kisindizi* [a house in the palace].

25. Kapodi Omweganywa's kondo: Kapodi Omweganywa was of the Bachwa clan, which produced the mother of Omukama Kyebambe III Nyamutukura. Omukama Kabalega gave it to his mother Duburwa.

26. Ntamara Omunyakitara's kondo: Ntamara belonged to the Banyonza clan. This crown had originally belonged to the Bachwa clan and was won by a man called Mwanga.

27. Mwenge's kondo: This crown was given to Mugarra. It
    had originally belonged to the Bafunjo clan, the clan of
    the mother of Omukama Nyabongo II Mugenyi.

28. Ruhonko was Bukya's kondo: This crown once belonged
    to the clan of the mother of Omukama Kyebambe IV
    Kamurasi. It was later given to Ruhonko of the Basiita
    clan.

29. Kikukuule kya Runego's kondo: Kikukuule kya Runego
    was of the Bairuntu clan. It was given to him by Omu-
    kama Kabalega.

30. The Kyambukya kondo belonged to Kabiri ka Rukoba. It
    is now in possession of Tibezinda, his son.

31. Kitanga's kondo: Kitanga was the ruler of Nsorro and
    belonged to the Bachwa clan. This crown was given to
    Ireeta by Kabalega, but Ireeta died without having won
    it. It also originally belonged to the mother of Omukama
    Kyebambe III Nyamutukura.

32. Mutunzi ya Munyara's kondo: Mutunzi was given this
    crown by the king. This crown originally belonged to
    Chope.

33. Komukibira Kabahinda's kondo: Komukibira Kabahinda
    was of the Bafumbya clan. This crown once belonged to
    the clan of the mother of Omukama Duhaga I. It was
    given to Komukibira Kabahinda by Omukama Chwa II
    Kabalega.

34. Nyakabango ka Rugwa's kondo: Nyakabango ka Rugwa
    was of the Bakurungo clan. He died without having won
    his kondo—he had been promised one by the king, though
    he died before having won it. He instead wore a bird's
    feather when there were *Empango* celebrations. This
    crown had originally belonged to the ruler of Butema.

35. Kasoro Rujara's kondo: [no further information supplied].

36. Rwabwongo's kondo: Rwabwongo came from Busesa and
    was a Royal Diviner.

37. Kaboyo Kabaitahona's kondo: Kaboyo Kabaitahona was
    of the Basiita clan. This crown was later given to the
    clan of the mother of King Chwa II Kabalega.

38. Ikwambu's crown: Ikwambu was the ruler of Bunyara.
    This crown originally belonged to the Babiito.

39. Kadyebo's kondo: Kadyebo belonged to the Badoka clan.
    This crown was made for him on the order of the king.

40. Olimi ya Kazana's kondo: Olimi ya Kazana was of the
    Badoka clan and the ruler of Kigaya.

41. Kagoro's kondo: Kagoro came from Kibiro [near Lake Albert]. This crown had been lost but has now been recovered.
42. Bikamba bya Kabale's kondo: Bikamba bya Kabale was of the Badoka clan.
43. Kabagyo's kondo: Kabagyo was the attendant to Omukama Rukidi.
44. Ndibalema's kondo: Ndibalema was of the Balisa clan, and a Saza Chief of Buhweju. He belonged to the clan of the mother of Omukama Winyi II Rubagiramasega.

We have now seen the number of the kondos of Bunyoro-Kitara. Later on I am going to explain to you about two things:

1. *Empyemi.*
2. *Enjeru.*

Traditional Government

Besides the saza chiefs, who ruled the country, there were:

1. Princes and princesses.
2. The mother of the king.
3. The head of the Babiito [princes].
4. The head of the Babiitokati [princesses] [Batebe, Kalyota, or Rubuga].

There was also a section of the Babiito known as the "Babiito of the Chair." This included the important Babiito, the king's wives, and some important chiefs. Besides these were the keepers of the king's regalia, etc., the king's minor chiefs, the clan heads, and the Bahuma [Bahima]. Their job was to settle minor cases. The Bamuroga was their leader or their Katikiro.

Geography

Kitara was surrounded by water on the right and on the left [east and west]. It extended to the boundaries of Busoga, Buganda, Nkore, and the Congo.

The people living near the lakes knew the skills of boat-building, fishing, and trading. They exchanged goods with other countries. They also provided the country with fish. The area between Lake Kyoga and Lake Albert was ruled by the Bakitara [Banyoro] chiefs who did not pay tribute to any ruler.

The lakes were also important as a source of different types of salt. From Lake Kyoga came a kind of salt known as *ebinyangurwe*, while from Lake Albert near Kibiro came a finer type of salt known as *enseru*. Tonya, Kaiso, and Buhuka also produced salt. A less fine type of salt came from Katwe and Busongora. The extracting of salt, fishing, and other jobs connected with the presence of water were done by the people of Kitara without the assistance of people from other areas. The salt was a very important item in the life of the Banyoro [Bakitara]. It was used locally for food and was also exported to the neighboring countries like Busoga, Bukidi [Lango], Teso, Acholi, Bulega, Buganda, Nkore, and Rwanda. It was even exported as far as Karagwe.

Land was of very great importance in Kitara. It was important for building houses, cultivating food, and grazing cattle, goats, etc. It was also important for extracting iron and clay for making pots. The iron was used for making hoes, knives, axes, and other things. It was also exported to other countries and in this way brought money into the country. Iron hoes were sold in Busoga, Lango, Acholi, Bulega, Buganda, and other countries. Kitara was self-sufficient in her requirements of iron implements. She was the sole maker of these. The Bakitara were well-skilled smiths, carpenters, potters, etc.

Clothing

Clothing was made of bark cloth, which was got from a type of tree known as *omutoma*. These were made by the people of Kitara themselves.[1] Besides the bark cloth, the people also wore skins of animals.

The Economy

This consisted mainly of cattle, sheep, and chickens. These were eaten as meat. The cattle also produced milk. They were also used for securing wives [bride price]. Ivory was also of economic importance to the country. It was got from elephants and was sold to Arab traders. The people in turn bought clothing [material], beads, guns, and shells from the Arabs [and, later, from the Europeans].

Kitara had many forests, whose trees were used for making boats, household utensils, and other things. There were many markets in Kitara. There was plenty of food and the country was self-sufficient in this aspect. She did not therefore need to import food from any neighboring country. There are many areas of fertile soil in Kitara.

CHAPTER 2

The King's Palace

The Buildings Found in the Palace

Let us now describe the setting of the king's palace and all the important buildings inside it.

The palace had to face the direction where the sun sets [west]. This was the custom from the time of Rukidi I [Mpuga] to that of Chwa II Kabalega. But with the coming of Christianity, the present kings do not follow this custom.

The Important Buildings Inside the Palace:

Karuzika	*Kasenda*
Kabagarama	*Kidoka*
Rwengo	*Kihukya*
Kadebede	*Kacwabwemi*
Kapeka	*Rwenyana*
Icwamitwe	*Karuhonko*
Kaitabadoma	*Kabarwaire*
Munkambi	*Kyambukya*
Bakutumaki	*Kyokya*
Kapanapa	*Ibandiro*

There were other halls, which were like courts. For example:

Nyamagambo was the hall used for secret talks. It was situated near *Ibandiro* house.

The *Bamwenagaho* was used for meeting people from other countries.

The other halls situated inside the palace included:

The *Rwabagara*	The *Kyarubanga*
The *Kaiohya*	The *Binyonyi*[1]
The *Barwara*	The *Kitanga*

The *Muchwa* hall was used as a court for the Batebe [the head of the princesses] and for the Babiitokati [princesses].

The *Kyamunuma*.

The *Kyakato* belonged to Kato Kimera, who rebelled against Rukidi I.

The *Kitogo* was a court belonging to the Okwiri [head of the Babiito princes].

The rest included the:

Kamurweya—Kacwa Magosi
Rwemigo—Kasenda-Akakoma
Mugabante [the main gate]
Manywayo
Bakutumaki [Kyokya]

The Royal Drums

The *Nyalebe* and *Kajumba* were left behind by the Bachwezi. The *Tibamulinde* once belonged to Rukidi I Mpuga.

There was also the:

Musegewa.
Mwiganjura—originally belonged to Duhaga I.
Galisoigana—originally belonged to Kyebambe III Nyamutukura.
Rugonya—originally belonged to Nyabongo II Mugenyi.
Aramutanga—originally belonged to Kyebambe IV Kamurasi.
Mugarra Nganda—originally belonged to Chwa II Kabalega.
Mpumuro—originally belonged to Duhaga II Andrea Bisereko.
Kalembe—belongs to Winyi IV Tito Gafabusa.

The Military Drums

Nyalebe—was left by the Bachwezi.
Kaijwire
Nkukumba
Nyambaga
Nyakangubi
Asindika ekitagenda
Macalya
Balyoga
Nigwaka
Kabatembe
Ntajemerwa
Kaliba Katoito

The Batebe [the king's official sister and head of the Ba-
    biitokati] also has a military drum, called *Asarra owabu*
    azikiza.
The Okwiri [the head of the Babiito] has also a military drum,
    called *Runyanya*.
The Bamuroga's military drum is called *Kanumi*.

The Royal Chairs

The *Nyamyaro* originally belonged to Rukidi I. This is found
    in the sitting room of the main house [*Karuzika*].
The *Kaizirokwera* was left by the Bachwezi and stays in a
    room known as *Nsika* in the *Karuzika*.
The *Kabwizi* was left by the Bachwezi, and
The *Maherre* was also left by the Bachwezi.

The Royal Spears

The *Kimuli kyokyamahanga* was left by the Bachwezi.
The *Kinegena* was left by the Bachwezi.
Maherre was left by the Bachwezi.
The *Katasongerwa mukuru atahwita* was left by the
    Bachwezi.

The Spears of the Babiito

The *Kaitantahi*
The *Galengera*

The *Dabongo*
Goti Ati [or *Goti Goti*]
The *Kaizireigo*—found in the sitting room of the *Karuzika*.
The *Nyamuhaibona Enganzi y'Okwezi*
The *Kirazankamba*
The *Mutasimburwa*

Other Regalia

These are as follows:

Rwobusungu: the chief crown or coronet, used to belong to Rukidi.

Kasunsu nkwanzi: also used to belong to Rukidi.

Karamaire: also used to belong to Rukidi.

Kabindango: also used to belong to Rukidi.

Nyamiringa: is a shield which once belonged to the Bachwezi.

Bisegege: is a shield which belonged to Rukidi.

Nyapogo obuta

Ndayampunu Omufuko

Busutama, Empirima [sword]

Kaguli Kidukuru: once belonged to the Abachwezi.

Nyamutungwa kisabu: once belonged to the Abachwezi.

Mugaju

Kyamusika [jar]

Hurru, Ebohera, Bagimbirwa

Kayanja [bowl]

Nyakabiito [bowl]

Malere yugi: water jug—supposed to have come from the sky.

Rwendero: a string of beads, also supposed to have come from the sky.

Ziribayo: a bangle, also supposed to have come from the sky.

Biganja: "shoes" which belonged to Rukidi.

Kaliruga: a walking stick which belonged to Rukidi.

And many more other things. It is very difficult to give the list of them all and also to explain their uses unless one got hold of all their keepers. However, it is very difficult to get hold of them these days. It would be worthwhile to write a separate book about the regalia of the kings of Kitara for the sake of the young generation who will never get a chance of seeing them.

The Royal Greeting

The king is greeted in this way:

"Engundu zona Okali." When the king appears, those present greet him, *"Kaboneke, Mwebingwa."* When the king is entering a house, those present greet him, *"Hamulyango Mbaire."* When he sits, they greet him, *"Kahangirize Agutamba!"* When he walks out, they greet him thus: *"Ha kyaro Nkya nungi."* When he is standing, they greet him thus: *"Omu byemo Wamara."* The king's subjects honor him with such sayings: *"Ha kyaro Rukirabasaija* [You who are better than all men in this village]"; *"Ha kyaro Agutamba* [The savior of the people in the country]"; or

Ha kyaro Mbaire.
"   "   Owa Kitara.
"   "   Nzaire.
"   "   Mwebingwa.
"   "   Ikingura.
"   "   Iguru Iyezire.
"   "   Kasorobahiga.
"   "   Kasura banyunya.
"   "   Nkya nungi.
"   "   Nzigu magana.
"   "   Kituli kinobere abeemi.
"   "   Wamara ya Bwera.
"   "   Rusenda mainaro.
"   "   Nyamunyaka.
"   "   Byoto kikekiire.
"   "   Bigere bisaga omu muhanda.
"   "   Lyogere.
"   "   Mbumba.
"   "   Ngabu ekamwa.
"   "   Ibuza bugyo.

The king's mother is also greeted in a special way. She may also be greeted in the same way as the king because she is a very important figure in the king's life. What pleases her also pleases her son.

Coronation of a New King

A king usually succeeded his father or his brother, who had died. He first had to perform the burial ceremony of his father's or brother's body before he could become king. In the case of a succession war, he had first to defeat his enemies before he could become king.

A new palace was built in preparation for the day of his accession to the throne.

When the day came the king's body had to be washed, his nails cut, and his hair shaved. These accession rites took place at the prince's maternal uncle's or any chief's house. In the afternoon around 3 P.M., he was carried by the chiefs and other people into the new palace. At the entrance of the palace, he was led by the Bamuroga, the Chief of the Palace, and Nyakoka and Kasoira, the diviners. Besides these was also a certain prince of Nyarwa's line. When they reached a certain part of the palace, *Mugabante,* the diviners killed a special cow called Rutale. Then the aforementioned prince spoke up in a loud voice, saying:

> Oh God of Gods, King of Kings, the king of the sky and the earth. I have brought this king to ascend the throne succeeding his father. Let the Royal Drum refuse to speak if he is not fit to be king or if he is not the rightful heir to his father's and grandfather's throne.

After saying this, the king and those leading him crossed the blood of the killed cow and chicken. The king entered the palace, being led by the Saza Chief Mugema, the head of all chiefs. When the king reached the doorway of his palace, or *Karuzika,* the aforementioned prince and diviners would repeat the same words mentioned above. Then the prince asked for a small drum known as *Nyalebe.* He then beat this drum nine times. Meanwhile all the people would be assembled in merriment. After this, the king jumped over a piece of ivory and then went and sat on the royal chair called *Nyamyaro.* Now he had become a real king and there were no longer any doubts. He was given the kingly possessions and his regalia the next day. He did not speak to anybody during the night and slept on one side of his body without rolling about in his bed. A man stayed all night at his side to see that he did not make any mistakes.

The Handing Over of the Crown and all the Royal Possessions to the New King

The king was woken up before dawn, at around 3 A.M. He then left the *Kabagarama* [house] and spent the rest of the night sleeping on the royal bed in the *Karuzika*. He then went to the *Kyambukya* and sat on another royal chair, known as *Kabwizi*. Then the king's washer-man brought water in a special jar known as *Mugaju* and put it in the bathroom and then the king had a bath. After bathing he left the *Kyambukya* and went back to the *Kabagarama*. Then one of the king's wives who stayed in the *Kabagarama* brought water in a jar and the king washed his face and mouth. Then the king's attendants brought bark cloth and dressed him. After being dressed, his wife at the *Kabagarama* would bring a basket of beads and then she would put strings of beads on the king's arms, feet, and round his neck.

After dressing, the king went to *Karuzika*. He first went to his bedroom and he then appeared in the sitting room, where he found every person in charge of a single royal possession ready. At this time, the aforementioned prince said once more:

> May God preserve our king and may he live for long. May he have children, riches, and may he die a very old man with white hair.

Meanwhile the crown-wearers would be ready to wear their crowns. The royal drum would be ready to be beaten by the new king while many people surrounded the king. Among these would be the keepers of the king's regalia and the king's musicians.

The Oathing and Anointing of the New King

The king then was made to take an oath by the following people: Bamuroga; Mugema; a prince of Nyarwa's line; Nyakoka and Kasoira; the king's chiefs; Iremera [the king's wife who lived in his bedroom]; Nyaraki; another wife, who lived in another house, called *Kapanapa;* and another wife of the Baitira clan, who looked after the beadworks in the palace. These people made him swear to rule his people bravely, to rule his people well, to welcome foreigners, to look after the interests of his people in an impartial way without making a distinction between the poor and the rich, to look after his people's fatherless children and to be just in settling the people's disputes or cases. The king also swore to do all these things accordingly. After swearing, the prince of Nyarwa's line annointed the king's head with the royal oil [ointment], which is kept in a special horn. This ointment distinguished him from the rest of the people, thus making him king. [This ointment was not from a cow's milk, but came from Lango and was extracted from a tree.]

The king was then made to wear a bangle round his arm, a royal string of beads called *Rwendero* round his neck. Then one of the king's wives who lived in his bedroom brought all sorts of small ceremonial items and handed them to the king. Then the prince of Nyarwa's line announced the king's royal name and royal pet name and put a royal crown called *Rwabusungu* on his head nine times and then put different crowns on the king's head. He then put a crown called *Kasunsunkwanzi* on the king's head and this one remained there.

Then shoes known as *Biganja* were brought and put on the feet of the king. The king would then be given a spear known as *Kinegena*. The handing of this spear to the king signified that he had to kill anyone who did wrong. He would then be given the royal shield known as *Bisegege*. This royal shield meant that the king must suppress any rising in the country in order to safeguard this country.

The king was then given a sword called *Busutama*, which meant that as the sword never misses its point [or cuts straight] the king also had to be upright in settling cases and to rule his country justly. He was then given a stick known as *Kaliruga*. This stick meant that though he was then the sole ruler, he should not kill everyone who wronged him, but could beat others with this stick. The king was also given a belt, which had the same meaning as the stick.

The king was next given a smaller stick [*orujunju*], which meant that he was not to give the same punishment to all wrongdoers, because some commit bigger offences than others, so the king should punish minor offenders by beating them with this small stick.

He was then given an iron hoe, which meant that he had now become the father of all his people and should order all of them to cultivate crops so that the country did not suffer from famine. The king was then given another spear, called *Nyapogo*, and another fighting implement, known as *Ndayampunu*. These meant that he should go and fight any enemy who threatened his country.

He was then given a royal bag [purse] known as *Endyanga Rutanga* made from leopard's skin. This meant that the king should trade, get rich, and give money or help to everyone who asked for help, taking this money from the royal bag.

The king would lastly be given a horn known as *Muserule* and a gourd, both of which meant that whenever he heard the sound of these two, he must go quickly to their help and defend them.

After the king had received these articles, the Bamuroga sent a message to Kakahuka of the Omubwijwa clan, who would be standing on the royal anthill. Kakahuka in turn shouted thus: "Why are the cursed rebels, witch doctors, foreigners, after you?"; and after this the royal ceremony formally began, while all the people shouted and rejoiced. Then the royal servants covered the paths from the *Karuzika* house to *Muchwa* house and from Kakato forest and Kyamunuma to Kamurweya with a long carpet. The path from Kamurweya forest past Kitogo forest to the kraal was strewn with special grass. In the kraal were prepared two young cows, a bull and a she-cow. The herdsman prepared a big fire for them.

After receiving the aforementioned royal implements, the king left the royal chair called *Nyamyaro*. He then met one of his wives, belonging to the Bakwonga clan, who held a small basket of coffee berries and sorghum before the king. He would pick two male coffee berries and two female coffee berries plus the sorghum and put them in his mouth and eat them. He did not throw away the husks from the coffee berries, but held them in his hands.

Omubiitokati [Princess] Kabatongole Smears the King with Water, Earth, and Clay

Then the king met Omubiitokati Kabatongole, who would be holding a jar of water, chalk and earth. This water was specially got from Ndahura's well [Ndahura, the Muchwezi king] on Mubende Hill. The princess mixed these two—the chalk earth and water—and smeared the king's forehead and both cheeks with them. She then got hold of other liquids from vegetables and sprinkled the king with them. She then sprinkled the people present with water. The purpose of this was to bless the king and his people. When sprinkling the king, the princess uttered the names of the king's ancestors. Besides this she also prayed that the king might have children, be prosperous, defend his country and his people, and that God might look down on him with a smile, and that his people and other countries might look upon him with love. The princess uttered all these words with her eyes closed and opened them after saying them.

Then the king gave the princess a chief who ruled the area where the princess chose to live. This chief was to build her a palace in the area she chose. Besides land, the king gave her many things—cattle, servants, etc. From then onwards this princess would never set eyes on the king. This vow she kept until she died.

The King Goes to the Royal Kraal and the Forests [Woods] [Found inside the Palace]

The king then went to the royal kraal, led by the chief palace musician, known as Enzini ya Rwotamahanga [the grandson of Nyakwehuta of the Muyaga clan]. This man was followed by his men playing flutes, etc. The king was followed by the people present and they sang his praise.

When the king came to the *Muchwa* house, he met its chief, known as Batebe or Kalyota [the head of the princesses]. He also met many princesses assembled there, who stood up at his arrival. Then the Kalyota and the princesses touched their heads on the king's shoulder. This was done while the king was standing on a cow's hide.

He then passed through *Kato* forest and, before reaching *Kyamunuma* forest, an elephant's horn and two wire strings were shown to the king. These were shown to him by a foreigner and were implements used by the rainmakers. The king touched the horn and wire strings. This action meant that he was now the boss of the rainmakers and whenever there was no rain in his country, he had the obligation of praying the gods to cause rain and so in this way save his people.

The king then passed through *Kaymunuma* forest and, leaving the forest, he found a spear known as *Kaitantahi* and other implements. These meant that the king had to defend himself from enemies with the aid of these weapons. From here he passed through *Kamurweya* forest [nothing was done in this forest]. He then entered another forest, where he met his "putters-on" [men who dressed the king], who straightened out the garments he was wearing. After this the king went to Kanaiguru [outside the palace enclosure] and the custodians of the royal spears brought the spears to the king, passing through *Rwemigo* forest. These brought the spears before him and held them with their sharp points facing the king.

At this time the keeper of the palace went to summon the king's chiefs, the crown-wearers, the Babiito, and other people, before the king. Then the crown-wearers put their crowns on their heads and all went to pay their respects to the king and to give him presents. It was customary for the king to settle two cases concerning debts at this time. He settled the cases quickly. Those who won their cases would kiss the king's hands. After this, every crown-wearer kissed the king's hands, thanking him for the special favor and honor shown to him.

Then the king retired to *Kamurweya* forest. At the same time, the royal drum left the royal anthill. It passed through *Mugabante* [the main gate to the palace] and was taken to *Kamurweya* forest, where the king was at that time. The royal drum was beaten nine times while at *Kamurweya*. After this a man from the Balisa clan sang a song in praise of Omukama Rukidi's shield [Rukidi was the first Biito king].

The King Comes Back to the Karuzika

Then the king left the *Kamurweya* forest, passing through all the aforementioned forests. The royal drum and all the people passed outside the forests. When the king reached *Karuzika* he would find that one of his wives, the one who belonged to the Bakwonga clan, had spread a white animal hide where he would stand, and would hand over to his queen the coffee husks he had carried in his hands all the way. Then he sat on the royal chair called *Nyamyaro*. Then one of his men took off the crown from the king's head and put it on the lap of the king's mother. He then moved it from the lap of the king's mother to the place where it was usually kept. Afterwards the king left the royal chair and went to the back of the house, where he met another of his queens, belonging to the Balisa clan, who would be ready holding a pot of milk for him to drink.

The king then sat in one of the rooms at the back of the house known as *Nsika*. He was later moved to another royal chair called *Kaizirokwera*. Then the queen handed him the pot of milk and he drank it. When he had drunk the milk, the queen handed him a piece of cloth with which to wipe his lips, and another one to clean his hands. After this, the king went and sat on his royal bed. He remained here only for a short time, and moved again back to the royal chair called *Kaizirokwera* in another room. While in this room his queen, belonging to the Baitira clan, brought a pot used for making milk into butter. She pointed this pot to the king nine times, which meant that "This pot was left to me by your grand-fathers, the Bachwezi, when they were leaving this world. I kept this pot and gave it to your grandfathers, the Babiito. I will always keep it safely for your sake. It is the one I am going to use to make butter which you will eat." She then brought a basket and pointed the basket at the king nine times. This meant that "This basket was left to me by your ancestors, the Bachwezi, and the Babiito. I will keep it well for your sake, as well as the other things kept in this basket."

The King Comes Back to the Sitting Room and Sits on the Royal Chair Called Nyamyaro

After this ceremony the king left the back room known as *Nsika* and went back to the sitting room and sat on the royal chair known as *Nyamyaro*. Meanwhile, the royal celebrations were going on in the sitting room. The crown-wearers left *Muchwa* house and came to the *Karuzika* and waited on the king. Then the prince belonging to Nyarwa's line, and the Bamuroga told the people that "This is your king who has been put on the throne. He is the grandchild of Rukidi Mpuga and let every man obey him. He who refuses to obey him or rebels against him will either be executed or exiled." After saying so, the mentioned prince disclosed the new king's royal name and pet name given to him on becoming king. On hear-ing the king's royal name and pet name, the people rose on their feet and praised the king. Then the royal drum [*Tibamulinde*] was brought near the king so that the king could beat it nine times. After this, he was given other drums belonging to his ancestors. He beat each of these four times. The king would then be given two chief flutes [*Amakondere*], one of which was known as *Nyamarra*. They were handed to the king four times. These flutes once belonged to Mpuga Rukidi. He had these two flutes with him when he was hunting in Bukidi, where he was found by Nyakoka and Karongo, who came to him and told him that he was to be king. On becoming king, Rukidi ordered these flutes to be covered with beads and to be included among the royal flutes. Then the king was handed bows and arrows. He shot four arrows in all directions—one arrow was shot in the direction where the sun rises [Buganda and Busoga]; the second one was shot in the direction where the sun sets; the third one was shot in the southward direction [Nkore and Rwanda]; the fourth one was shot in the northward direction [Bukidi and other countries]. This action meant that every rebel [rival] who came from any of these directions would be killed with an arrow. After this, the king was handed the chief *entimbo* [a small drum], known as *Mutengesa*. This *entimbo* was left behind by the Bachwezi. This small drum was used to lead the king into the palace. The king was then given the chief *engaija* [also a small drum], called *Tomunju*. Meanwhile other *engaijas* were beaten in front of the king. The *engaija* has the same use as the *entimbo*. After this, the keepers of spears brought the royal spears—*Maherre, Kimuli, Kaizireigo, Mutazimbwa, Gotigoti*, etc.—before the king and pointed them at him. This signified that these spears were the ones the king's forefathers—the Bachwezi and the Babiito—had used in their conquest of other countries and if the new king wished also to conquer countries they were at his disposal and were kept safely for his use. The king was next handed a hammer and a stone used for making iron implements. These were put on the ground in front of him. Then the king imitated a smith working on this stone four times. This meant that the king was now the chief of all the smiths. The hammer in front of him was the one used for making spears used by his subjects for fighting and the hoes used by his subjects. The other meaning attached to the hammer was that the king should live for long like the hammer and also like the hammer speak straight [speak the truth], because a hammer always cuts straight and is loved by all.

At this point there came a diviner called Kasoira Omutwairwe, who squatted on the floor in the sitting room in front of the king. Then the Bamuroga went to the *Kasenda* forest and got a smoking pipe with an iron handle. He handed this to Kasoira, who smoked it in front of the king. This action of the diviner signified the power and honor given to this diviner by Rukidi. This diviner had been delegated by the Bachwezi to go and tell the Babiito that they were to take their place as rulers. Kasoira was also the one who explained the loss of respect for the Bachwezi as the cause of their going away and leaving the throne vacant for the Babiito. After this ceremony, another diviner, Nyakoka Omusuli, brought a stick and four knives—*Kabutika, Kyeraigongo, Nyamahunge,* and *Kyebagira*. He handled these nine times saying: "I am the diviner of the Babiito and I am also the one who divined for Rukidi that he would become king of Kitara." At this time Kadongolima, the Chief of Matiri, of the Bakwonga clan, wore a crown covered with chicken feathers on his head. He then turned the other way with his back facing the king and greeted the king with the royal greeting of "Zona Okali," saying, "I am the maternal uncle of Rukidi."

The King Returns to the Ijwekero

[A room in the *Karuzika*—the main house—where the king dressed and undressed]

After all these ceremonies, the king went to the back room *Ijwekero* and changed his clothes. He then went and sat in a room called *Ihundiro,* also at the back of the *Karuzika*. All the queens brought baskets of beads for him to wear round his arms and feet. They also brought charms, fingers of a lion, and fingers of an elephant covered with beadworks, and other things. These things were made by the king's wives. The king went back to the *Ijwekero* room after this and changed his clothes once more. He then came back to the sitting room of the *Karuzika*. The royal drum and the celebrants left the *Kyawairindi* and came back to where the king was. Then the chiefs, princesses [but not princes], and other people came to pay their respects to the king. The smaller drum before the king was beaten nine times by its keeper. He then handed it to the king, who also beat it nine times and handed it back to its keeper, who once more beat it four times this time. Then Kakahuka [a man who played some part in the ceremony] shouted in honor of *Mugiddo* shield. After this, the keeper of the small drum—Omujaguzo—who belonged to the Basiita clan, beat the drum once more four times. The royal drum was then moved back to the *Kyawairindi*. The king left the room to go and have some rest and see that the people in the palace got enough food.

Enkorogi[2] Brought Before the King in the Afternoon

The king went back to the *Ijwekero* room to change his clothes once more. From here he went to the *Kyawairindi,* where he found a chair called *Kibwizi,* which had been moved from the *Ijwekero* room ready for him. He sat here for a while and the royal drum was also moved to where the king was. The crown-wearers, Ababiitokati, and other people also came and sat round the king. Then some people started dancing the royal dance called *empango* to the rhythm of the drum and the music provided by the royal musicians. The people also brought their presents to the king. The king spent about an hour here and then went back to the *Ijwekero* room to change his clothes again. After changing he would go to the sitting room, where the royal cows were brought before him for milking. These *enkorogi* were brought by a young man who had not yet grown any hair on his body. He came shouting, warning the people to move away so that they did not set their eyes on these cows. These cows came running slowly on their way with the young man in front of them. When this young man developed hair on his body he no longer performed this job. Such young men came from special clans —Abalisa, Abasambu, Abasiita, Abaitira, and Abayaga. Then a certain man from the Bakwonga clan spread a rug where the cows were to stand while being milked. Then two of the king's wives, one of the Balisa clan and another of the Baitira clan, came forward smeared with chalk, one holding more chalk and a bowl and another holding a horn containing water. Then a man from the Bahango clan milked the cow by holding its front teats and pulled them four times and then held the back ones and pulled them four times, too, until the milk bowl was full. The person milking the cow had to take special care. He first cleaned the cow's teats and the area between its legs with leaves known as *enkuyo* so that no dirt fell into the milk. The milkman also said nice words to the cow to make it stay steady and facilitate the milking process. The milkmen abstained from sexual intercourse during this period and had to avoid women in general. They had also to be merry all the time with no moment of sadness. No one was allowed to cough or sneeze while this cow was being milked.

The King Eats

After taking back the cow, a royal dish called *Nyakabiito* was brought by Nyakabango of the Bakurungo clan, helped by other people. They wore two new bark cloths and smeared themselves with chalk. One of them came carrying the royal dish lying between two bark cloths. Another held a jar of water called *Malere*, a dish, and a very small water jar. All these were brought covered with bark cloth. At this time, the king was seated on his royal chair called *Nyamyaro*. He was given water with which to wash his hands. He was then handed small knives [four of them, all different in make, with sharp ends]. He was also given two other bigger knives.

Then the king got hold of one small knife and one big one and cut the meat [brought to him] into pieces. He then threw the pieces of meat to the different points of the compass, the direction where the sun rises, where the sun sets, on the right, and on the left. He then cut the remaining meat into nine pieces and ate these. All those present had to look downwards so that they would not stare at the king while eating. After eating the king was then given water to wash his hands. After washing his hands he was given water to drink. After this meal one of the servants, named Nyakabango, announced to the king that he was his waiter and that his job was hereditary and that his ancestors had been in the service since Rukidi's time. This man swore to do the job faithfully. He then told the king of the land he had been given for his office. The king answered him confirming what the waiter had said. The king then promised the waiter the honor of washing his hands the next morning in front of all the king's chiefs as witnesses. After this, the waiters cleaned the dishes and the king left the room to go to another room at the back of the house, called *Nsika*. The succession ceremony ended this day.

The King's Day-to-Day Functions

Early every morning, around 3 A.M., the king was woken up by his bathers and taken to the *Kabagarama*. Having had his bath, he would go back to the *Karuzika* to have more sleep [on the royal bed] and slept until daybreak. He then went back to the *Kabagarama* to wash his face. Then his dressers brought fresh bark cloth and dressed him, taking off those he had been wearing while at the *Karuzika*. Then one of his wives who resided at the *Kabagarama* and who belonged to the Bapopi clan brought a basket of beads. She would tie the strings of beads round the king's arms, feet, and neck. Then the king would go to the *Karuzika*—to the *Nsika* room to drink milk.

After drinking milk, he would retire to the sitting room and sit on the royal chair known as *Nyamyaro*. From here he watched his herdsmen milking the cows. After the milking these herdsmen brought their cases before him [if they had any] for settlement. Besides cases, personal troubles were also brought before the king so that he could help solve them. After settling the cases and troubles of his herdsmen, the king would pass through the dressing room and would go to the *Barwara* forest [a kind of High Court] and would sit on a chair made of skin straps called *Ekirangira*. Here he found a different type of cows, known as *embamba*, looked after by Kalyegira of the Bayaga clan, being milked. The milk of these cows was the one which was given to the king's wives, the king's children, and the princes. After milking these cows, the king heard the herdsmen's cases and settled them. The cows were then taken away and the doorkeepers opened the doors to let the king's chiefs and other people into the *Barwara* compound to pay their respects to him. The saza chiefs were allowed to enter the forest [wood] and sat near the king. This was the place where the king heard the cases and troubles of all the people of Kitara [High Court] and this was the place where all the people who wished to see the king could see him. The Babiito could also see the king on this spot if they wished. The king remained in the *Barwara* until around 11 A.M.

On leaving the *Barwara*, he returned to the *Karuzika* and went to his dressing room, where he found one of his wives sitting on a mat [or rug] and ready with her basket of beads. The king's wife was dressed in two pieces of bark cloth with a string of beads round her neck. When the king arrived in the dressing room, he sat with his wife on the mat, where he would spend about half an hour resting.

The king then called his servants to bring another set of clothes and changed the clothes he had been wearing for the new ones. Then the wife put beads on his arms and around his neck. The king left his dressing room and went to the place where the cows are milked. This was around midday.

On leaving the *Karuzika*, he would meet one of his servants, who smeared him with chalk and other substances and tied a charm round his body. This was where he met the Babiito who had cases to bring before him or anyone who had a case against a Mubiito. The king left this place at around 1 P.M. and retired to the *Nsika* in the *Karuzika* to drink milk.

He then proceeded to his sitting room, where he spent about two hours. While here, the king would hear and settle about four cases. After this judicial function he left the sitting room and, passing through his dressing room, went to the *Kabagarama* house, where he took off the beads round his neck and arms. He then went to another house, called *Kyokya*, to eat lunch, after which he returned to the *Kabagarama* and changed again. At around 4 P.M. one of the king's wives brought him beer, which he drank until around 6 P.M. The king then went to the sitting room of the *Karuzika* house to see the milking of his cows. From here he went to have his supper. After supper the king met his people, who had come to pay their respects. All these functions were performed every day of the week.

The King's Court

1. The king's main court was the forest called Barwara, where he heard the cases brought by chiefs and other people of Kitara, including the Bahuma.
2. The *Bamwenagaho* forest was where he met the people from Buganda and those sent by the Kabaka of Buganda to deliver presents to the king. He also met the Basoga in this place.
3. The *Binyonyi* forest was the place where he met delegates from his colonial territories of Ganyi, Madi, and Bulega.
4. The *Kyamunuma* forest was where he met delegates or visitors from Nkore and Karagwe who had been sent by their kings. This was the main forest and it was where the Chief Royal Spear, known as *Kaitantahi*, was kept. It was also where the heirs of the crown-wearers drank their milk during the milk-drinking rite when they were being confirmed as the rightful heirs of their fathers. Here, too, the king settled their disputes over succession as crown-wearers.
5. The *Munkambi* forest was situated at the back of the palace, in front of the *Kaitabasiru* house. Inside this wood

there was a house where the royal goods and property were kept, e.g., ivory, shells, bundles of bark cloth, materials, and many other things.

The Empyemi Rite

Empyemi is the succession rite. The performance of this rite necessitated the presence of all the royal servants—custodians of spears and stools, cooks, bath attendants, etc. The king had first to order the execution of many people for the occasion. Besides these people he also executed many of the royal servants. A cow was also to be killed. After the execution of these people their blood was allowed to flow over a large area and the king was required to pass through the bloody ground. He then climbed on top of a hill called Eburu, which is found in Buhekura County. The royal drum was sounded while the king climbed the hill. When the king got down, he went back to his headquarters, which he had built near the hill. In the afternoon, the military drum was sounded and the king led a raiding expedition into Nkore, where he captured many cows and brought them to his father's burial place. The king had these cows milked.

Then the king visited all the tombs of his ancestors and had the cows he had captured from the raids milked. The milk was given to these ancestors. By so doing he would confirm his succession. He now took to wife all the young wives guarding these royal tombs who belonged to his father. Afterwards he proceeded to his mother and offered her the milk from the captured cows. From this day onwards, the king was no longer permitted to set eyes on his mother.

After performing all these rites, the king would go back to his capital. And the succession would be completed and confirmed. He then nominated other people to replace the royal servants who had been killed during the succession rite. The king was given cows and many presents by his chiefs as well as by other subjects. He, in turn, prepared a feast for his people.

This is the ceremony called *Empyemi*. It was performed on a hill called Buru found in the area where Omukama Rukidi built his first capital. This is the same ceremony as that done in Buganda on Budo hill.

The Omukama Makes Enjeru[3]

This ceremony was performed as follows:

The white bull called Rutale was produced. It was first given milk and then killed, and its insides examined. Then the king put on his royal robes, which consisted of two new pieces of bark cloth. Then his sister—who was roughly of the same age and size—was also dressed like the king. But a special animal skin was made for her as well. She wore this on her shoulders. She was then carried by the people while the royal music was being played.

Then the insides of the bull were removed and put in a pot. This pot was then given to the most beautiful of the king's wives to hold. Thereafter the king and his sister and his chiefs dressed for the occasion, and proceeded to the *Mugabante* [the main gate to the palace] while the royal drum was being sounded. The people got hold of two pieces of bark cloth, wrapped them around the pot full of the animal's intestines and buried it near the gate. A *mutoma* tree was planted on the spot. These celebrations went on for nine days. Different types of food crops were also planted on the spot and it is said that the crops took a very short time to grow.

Enjeru, or Jubilee, was associated with an oath of "peace." This was done by kings who had reigned for a long time and who had experienced a reign of peace [without any wars or rebellions]. The killing of the bull and the examination of its entrails was done to investigate whether the king had been accepted by higher powers or not. It will be remembered that the precursor of the fate of the Bachwezi was a bull without entrails. Its non-possession of entrails meant that the Bachwezi had been shorn of their power by a higher power and so had to leave the throne. The *enjeru,* or Jubilee, could only be done by kings who had reigned for more than nine years. When the king had made an *enjeru,* or Jubilee, he handed over all responsibility of governing the country to the Mugema [the chief of all chiefs], the Bamuroga [the Katikiro of the palace], and to the Okwiri [the head of the Babiito clan].

The king had also to observe certain stipulations after making an *enjeru,* such as the following:

1. He should never quarrel.
2. He should never kill anyone.
3. He should never become angry.
4. He should not be unwilling to give [in other words he was to be generous to his people].
5. He should not punish his people.
6. He should not settle cases or pass judgment over his people.
7. He was forbidden to lead expeditions [raids or wars] into other countries.

All these were either done by the Bamuroga, the Mugema, the Okwiri, or other important chiefs. But they were done in the name of the king.

Part VI

KINGS OF BUGANDA, TOORO, NKORE, AND KOOKI

CHAPTER 1

The Kings of Buganda

In explaining the origins of Kiganda monarchy one has to tell the truth irrespective of what Baganda might say. Banyoro are all aware of the story of the coming of the first Babiito, Isingoma Mpuga Rukidi and Kato Kimera. However, Baganda texts try to distort the story. In Sir Apolo Kaggwa's book [who was the Katikiro of Buganda] we read that Kintu is the forefather of Omukama Winyi of Bunyoro. In John Sabalangira's book entitled *Magezi Ntaiki* we read that Kato was a brother of Rukidi. But he then says that these two came from the direction of Busoga. Other Baganda writers say, however, that Kimera was the son of Prince Kalemera Muti [a Muganda prince]. They also assert that Kiiza Nkumbi was the illegitimate child of a Muganda prince and Wanyana, the wife of Winyi I of Kitara. However, this was impossible because a king's wife could never have a child from another man. If this was known she [the queen] was thrown into the lake and all the people of her clan were destroyed. It is clear that Baganda writers have attempted to distort history to boost up their claim that they were the first people to establish a ruling dynasty in Uganda. But we cannot be deceived in this way, because we have the royal tombs, which can be identified. So far no tomb bearing the remains of Kintu is known. It is also very difficult to believe that Kabaka Chwa got lost in Davula. On the other hand, evidence may be found through Kabaka Mukabya.[1] On becoming a Muslim, he collected all the remains [jawbones] of all the kings of Buganda and had them buried. But no jawbones of Kintu and Chwa

Nabaka were found. Many European writers on the history of Buganda regard Kimera as the first king of Buganda.[2] I have used these European books in my research into the names of the kings of Buganda. These European writers got their information from the Baganda and not from European sources.

1. KATO KIMERA

His mother was the lady Nyatworo of the Bakwonga clan. Kato Kimera came from Bukidi with his brother Rukidi Mpuga. He was given Buganda to rule by his brother Rukidi Mpuga, who was then king of Kitara. Kato Kimera rebelled against his brother and declared himself king of Buganda. His tomb is at Lunnyo. The Baganda historians try to distort his real identity. They deny that Bunyoro-Kitara was the first to have a ruling dynasty.

2. TTEMBO

He became King of Buganda in succession to Kimera. It is said that he was a mental case and this eventually caused his death. His mother was the lady Nattembo of the Mmamba clan. His tomb lies in Luwoko.

3. KIGGALA MUKABYA KUNGUBU

He succeeded his father Ttembo. His mother was the lady Najjemba. We are told that this king reigned for a very long time. His tomb lies in Ddambwe.

4. KIYIMBA

He is not really counted among the kings of Buganda because he became king while his father was still alive and died before his father did. His father became king once more. Kiyimba was very much hated by his people because he was a very bad man. His body lies in Ssentema. His mother was the lady Nnabukalu.

5. KAIMA

He was a son of a mere prince called Wampamba. His mother was the lady Nnabuso. He was the first king to lead an attack on Kitara and lost his life in the undertaking when he was fighting against the saza chief of Bwiru [Buddu]. He died in Isunga after being wounded. He died during the reign of Winyi I. His body lies in Kkongoije.

6. NNAKIBINGE

He succeeded Kabaka Kaima, his father. He was the son of Nnababinge. He is mostly remembered for his bravery. He was killed by Olimi I, the Omukama of Bunyoro-Kitara. Omukama Olimi I wanted to reconquer Buganda but he was advised against this undertaking because it was not good for one kingdom to swallow another. He therefore gave up the idea. The Baganda put his wife Nnannono on the throne. Nnannono was pregnant at the time and it was hoped that the child she bore would become king. But she was, however, unfortunate because she had a baby girl and not a boy.

7. MULONDO

He succeeded his father Nnakibinge and became King of Buganda while a baby. His mother was the lady Nnamulondo. He lived to a ripe old age. The royal chair of Buganda started to be called *Nnamulondo* [after his mother] during the reign of Kabaka Mulondo. His tomb is found in Mitwebiri.

8. JJEMBA

This king succeeded his elder brother, Mulondo. His mother was the lady Nnajjemba. He did not reign for long because he had come to the throne while already an old man. His body lies in Mubango.

9. SSUNA I

He came to the throne while already a very old man. He was a son of Kabaka Nnakibinge. He succeeded his elder brother, Jjemba. His mother was the lady Nnasuna. Ssuna I did not reign for long because of old age. His body lies in Jiimbo.

10. SSEKAMANYA

He became king while a very young man and succeeded his father, Ssuna I. His mother was the lady Nnakku. He did not reign for long. His body lies in Kkongoije.

11. KIMBUGWE

He became king in succession to his elder brother, Ssekamanya. He was also a son of Ssuna I. His mother was the lady Nnalugwa. Kimbugwe also did not reign for long. He died soon after being poisoned by Kateregga, his young brother. He was buried in Bugwanya. He was the one who captured the county of Kaima from Kitara and gave it to Omulangira [Luganda word for prince] Mpandwa.

12. KATEREGGA

He became king in succession to his elder brother, Kimbugwe. He was also a son of Ssuna I. His mother was the lady Nabuso-Nabagereka. He was buried in Mitwebiri. He was the man who began the process of seizing areas of Kitara and adding them to Buganda. He captured Butambala County and gave it to Maganyi. He also captured Kitunzi County and gave it to Kawewo. This happened in the reign of Winyi II.

13. MUTEBI

He succeeded his father, Kateregga. His mother was the lady Nnamutebi. His body lies in Kkongoije.

14. JJUKO

This king succeeded his elder brother, Mutebi. He had the same mother as Mutebi. He commissioned his young brother Kayemba to conquer Buvuma, which was also added to the kingdom of Buganda. He was buried in Bujuko.

15. KAYEMBA

He was also a son of Kateregga. He succeeded his elder brother, Jjuko. He came to the throne while a very old man and was buried in Lunnyo.

16. TEBANDEKE

He succeeded his uncle, Kayemba, and was a son of Mutebi. He is said to have been a man of very bad temper. He killed all the witch doctors [who were regarded as small gods—or *Embandwa*] and he himself became the only witch doctor in the country. He was buried in Merera. His mother was the lady Nabuto-Nnabukulu.

17. NDAWULA

He succeeded his cousin, Tebandeke. Ndawula was the son of Jjuko. He is mostly remembered for his peaceful reign. His mother was the lady Nandawula. He died a very old man. He was buried in Musaba.

18. KAGULU-TIBUCWEREKE

This king succeeded his father, Ndawula. He is said to have been a man of difficult nature. He ordered all his people to kneel on knives [with sharp ends] when they came to greet him. But the people rebelled against him. His mother was the lady Nnagujja. He was not given a royal burial like other kings because of his evil character. His body was thrown into Bukule River Valley.

19. KIKULWE

He succeeded his elder brother, Kagulu-Tibucwereke. His mother was the lady Nnamirembe. He did not reign for long. His body lies in Kaliti.

20. MAWANDA

He succeeded his elder brother, Kikulwe. He was also a son of Ndawula. He was the one who conquered the Basoga and it was during his reign that Busoga first became a colony of Buganda. His mother was the lady Nnakidde. He was buried in Sserinnya. He was the Kabaka who cut off Kyaggwe from Kitara, and made it part of Buganda. This happened during the reign of Kyebambe II.

21. MWANGA I

He succeeded his uncle, Mawanda. He was a son of Prince Musanje, the young brother of Mawanda. Musange and Mawanda had one mother—Nnakidde. Mwanga I is not really counted among the lists of the Kabakas of Buganda, because he only spent nine days on the throne. He was killed by his [maternal] uncle called Nkunnumbi. His mother was the lady Nnalugwa. He was buried in Kavumba.

22. NNAMUGALA

He succeeded his elder brother, Mwanga I, with whom he had the same mother—Nnalugwa. He is said to have been a drunkard. He is said also to have been the first king to start the ceremony of the succession rite which takes place on the Budo hill [like that of Kitara which takes place on the hill of Buru]. Kabaka Nnamugala did not die a king, having been dethroned by his young brother, Kyabaggu.

23. KYABAGGU

This Kabaka succeeded his elder brother, Nnamugala, from whom he had usurped the throne. He too was the son of Prince Musanje [like Mwanga I and Nnamugala]. His mother also was the lady Nnalugwa. Kabaka Kyabaggu is also counted among the brave kings of Buganda. He was the one who finally defeated and conquered Busoga and built his capital at Jinja in Busoga. His body lies in Kyebando.

24. JJUNJU

This Kabaka succeeded his father, Kyabaggu. He is also counted among the brave kings of Buganda. His mother was the lady Nnanteza. He is the one who captured Bwiru [Buddu] and Kooki counties from Kitara and added them to Buganda. His body lies in Luwunga.

25. Ssemakokiro (1796–1818)[3]

He became king in 1796 in succession to his elder brother, Jjunju. They had the same father and the same mother [Kyabaggu and Nnanteza]. From this came a proverb which says: "A banana tree does not bear fruit twice except the womb of Nnanteza," meaning that she provided two kings. He was also brave like his brother. Ssemakokiro killed his brother Jjunju and usurped the throne. But Ssemakokiro turned against his agents who had helped him to kill Jjunju and these escaped death by fleeing to Bunyaruguru. Ssemakokiro's tomb is in Kisimbiri.

26. Kamanya (1818–32)

This Kabaka succeeded his father, Ssemakokiro. His mother was the lady Ndwaddewazibwa. Kamanya was also very brave. He was the Kabaka who extended the Kitara-Buganda border to Wesigire near Mubende. From this time onwards no other king of Buganda annexed big chunks of Kitara territory until the advent of the Europeans. It was these Europeans who annexed large areas of Kitara to Buganda during the close of the last century.

27. Ssuna II Semunywa Kalema Kansinjo (1832–57)[4]

He succeeded his father, Kamanya. His mother was the lady Kannyange Nnakkazi. It was during Ssuna II's reign that foreigners [Arab slave traders] started coming to Buganda. He was the first king to receive clothing [cotton cloth] from foreigners. He is said to have married very many wives. He died in Bwiru [Buddu] when he was on his way back from Kiziba, where he had gone on a raiding expedition. His body lies in Wamala.

28. Mukabya Muteesa Sewankambo Walugembe (1857–84)[5]

He succeeded his father, Ssuna II. His mother was the lady Muganzirwazza. This king was a good and wise man and ruled prudently. He was the first king to meet Europeans, in February 1862 in the persons of Captains Speke and Grant.

Christianity also arrived in Buganda during his reign. He was on good terms with the Christian missionaries and did not try to fight them. The Protestants were the first to arrive in Buganda, in 1877. They were followed by the Roman Catholics in 1879. The king himself was a Muslim. But it is not known whether he was ever circumcised, because a king's blood could not be shed. He had very many children but many of them were burnt to death by his brother, Kalema. Kabaka Mukabya died in 1884, and his tomb is found at Kasubi.

29. MWANGA II BASAMMULA-EKKERE (1884-97)[6]

He became king on 24th October 1884 in succession to his father Mukabya. Mwanga II did not have the goodness and wisdom of his father, for he was unstable in character. And for this reason Mwanga II did not enjoy the throne peacefully, for he was on and off it. He was driven away from the throne twice, first by Kiwewa and then by Kalema. He, however, struggled back to power again but was finally deposed on 6 July 1897, when he revolted against the Europeans. He fled through Kiziba, Bwiru, and finally reached Kitara. He again moved on through Kitara to Bukidi, where he met his uncle Kabalega of Kitara. These two followed the path which Isingoma Mpuga Rukidi and Kato Kimera, their ancestors, had followed on their way to Kitara. These two kings were arrested by the British in April 1899 and were exiled to the Seychelles Islands, where Mwanga II died in 1908.[7] His body was brought back to Buganda and was buried with his father's at Kasubi. His mother was the lady Abisagi Bagalyaze.

Kiwewa

In our custom [Banyoro custom] Kiwewa should not have been counted as king because he came to the throne while the rightful heir, Mwanga II, was still alive. Kiwewa spent only seventy-two days on the throne and was killed by another brother of his. But in the custom of the Baganda, Kiwewa is counted as king and that is why he has been included in this list of Baganda kings. He was the father of Prince Augustini Tibandeke. His tomb is found in Masanafu. His mother was the lady Kiribakka.

Kalema

He is also counted among the rebel princes against their brother kings. He became king in succession to his brother Kiwewa, whom he killed. He is the one who sought help from Kabalega. He appealed to Kabalega for help and was given an army led by Rwabudongo. The army helped to put Kalema on the throne of Buganda. Kalema spent more days on the throne than his brother Kiwewa. He ascended the throne on 12 October 1888 and was driven off on 5 October 1889. He thus spent almost a year on the throne. He was the father of Princes Yozefu Musanje Walugembe and Edimond [Edmund] Ndawula, now deceased. Prince Edmund Ndawula was first a Muslim by the name of Aramanzani but later became a Christian. Kalema was also the father of Maria Kamuhanda, the Rubuga, or official sister, of Sir Daudi Chwa II. Kalema died in Kitara when he had fled to Kabalega asking for help. Kabaka Kalema is said to have had a very bad temper and also to have burnt to death his brothers, thus destroying the royal clan because he feared that they might one day rebel against him and usurp his throne.

His mother was the lady Ndikubwani. His body lies in Mmende. His body was removed from Kitara to Buganda to be buried as was the custom.[8]

30. Sir Captain H. H. Daudi Chwa, K.C.M.G. (1897–1939)

Kabaka Chwa is the present king in Buganda at the time I am writing this book. He is counted among the very powerful and honorable kings of Buganda. He succeeded his father, Mwanga II, on 14 August 1897, while his father was still alive and still fighting against the Europeans. His mother was the lady Everini [Evelyn] Kulabako. Daudi Chwa's ability was very much tried by the wisdom of the Europeans. Buganda progressed during his reign and was peaceful. His people are very rich. They have built nice and strong houses made of stone and iron roofs or tiles. Things seem to be going well in his reign. At present, Buganda has twenty big counties with many people living in them.[9]

The Counties of Buganda

1. Kyaddondo—ruled by Kaigo [official title] with headquarters at Kasangati.
2. Ssingo—ruled by Mukwenda with headquarters at
   Mityana.
3. Kyaggwe—ruled by Sekiboobo with headquarters at
   Mukono.
4. Bulemezi—ruled by Kangawo, with headquarters at
   Bbowa.
5. Egomba—ruled by Kitunzi, with headquarters at Mpenja.
6. Mawokota—ruled by Kaima, with headquarters at Butolo.
7. Buddu—ruled by Pokino, with headquarters at Masaka.
8. Busiro—ruled by Mugema, with headquarters at Kitala.
9. Butambala—ruled by Katambala, with headquarters at
   Bweya.
10. Busujju—ruled by Kasuju, with headquarters at Mwera.
11. Ssese—ruled by Kkweba, with headquarters at Kizzi.
12. Kooki—ruled by Kamuswaga, with headquarters at Rakai.
13. Buvuma—ruled by Mbubi, with headquarters at Majyo.
14. Mawogola—ruled by Mutesa, with headquarters at
    Makole [Ssembabule].
15. Kabula—ruled by Lumama, with headquarters at Kabula.
16. Bugangaizi—ruled by Kayimba, with headquarters at
    Kakumiro.
17. Buyaga—ruled by Kyambalango, with headquarters at
    Kibale.
18. Buwekula—ruled by Luwekula, with headquarters at
    Kaweri [Kiryannongo].
19. Buruli—ruled by Kimbugwe, with headquarters at
    Nakasongola.
20. Bugerere—ruled by Mugerere, with headquarters at
    Ntenjeru.

Kabaka H. H. Sir Daudi Chwa died on 23 November 1939,
before this work was completed.

31. MUTEESA II, EDWARD, S. M. LUWANGULA

He succeeded his father, Sir Daudi Chwa, on 24 November
1939. The Second World War had begun at this time. He is
the one who sent a section of the army, the 7th K.A.R., to go

and fight in other areas. During his reign, a strike broke out on 11 January 1945. This resulted in the arrest of Samuel Wamala, who was then Katikiro of Buganda, and he was exiled to Bunyoro. P. Kitaka and Ganya, the Assistant Katikiro were arrested and exiled to the Seychelles Islands. S. Bazongere, Saza Chief of Kyaddondo, Njuki, Saza Chief of Ssingo, and sixteen others were detained in Kitgum and other parts of Uganda. Muteesa II went abroad for further studies and stayed there for two years from 1946–47. His country is progressing. His mother is the lady Airene [Irene] D. Namaganda, the daughter of Reverend Jonasani Kaizi.[10]

CHAPTER 2

The Kingdom of Tooro

The kingdom of Tooro was established at about 1830 because only five years had passed [with Kaboyo as king of Tooro] before his father, Kyebambe III Nyamutukura, died.

OMUKAMA OLIMI I KABOYO

He was the first son of Omukama Kyebambe III Nyamutukura, the King of Kitara. He was honored thus: "He who refuses to budge, he of Myeri [Mwenge]." A song was formed out of his action of rebelling against his father which says: "People thought that he had gone to look after his father's cows while he went to rebel."[1] Kaboyo decided to cut off part of his father's kingdom mainly because his father had reigned for too long and because also the part of Tooro he carved out was ruled by the chiefs [the king ruled it indirectly through the chiefs]. Kaboyo had first gone to Tooro when his father sent him there to collect taxes [in the form of cattle] from Tooro and Busongora. It was at this time that he schemed to rebel against his father, having seen how beautiful and far away this area was. He therefore approached some brave men and spoke to them in secret and asked for their support. These men gave him their support and said to him, "Come and rule us because the kingdom of Kitara is too far away." After this, Kaboyo brought back the cattle to his father as he had been asked to do. He then went back to Tooro, passing through Mwenge. There happened to be his sisters, Princesses Mpanja and Batebe, in Tooro. These ladies came to learn of their brother's schemes and reported to their father, Kyebambe III. But because Kyebambe loved his son too much, he could not believe his daughters' report. When Kaboyo knew that his father had found out, he lied to him, saying, "My wife has had twins and therefore I would like to go and see her." So Kyebambe allowed him to go to Tooro, but when Kaboyo arrived in Mwenge, he called on his men and told them that he had rebelled against his father. No one raised a cry against his action. So Kaboyo and all his men moved on to Tooro and took his father's cattle which were in Mwenge.

But before Kaboyo reached Tooro, his wife gave birth to a baby boy [but not twins]. Kaboyo therefore named the boy Barongo, which means twins in Runyoro, in commemoration of his lie to his father. So from this time Tooro became a separate kingdom from that of Kitara until Kabalega reconquered it. Its border with Kitara was near the Munobwa River.

When Kyebambe III died, Kaboyo was summoned to go and become king of Kitara but he rejected the offer, saying: "I cannot do so because I rebelled against my father while he was still alive." The kingmakers instead chose his young brother, Mugenyi Nyabongo II, to succeed Kyebambe III.

Omukama Kaboyo reigned for a very long time. His body lies in Burongo in Bunyangabu County in Tooro. He was succeeded by his son, Kazana Ruhaga.

OMUBIITO KAZANA RUHAGA

He succeeded his father, Olimi Kaboyo. But Kazana did not stay on the throne for long. He was soon killed by his brother, Nyaika Kasunga, who became king. He is not really counted as king because he spent only a short time on the throne.

OMUKAMA NYAIKA KASUNGA

He became King of Tooro after killing his brother, Kazana Ruhaga. Soon after ascending the throne, he was attacked by his brother Kato Rukidi, who also wanted the throne. Kato Rukidi went to Nkore to Omugabe Mutambuko and asked him for an army. The Omugabe agreed and he came back to Tooro with a strong force, and attacked his brother. But Nyaika Kasunga managed to defeat him. Kato was not satisfied. He went to Buganda and asked Kabaka Muteesa to give him an army. Muteesa did give him an army led by Pokino Mukasa. So when Omukama Nyaika Kasunga saw Kato's strong forces, he fled to Mboga, but left a delegate to lead his forces. There was a lot of fighting. Kato and his Baganda forces were victorious and Kato became king and the Baganda auxiliaries went back to their country.

OMUBIITO KATO RUKIDI

Kato became king after defeating Nyaika Kasunga, his brother. But when Nyaika Kasunga, who had fled to Mboga, heard that the Baganda forces had returned home, he decided to attack Kato and recover his throne. A serious battle was fought in which Kato Rukidi was killed. Nyaika became King of Tooro for the second time. Kato is counted among the rebel princes.

OMUKAMA NYAIKA KASUNGA [*king for the second time*]

Omukama Nyaika soon settled on his throne. After a short time, he sent an expedition into Mwenge which captured a lot of cattle belonging to Kabalega of Kitara. Among these cows was Kabalega's favorite cow, called Rwakoma. When Kabalega heard of Nyaika's action, he was very angry and sent Tigulekwa to go and capture Nyaika alive so that he [Kabalega] could kill him with his own hands. S. Tigulekwa led an expedition to Tooro. Among these were about forty Nubian soldiers, who were led by Zeni, and many people from Bukidi. Regardless of the big forces of Kabalega, Nyaika was able to defeat them during the first encounter. Another battle was fought the next day and many Batooro lost their lives during this encounter. But Kabalega's forces failed to capture Nyaika and went back, taking many cows with them. Two years later, Nyaika died. He was succeeded by his son Olimi Mukabircre. Nyaika was buried in Kagoma in Bunyangabu County in Tooro.

Omubiito Olimi II Mukabirere

Olimi II became king, succeeding his father, Nyaika, at his death. After he had spent one year on the throne, Kabalega, who hated rebels and who did not wish Tooro to have another king, sent Matebere, son of Ndyaki, to lead his forces against Tooro. When Matebere reached Tooro, he discovered that the kingdom had disintegrated into two parts, with Olimi II Mukabirere as King of Tooro, while Prince Mukarusa had declared himself ruler of Busongora County. There was a certain chief in Olimi's area called Rwomire, who went to Matebere and promised to capture Olimi II for him. Rwomire went to the king [Olimi II] and told him that Kabalega's forces were very far. While they were thus talking, Matebere [Kabalega's army leader] came and surrounded Olimi's palace. Olimi II was captured together with other princes. Matebere also captured many of Olimi's possessions and took them to Kabalega. The elders of the Babiito and other people of Tooro held a meeting. They decided to send off the king's son, Kasagama, and his brothers, Musuga and Kamurasi, to Nkore. So they took Kasagama and his brothers to Nkore.

Omubiito Mukarusa

When Omubiito Mukarusa [who had declared himself ruler of Busongora County] heard of the capture of Olimi II and of his being taken to Kitara, he declared himself King of Tooro. But when Kabalega heard that Mukarusa had become king, he sent another force, led by Kikukuule, to attack him. Kikukuule and his forces, however, could not find Mukarusa and his men because they had fled and were hiding in the mountains of Ruwenzori. So Kikukuule had to go back to Kitara, capturing many cows from Tooro. He left Rusongoza as his representative in Tooro. Now, Rusongoza, in Tooro, thought out ways through which he could capture Mukarusa. So he made friends with a certain man called Kalikula, who was an attendant to Mukarusa. Rusongoza prayed Kalikura to show him where Mukarusa was hiding. Kalikura did as he was asked and, in this way, Rusongoza was able to take the king and other Babiito unawares. He captured them and took them to Kabalega.[2]

After the capture of Olimi Mukabirere, Kabalega divided Tooro into counties such as those which had existed during the time of his grandfather, Nyamutukura. This arrangement lasted up to 14 August 1891, when Captain Lugard restored the kingdom of Tooro and made Kyebambe Kasagama Daudi, M.B.E., the King of Tooro. There were other rebel princes who reigned for some time in Tooro—Katera and Rububi.

OMUBIITO NYAMUYONJO KAKENDE

At this time there arose a prince named Nyamuyonjo Kakende, the grandson of Omukama Olimi I Kaboyo. This prince went to Muteesa of Buganda and asked him for help. Muteesa gave him an army and Nyamuyonjo attacked Kabalega's forces in Tooro and defeated them and became King of Tooro as the rightful heir of his grandfather. After two years [with Nyamuyonjo as ruler] Kabalega sent an expedition against him and defeated him. Nyamuyonjo fled to Buganda, where he died of smallpox after a short time. His bones were afterwards removed to Tooro and buried at Mperre in Burahya County.

OMUKAMA DAUDI KYEBAMBE KASAGAMA, M.B.E.

He became king on 14 August 1891. He was the one who restored the kingdom of Tooro by cutting it off once more from Kitara, with the help of Europeans. He was brought to Tooro by the Europeans who found him in Buddu in Buganda. Omukama Kyebambe looked an impressive king in physique and speech. Under his reign the kingdom of Tooro was extended to Mwenge, Kyaka, Nyakabimba, and Kitagweta.

Omukama Kyebambe received many honors from both the local and colonial governments. He first got a medal with his name written on it. It was given to him by Queen Victoria as a reward for his refusal to join the Nubian soldiers in Busoga who had risen against the Colonial Government in 1897. In 1900 he signed an agreement with Sir H. Johnston making Tooro part of the British Protectorate. In 1914, when the First World War had broken out, he supported the Protectorate Government with his decision to send an army to help with fighting on the Allies' side. At the end of the war, in 1918, he was awarded the M.B.E. as a reward for his help.

He ruled his country well and with honor. He was friendly with the people of other kingdoms. He was sympathetic to all the different religions and allowed the teaching of all of them in his kingdom. He also became a Christian on 15 March 1896 in Buganda. He took an interest in education and asked his chiefs to send their children to schools. He sent his children [sons] George Kamurasi and Hosia Nyabongo to schools. Prince Nyabongo is still in England pursuing further studies at this moment.

Omukama Daudi Kyebambe Kasagama ruled for thirty-seven years and four months, and seven days. He had a number of children, including George Kamurasi, Ruth Komuntale, Keesi Bahindi, and many others. He died on 31 December, 1928. He was buried at Karambi, Burahya County.[3]

Omukama Rukidi III George Kamurasi [*Lieutenant*]

Omukama Kamurasi became king on 29 January 1929, succeeding his father, Daudi Kasagama Kyebambe I. He is honored in this way: "He who sleeps among guns, the brave son of Kyebambe."

George Rukidi is counted among the educated kings ruling at this time. He went to England in 1924 together with Prince Ssuna of Buganda, while still a prince. These two princes spent one year pursuing further studies in England. He was a soldier in the fourth battalion of the K.A.R. and later became a lieutenant.[4] Tooro now consists of the following counties:

1. Burahya, ruled by Omuhenda [official title], with headquarters at Butebe.
2. Mwenge, ruled by Omutaleesa, with headquarters at Butiiti.
3. Bunyagabu, ruled by Omunyaaka, with headquarters at Kibiito.
4. Busongora, ruled by Omujwisa, with headquarters at Kaseese.
5. Kibaale, with headquarters at Kamwenge, ruled by Omuhukya.
6. Bwamba, ruled by Omukumbya, with headquarters at Bundibugyo.
7. Kyaka, ruled by Omutaizibwa, with headquarters at Kyegeegwa.

8. Bukonjo, ruled by Omulemansozi, with headquarters at Nyabirongo.

POSTSCRIPT

OMUKAMA PATRICK MATTHEW KABOYO OLIMI III

Omukama Kaboyo succeeded his father, George Rukidi, on 2 March 1966. He is also counted among the educated kings because he was abroad in England pursuing further studies at the death of his father. Omukama Kaboyo did not reign for a long time on the throne of Tooro. He was king only for one year and a half [1966–67]. He had to abdicate due to the changes brought about by the coming of Independence to Uganda. He abdicated while a very young man and unmarried. He was given compensation amounting to Shs. 250,000. All royal regalia were taken by the central government and are displayed in the Uganda Museum. Omukama Kaboyo was honored this way: "He who gives light to the left son of Rutabingwa Rusasuka."

CHAPTER 3

The Kings of Nkore (The Bahinda Dynasty)[1]

Nkore was originally known as "Karokarungi," or the beautiful village. The following account of the history of Nkore is based on Nkore tradition.[2] Nkore was originally a county of Kitara. This county was given to a man called Macumulinda by the Kitara king. Later on Omukama Ndahura [a Muchwezi king] gave it to Isimbwa, his father. Later on still, Omukama Wamara gave it to a man called Katuki [or Katukuru], son of Rubango.

However, Omukama Wamara was very worried because he had no son. So he called his fellow Bachwezi and said to them: "Let us call Omuchwezikati[3] [a female Muchwezi]

named Kaikara, daughter of Kasagama, a diviner, so that
she may divine who among my wives can bear me a child."
His fellow Bachwezi discouraged him, arguing that Kaikara
was no diviner but only a liar. But Wamara would not be persuaded and so the people decided to test her ability. So they
hid certain objects in Kaikara's way as a test. They wanted
to see if she could detect their presence; and if she did, they
would then accept her as a true diviner.

The objects they hid in chosen places were an ax, a shaving
knife, and a wire. But their plans were betrayed. There happened to be a maid named Njunaki, who heard all their plans
and went and told Kaikara everything. She said to the maid:
"Now that you have told me everything, I will reward you
with big things and you will be the king's wife." So Kaikara
went to perform the test. She was invited to enter the palace,
but she said: "There is something hidden to trap me into
death." The Bachwezi laughed and removed the ax from the
path and she was able to pass. When she reached the doorway, they asked her to enter the house but she hesitated,
saying: "There is something in the doorway which will kill
me." The Bachwezi laughed and then removed the shaving
knife. Then they brought her some beer to drink, but she
also hesitated and said: "You had better put the beer away
because there is a snake of iron [a wire] in the beer which
will bite me." So they took away the beer and brought her
some other beer to drink. So the king appeared to have won
over the others [because Kaikara had apparently shown that
she was a real diviner]. So Kaikara was given the necessary
items for her assignment to divine whether or not the king
could have children. This was to be done the next morning.
During the night Njunaki [the maid] went to Kaikara and
asked her: "Adyeri [Kaikara's pet name], did you see all that
I told you?" Kaikara confirmed that she had done so and
said to Njunaki: "Tomorrow at sunrise, while I am divining
for the king, pretend to pass by us. You will see what I am
going to do for you." The following morning Omukama
Wamara and some of his brothers went to hear the verdict of
the diviner. Kaikara's hands were smeared with ointment in
readiness for her job. At this juncture, Njunaki, the maid,
pretended to be passing by. Whereupon Kaikara said to
Wamara: "You will have children by that maid." But
Omukama Wamara was angry at her statement and took her
words as an insult. "How can a king have children by a maid?

I already have my wives," he reprimanded Kaikara. But Kaikara told the king that it did not lie in his power to choose which woman would bear him a child. Wamara therefore agreed to do as he was told. He annointed the maid with ointment and ordered that a house be built for her on that day and Njunaki moved in as soon as it was completed. She was to take her bath, and from that day she became one of the king's wives. She was also given milk to drink. Njunaki gave birth to a baby boy after some time. This baby was born with a mark on his brow and was therefore named Ruhinda. He was called Ruhinda rwa Muchwa Omukumirizi because he was Wamara's only child, and because his mother's house became the *Muchwampaka*, which is ruled by the Batebe or the Rubuga in Bunyoro-Kitara and Buganda respectively.

Ruhinda grew up and showed great love for cattle and for this reason went to Karagwe and remained there up to the time the Bachwezi left the country. He was rescued and brought back to Kitara by his relations, Rukidi Mpuga and Kato Kimera, who sent Saza Chief Kakwenda to bring him back. Ruhinda was given the area of Nkore [Karokarungi] to rule. He was of the same stock as the Bachwezi, but because the Bachwezi had no clans, he chose to take that of his mother [Muhinda]. Abahinda were also Babiito. Ruhinda is regarded as the first king of Nkore and he was the one who provided sons who became rulers of areas north of the Kagera River—such as Karagwe, Kyanja, Ihengiro, Usui, Rwanda, and other small areas.

1. OMUGABE RUHINDA RWA MUCHWA OMUKUMIRIZI

Kinyoro tradition is firm on one point, namely, that Ruhinda was the first man to become Omugabe of Nkore, which was at the time known as Karokarungi, and that he was a Muhinda during the reign of the Bachwezi. It may be recalled that the Bachwezi loved cattle very much. But when they left the country, Ruhinda, who was residing in Karagwe, captured all the cattle which had belonged to the Bachwezi and took them to Karagwe. The new arrivals, the Babiito who replaced the Bachwezi, did not attempt to fight against Ruhinda because he had agreed to send them cattle whenever they asked him to do so. He became friendly to the Omukama Rukidi I Mpuga and agreed to move to Karokarungi. He built his capital at the hill called Mweruka. Rukidi I had at this time moved from Bwera to Bugangaizi near Mubende and the Buru hill. Omugabe Ruhinda died a very old man. He was honored with many sayings, which it will not be necessary to recite here, but which will be found in the book which the Banyankore are writing now.

2. OMUGABE NKUBAYARURAMA

He succeeded his father, Ruhinda. He also reigned for a very long period and died a very old man. He was buried in Sanze in the royal burial place.

3. OMUGABE NYAIKA

He succeeded his father, Nkubayarurama. He built his capital at Kicwekano hill. His reign is mostly remembered as a reign of peace. He died a natural death while a very old man.

4. OMUGABE NYABWIGARA

He succeeded his father, Nyaika. He built his capital at Kakukuru. This king did not get the chance of a peaceful rule in his country as his three predecessors had had. It was during his reign that Olimi I of Kitara was fighting with Nnakibinge of Buganda. After killing Nnakibinge, Olimi I was determined to restore the kingdom of Kitara as it had been in the time of the Bachwezi. So he turned against Nkore and defeated Omugabe Nyabwigara. Olimi I decided to remain in Nkore, which he had conquered.

But after some time there came darkness in the country [eclipse] and Olimi I was advised by his diviners to leave Nkore and go back to Kitara. So he left the country and went back to Kitara, leaving his chiefs to take charge of Nkore. When Omugabe heard that Olimi had left the country, he left the place where he had been in hiding and gathered an army around him. He then moved against the people Olimi I had left behind and nearly killed them all. Those who survived fled the country. Then Omugabe Nyabwigara became king again. Nyabwigara was left to rule in peace because Omukama Olimi I had already performed the *Enjeru* rite. Nevertheless, the Bagabe of Nkore had not yet gained the kingly confidence and had not been regarded by other people as real kings at that time.

5. OMUGABE RUSANGO

He succeeded his father, Nyabwigara. He did not reign for long. He built his capital at Kibaale hill. He had only two sons—Kagwijagirra and Makobera. He was buried at Sanze.

6. OMUGABE KAGWIJAGIRRA

He succeeded his father, Rusango. He built his capital at Buhandagazi hill. He had only two sons—Rugamba and Butiti. He spent a long time as an invalid and died in the end.

7. OMUGABE RUGAMBA

He succeeded his father, Kagwijagirra. He built his capital at Kitamba hill. It is said that during Rugamba's reign there came a great hailstone which turned one part of the country into a lake. This lake still remains up to this time. It is also said that those who went to see this extraordinary event perished at the spot. It is also said that the smell from the many rotting bodies on this spot was to cause smallpox in the country. Omugabe Rugamba died a fairly old man and was buried in Sanze.

8. OMUGABE KASASIRA

He succeeded his father, Rugamba, and built his capital at Bweyolere hill. He had only two sons, Lumonde and Kitera. He reigned for a very long time. He was buried in Sanze. However, at his death, his two sons did not come to any agreement as to which of them would become king and fought against one another for the throne. The younger brother proved stronger and became king.[4]

9. OMUGABE KITERA

He succeeded his father, Kasasira, after defeating his elder brother, Lumonde. He built his capital on Buhungura hill. After a short period, Lumonde, his elder brother, closed upon him, killed him, and became king.

10. Omugabe Lumonde

He succeeded his younger brother, Kitera, whom he had killed. Had he been a Munyoro king, he would have been given the name of Kyebambe—meaning usurper. He built his capital at Kagarama hill. He only had one son, Mirindi. He lived for quite a long time. He was buried in Sanze.

11. Omugabe Mirindi

He succeeded his father, Lumonde. He chose to stay in his father's capital of Kagarama. He had three sons, Ntare, Rugamba, and Nsiga. He also reigned for quite a long period and was buried in Sanze.

12. Omugabe Ntare I Kitabanyoro

He succeeded Mirindi, his father. He built his capital at Byanganga hill. But Omugabe Ntare I did not enjoy a reign of peace as the other Bagabe before him had done because he had to face an attack—from Kitara sent by Omukama Chwa I. Chwa I attacked Nkore and there was serious fighting in which Omugabe Ntare was wounded and fled to a hiding place on an island in the Kagera River. Omukama Chwa I remained in Nkore for a long time. While there he decided to attack other countries south of Rukiga [Kigezi]. He died in Rwanda. At this time the border between Kitara and Nkore was the Rwizi River [Rwizi River now near Mbarara town]. But when Omugabe Ntare heard of the death of Omukama Chwa I, he left his hiding place and came back to his kingdom and destroyed all the forces which Chwa I had left behind in Nkore. That was why he was honored with the name of Kitabanyoro—meaning, the destroyer of Banyoro. It was from this time that his country came to be known as Nkore and not as Karokarungi as it was originally known. The name Nkore was taken from Chwa I's mother's lament at his death: *"Ente zankora omuliso,"* meaning that it was her son's love of cattle that had caused his death and from the word *zankora* came the name Nkore.[5]

Omugabe Ntare captured Chwa I's cattle after killing his people and became king once more. He had four sons, Macwa,

Buzuga, Murali, and Kakonko. He died a very old man. He
was also buried at Sanze.

13. Omugabe Macwa

He succeeded Ntare, his father. He built his capital at
Omubinabiro. Omugabe Macwa had more children than any
other Mugabe before him. He had fifteen sons, Kahaya,
Karara, Rwebirere, Karaiga, Kimina, Tabairwa, Rwakai-
zumba, Bunyere, Nyabinyege, Nyabwimbe, Rwakoma,
Buranda, Karugende, Bunyonyo, and Bukirenge. Omugabe
Macwa died a very old man and was also buried at Sanze.

14. Omugabe Rwebirere

He succeeded his father, Macwa. He only spent about three
months on the throne. He died soon after from a fall when
he was coming home after watering his cattle. He was buried
at Kabanyiginya.

15. Omugabe Karara

He succeeded his father, Rwebirere. He built his capital
at Bweyogerere hill. Karara spent only about three years on
the throne. He was killed by his younger brother, Karaiga,
who came upon him at night while he was drunk. He set the
house [where the king was] on fire after killing him, and
therefore the king's body was burnt within the house.

16. Omugabe Karaiga

He was the one who killed his brother, Karara. He built
his capital on Mabale hill. After some time he grew afraid of
his young brothers because he was tormented by the thought
of his brother's death. So he decided to prevent such an
eventuality. He asked Ruhigara, the king of Igara, to give
him poison. He mixed this poison in beer and gave it to his
elder brother, Kahaya, to drink. Fortunately Kahaya did not
die from the poison, but suffered greatly from it. Kahaya
learnt of his brother's evil plans and hated him for that. So
when he got better he decided to rebel against Karaiga. He
collected an army and gave it to his son, Rwebisengye, to
lead the attack against his uncle, the Omugabe Karaiga.

Rwebisengye was victorious and deposed Karaiga, who fled to Buganda. The place where Karaiga died is not known. However, many think that he was killed by Omukama Duhaga I of Kitara.

17. OMUGABE KAHAYA

He succeeded his younger brother, Karaiga, whom he kicked off the throne. Kahaya built his capital at Nyabikira hill. Here he was attacked by the King of Rwanda, Kigere, and Omugabe Kahaya was forced to flee and hide in Rwamahungu. He left his son, Rwakyendera, to lead his forces against Kigere of Rwanda. Kigere was defeated and Omugabe Kahaya left his hiding place and was once more king. He moved his capital to Byaki hill, and moved again and built his capital on Buhandagazi hill. Omugabe Kahaya became king when already an old man. He therefore died a very old man. He was also buried in Sanze.

18. OMUGABE NYAKASAIJA

He succeeded his father, Kahaya I. He built his capital at Mabale hill. Omugabe Nyakasaija did not enjoy peace on the throne. He was soon attacked by his elder brother, Rwebisengye, who went to Buganda and secured an army from Kabaka Kamanya, with which he attacked his brother. Rwebisengye defeated Nyakasaija and killed him. But Rwebisengye did not become king. The people's choice fell on his younger brother, Bwalenga.

19. OMUGABE BWALENGA

He succeeded Nyakasaija, his elder brother, who was killed by another brother, Rwebisengye. Bwalenga did not stay on the throne for long. While in his capital of Kikakalabwa hill, he was taken ill and died soon afterwards. It is said that when his body was on its way for burial, it rained a great deal. There came thunder and lightning and the people carrying the body were frightened and scared. It is claimed that when the lightning and thunder stopped, the king's body could not be seen. It had disappeared! No one up till this day knows what had happened to it.

20. Omugabe Rwebisengye

He succeeded his young brother, Bwalenga. He became king while already an old man. He built his capital on Kakukuru hill. He already had two sons, Gasiyonga and Kayungu. He got two daughters while on the throne. They were called Kyazanga and Nyanziringa. He was buried in Sanze.

21. Omugabe Gasiyonga

He succeeded Rwebisengye, his father. He built his headquarters on Lukoma hill. He had many children, Mutambuko, Kigamba, Munaningo, Rukuta, Lwakimete, Mananate, and Kibangura. He was taken ill and died soon afterwards. He was also buried in Sanze.

22. Omugabe Mutambuko

He succeeded Gasiyonga, his father, and built his capital on Bisarera hill. Just after a year, Mutambuko was attacked by his younger brother, Kigamba. But Kigamba failed to capture and kill the king at the first attempt. However, he succeeded in killing him afterwards. Mutambuko had the following children: Bachwa, Mukwenda, Ntare, Makumbi, Eria Kaisi, Mazinyo, Kyetoba, and Bitojwa. Bachwa, his eldest son, died while fighting in one of the numerous battles he fought. Bachwa was the father of Igumira and Bikwaso. Omugabe Mutambuko died while on his way back from Buhweju, where he had gone on a raid. He was taken ill and died as a result. He was buried in Sanze.

23. Omugabe Mukwenda

He succeeded Mutambuko, his father. He built his capital on Mabale hill. Omugabe Mukwenda did not enjoy peace on the throne, for he was attacked by his young brother, Ntare. Omugabe Mukwenda failed to get any help from Buganda and so decided to fight with his own small forces. Serious fighting continued and it was during this fighting that Lwambubi, the father of Nuwa [Noah] Mbaguta, the Katikiro of Nkore, was killed. Ntare managed to kill his brother, Mukwenda, and became king.

24. Omugabe Ntare II[6]

He succeeded Mukwenda, his elder brother, whom he had killed. He built his capital on Kitoma hill and later moved it to Kagosora and again to Bugabe. He once more moved it to Nyakakoni, and then to Ruhunga. It was when he was at Ruhunga that his son, Kahaya, was born. He then moved to Kabunyonyi, where he himself died. He was buried at Tete. It is said that Omugabe Ntare II was so much loved by his people that many people cut themselves to death as a sign of their love for him when he died.

25. Omugabe Kahaya II Edward Sulemani, M.B.E. [1895–1944]

Kahaya II succeeded his father, Ntare II. These were the counties of Nkore in the reign of Omugabe Kahaya II:

1. Shema, ruled by Kaigo [official title], with headquarters at Kibingo.
2. Rwampara, ruled by Mukwenda, with headquarters at Kinoni.
3. Igara, ruled by Pokino, with headquarters at Bushenyi.
4. Mitoma, ruled by Sekiboobo, with headquarters at Kitwe, Ibanda.
5. Buhweju, ruled by Kangaaho, with headquarters at Nsika.
6. Nyabushozi, ruled by Katambaara, with headquarters at Rwentsinga.
7. Nsala, ruled by Kaima, with headquarters at Kibaruko.
8. Isingiro, ruled by Mugema, with headquarters at Kyairumba.
9. Kashara, ruled by Kasuja, with headquarters at Rwashamaire.
10. Bunyaruguru, ruled by Kitunzi, with headquarters at Rugazi.
    Edward Sulemani-Kahaya died on 10 October 1944, in Mbarara.

POSTSCRIPT

26. CHARLES G. RUTAHABA GASIYONGA II

He succeeded his uncle, E. S. Kahaya II. He reigned for twenty-two years and six months (1944–67). He also was forced to abdicate the throne due to the political changes brought about by the coming of Independence in the country. He was still strong when he was made to leave the throne. He was given compensation amounting to shillings 432,000, while the Omwigarire [his wife] received shillings 42,000.

CHAPTER 4

The Kings of Kooki

1. OMUKAMA BWOHE

He was a true Mubiito, for he was the son of Omukama Isansa of Kitara. Prince Bwohe had gone on a raiding expedition with his father to Nkore. This was during the reign of Omugabe Karaiga. On their way back, they passed through Kooki and on seeing the beauty of this country and its remote position, Prince Bwohe became fascinated by it. So he said to his father, "My Lord, let me stay in Kooki so as to prevent enemies from coming to spoil our kingdom." His father [Isansa] allowed him to do so and made him ruler of Kooki. But because of its remote position from the center, Bwohe declared himself King of Kooki and started sending out expeditions into Kiziba to attack the rulers of that country—his fellow Babiito, the grandchildren of Kaganda-Kibi—who had been given Kiziba by Winyi I. Prince Bwohe of Kooki sent these raiding expeditions which captured many things from Kiziba. Bwohe distributed this booty to his subjects. He then began to have dealings with the Baganda. But because Bwohe kept on communicating with his father and because

Kitara was still very extensive, no one paid much attention to
him. So Bwohe was left in peace as ruler of Kooki until he
died. The King of Kitara never suspected that the ruler of
Kooki could rebel and declare Kooki a separate kingdom from
that of Kitara. Bwohe had the following sons: Kitahimbwa,
Majwiga, Mugenyi, Ndahura, and many daughters.

2. OMUKAMA KITAHIMBWA I

He succeeded Prince Bwohe his father. Prince
Kitahimbwa's succession ceremony confirmed beyond doubt
that Kooki had in fact seceded from Kitara. This showed
clearly how the princes of Kooki had rebelled against their
overlord, the Omukama of Kitara, by making themselves independent kings. This report first reached the King of Buganda, who disapproved of their action. The King of Buganda
sent an army against Kooki. However, Kitahimbwa managed
to defeat the forces sent by the King of Buganda against him.
The Buganda army fled and left many spears behind which
were captured by Kitahimbwa. At this time, Duhaga I,
Kitahimbwa's uncle, was the King of Kitara. Kitahimbwa sent
him all the spears he had captured from the Baganda to
demonstrate to him that he was still loyal to Kitara. But some
people went to the king and told him of Kitahimbwa's dis-
loyal actions in Kooki and interpreted the sending of the
spears as Kitahimbwa's way of showing off his strength. They
warned the king that Kitahimbwa meant to seize the crown
of Kitara. Omukama Duhaga I had a very bad temper and
when he heard of this, he summoned his forces and with himself as commander, moved against Kitahimbwa. He attacked
the prince and captured him. But while on his way to be
killed, Kitahimbwa's last words were:

> Let those of my children and grandchildren who will
> succeed to the throne of Kooki be loyal and put trust in
> the King of Buganda, their uncle, and not in Kitara. The
> King of Buganda will look after and care for you.

From that time, Kooki became separated from Kitara and
became an independent kingdom.

3. OMUKAMA MUJWIGA

He succeeded his elder brother, Kitahimbwa I, who was killed by the King of Kitara. After becoming King of Kooki he requested an army from Jjunju, the Kabaka of Buganda, with which to attack and conquer the forces belonging to the chiefs who had been given Bwiru [Buddu] to rule. His aim was to conquer Bwiru and incorporate it into Kooki. Kabaka Jjunju gave him the necessary men and they were led by Luzinge. Mujwiga was therefore to conquer Bwiru and then drive the King of Kitara's agents from this county. Mujwiga made Luzinge Saza Chief [Pokino] of Bwiru and from that time Bwiru became separated from Kitara. Mujwiga died a short period after this incident.

4. OMUKAMA MUGENYI

He was also the son of Omukama Bwohe. He succeeded Mujwiga, his elder brother. Mugenyi was not an independent king because he had the King of Buganda as his guardian. He died after some time.

5. OMUKAMA NDAHURA I

He was also a son of Bwohe and succeeded Mugenyi, his elder brother. We shall not go into details about the kings of Kooki. You will find these in their book, which is being written now. This book will give you all the details relating to the achievements of the kings of Kooki.[1]

6. OMUKAMA KITAHIMBWA II

He was the son of Omukama Ndahura and was the one who succeeded him on the throne. He became king while a middle-aged man because he was born when his father was still a mere prince. He died an old man.

7. OMUKAMA ISANSA I

Isansa succeeded his father, Kitahimbwa II. The royal regalia increased during his reign. He was an arrogant man who boasted of his own power and prestige. He one day sent an abusive message to the Omugabe Mutambuko of Nkore, saying that he [the Omugabe] had protruding teeth. Mutambuko was very much annoyed at this insult and therefore organized a punitive expedition against Isansa. Mutambuko himself led his forces against the enemy while his son, Bachwa, led part of the forces. Omugabe Mutambuko only wished to capture Isansa and not to kill him. But his son, Bachwa, due to his youth, attacked and killed Isansa. Ssuna was the Kabaka of Buganda at this time.

8. Omukama Rubambura

He succeeded his father, Isansa, who had been killed by Mutambuko, the Omugabe of Nkore. He had a brother [a full brother] called Ndahura. Omukama Rubambura died after some time had passed.

9. Omukama Ndahura II

He succeeded Rubambura, his elder brother. It was during Ndahura II's reign that the Europeans came to this part of Africa. He was the ruling King of Kooki when the Europeans arrived in this country. Ndahura II agreed to have Kooki made into a county of Buganda and he the saza chief of Kooki, which was now part of Buganda. It became part of Buganda on 14 November 1896. His important chiefs became gombolola [sub-county] chiefs. Ndahura II became a Christian and was baptized Edward Kezekia Ndahura.

10. Omukama Kabumbuli Isansa II

His full names were George Sefasi Kabumbuli Kamuswaga. This prince succeeded to the throne of Kooki after Kooki had been made into a county of Buganda. After his death, he was succeeded by his son, who did not carry out the royal ceremonies of succession. He remained a saza chief of Buganda and was treated like the other saza chiefs of that kingdom.

EXPLANATIONS

Now we have seen how the kingdom of Kooki broke away from that of Kitara. In spite of this, Kooki retained one custom—that of sending a message to the King of Kitara at the accession of a new king to the throne of Kooki. The Omukama of Kitara would send a Mubiito, who performed the coronation rites such as sitting the new king on the throne, handing him the royal spear, etc. This connection with Kitara had always been retained in Kooki up to the time of Omukama Kabumbuli. It was done at the coronation of Kabumbuli when Omukama Duhaga of Bunyoro sent his brother Prince Nyakana Basambaagwire to perform these rites. He was also the one who gave him the royal name of Isansa. The Kitara kings performed these rites for other kings, too.

Epilogue

Since this book was published in 1947, certain important developments have taken place in Uganda. The most important of these was the achievement of independence in 1962. This is an event which should be remembered at all times in the history of Uganda.

It will be remembered that in 1894, Buganda was declared a Protectorate by the British Government and by the end of the century, the whole of Uganda had come under British protection. In 1906, however, the country was made into a colony of the crown, thus transferring its administration from the Foreign Office to the Colonial Office. Now, in 1962, the British Government ceased to be responsible for Uganda with the achievement of independence on 9 October. But this independence brought many changes in the country.

When the British Government took control over what later came to be called Uganda, it curtailed the powers of the existing monarchs in that part of the empire but did not abolish the monarchical institution. These monarchs became mere leaders of their kingdoms though they still retained powers over the respective councils within their kingdoms, as well as the appointment of traditional chiefs.

The first issue of this book came out when the hereditary monarchies still held power—albeit in a limited form—in their respective kingdoms. The kings who were reigning in 1947 were: C. G. Rutahaba Gasiyonga II [Nkore]; Edward Muteesa II [Buganda]; Tito G. Winyi IV [Bunyoro-Kitara]; and George Rukidi III [Tooro], who died on 21 December 1965, and was succeeded by his son, Patrick Matthew Kaboyo Rwamuhokya Olimi III.

There are no more copies of the original book to be found and since it has become a standard history for schools, it has been found necessary to have a second edition and more particularly in English.

History is a continuous process and many things have happened since this book was written. These have necessitated certain additions to the original work to make it up-to-date. One of these important developments was the abolition of the kings by the Republican Constitution of 1967, and the new system of government introduced in the country.

Originally the four kingdoms were ruled separately, each kingdom possessing its own ruler and its own language. Now it has been found necessary to have a unitary form of government for the whole of Uganda and to abolish the system of government by different entities. The new system, it is hoped, would eradicate tribalism and clanishness and stimulate Ugandan nationalism. It was realized also that Ugandan independence would be of no use if the different areas of the country still thought solely in terms of the interests of their ethnic groupings. This is important, for though colonial rule brought Christianity, which taught us to love one another, it failed to erase the idea of separatism. In fact, colonial rule caused more friction by its system of creating different districts and defining new boundaries. This system resulted in people of different ethnic groups being handed over to be ruled by people of another group. In these ways sectional differences were exacerbated.

But with the coming of independence all the people of Uganda came to regard themselves as Ugandans and not merely as members of different ethnic groups. But equally our new rulers after independence tried to make sure that our representatives in the National Assembly came from all parts of Uganda. To further make for unity it was found necessary to abolish the kings and the traditional chiefs and to create a unitary form of government. Uganda therefore became a republic in 1967 headed by a President elected by all the people of Uganda. It has a National Assembly and the country is divided into districts, which are under the Ministry of Regional Administration. This is the best way to unite the country.

Uganda therefore is today ruled on three levels—the national level, the regional level, and the district level. It comprises four regions—Buganda, Eastern, Western, and Northern regions. Each region is further divided into districts.

The Buganda Region consists of:

1. East Mengo District, with headquarters at Bombo.
2. West Mengo District, with headquarters at Mpigi.
3. Masaka District, with headquarters at Masaka.
4. Mubende District, with headquarters at Mubende.

The Eastern Region consists of:

1. Busoga District, with headquarters at Jinja.
2. Bugisu District, with headquarters at Mbale.
3. Bukedi District, with headquarters at Tororo.
4. Teso District, with headquarters at Soroti.
5. Sebei District, with headquarters at Kapchorwa.

The Western Region consists of:

1. Nkore District, with headquarters at Mbarara.
2. Tooro District, with headquarters at Fort Portal.
3. Bunyoro District, with headquarters at Hoima.
4. Kigezi District, with headquarters at Kabale.

The Northern Region consists of:

1. Acholi District, with headquarters at Gulu.
2. Lango District, with headquarters at Lira.
3. West Nile District, with headquarters at Arua.
4. Madi District, with headquarters at Moyo.
5. Karamoja District, with headquarters at Moroto.

Kampala is the capital of Uganda as well as the seat of government. The National Assembly is also at Kampala. The President and the ministers live at Entebbe. The President's residence is known as the State House.

Notes

The notes and comments have been deliberately reduced to the minimum to avoid making the book very unwieldy.

AUTHOR'S PREFACE

1. *Kimbugwe* is the hereditary title of the saza chief of Busindi [Masindi]. The title, however, was introduced by Baganda at the beginning of this century.

INTRODUCTION

1. Buyaga was one of the most important counties of Kitara precisely because of its great historical importance. Many of the *amagasani* (tombs) of the kings of Kitara are situated there. *Vide* K. Ingham, "The *Amagasani* of the Abakama of Bunyoro," *Uganda Journal* (henceforth, *U.J.*), 272 (1953). At the moment one of my students is researching into "Some Sacred Places of Historical Interest in Buyaga."
2. *Vide* H. Colvile, *The Land of the Nile Springs* (London, 1895); A. D. Roberts, "The Lost Counties of Bunyoro," *U.J.* 26 (1962); Lord Molson, *Uganda: Report of a Commission of Privy Counsellors on a dispute between Buganda and Bunyoro*, C.M.d.1017 (London: H.M.S.O., 1962).
3. M. S. M. Kiwanuka, "Bunyoro and the British: A reappraisal of the causes for the decline and fall of an African Kingdom," *Journal of African History* (henceforth, *J.A.H.*), IX, 4 (1968), pp. 603–19.
4. Entebbe Secretariat Archives, A33/2/1896, F.O. to Berkerley, 8 August 1896, No. 115 and Tel. No. 120.
5. *Vide* Molson, op. cit.

6. P. Bikunya, *Ky'Abakama ba Bunyoro* (London, 1927).
7. H. K. Karubanga, *Bukya Nibwira* (Nairobi, 1949).
8. This short biographical sketch is based on a series of interviews which the editor has had with the author since 1967.
9. *Vide* J. W. Nyakatura, *Aspects of Bunyoro Custom and Tradition*, translated and annotated by Zebiya Rigby. Mrs. Rigby was kind enough to allow me to read parts of this book in manuscript form.
10. Sir Apolo Kaggwa, *Basekabaka be Buganda* (Kampala, 1953); *Empisa za Baganda* (Kampala, 1952).
11. A. G. Katate and L. Kamugungunu, *Abagabe b'Ankole, Ekitabo I & II* (Kampala, 1955).
12. Sir Tito Winyi, (or K.W., meaning Kabalega and Winyi), "Abakama ba Bunyoro-Kitara," in *U.J.*, 1935, 1936, and 1937.
13. Bikunya, op. cit.
14. M. Posnansky, ed., *Prelude to East African History* (London, 1966), p. 138.
15. M. S. M. Kiwanuka, "Sir Apolo Kaggwa and the Pre-Colonial History of Buganda," *U.J.*, 30 (1966), p. 148.
16. Opinion formed after several interviews with Nyakatura.
17. Kiwanuka, *loc. cit.*
18. J. A. Rowe, "Myth, Memoir And Moral Admonition: Luganda Historical Writing 1893–1969," *U.J.*, 33 (1969), p. 21.
19. It is worth remarking that the first edition of *Basekabaka* did not carry the list of Kaggwa's informants. This omission was rectified in the 1927 edition probably due to the advice of the literary circle which surrounded him. There was hardly any such circle in Bunyoro at the time Nyakatura wrote. But he should have at least taken a hint from the 1927 edition of *Basekabaka*.
20. R. Oliver, "Ancient Capital sites in Ankole," *U.J.*, 23 (1959), p. 52.
21. Idem.
22. Kiwanuka, op. cit., p. 150.
23. Ibid., p. 147.
24. Kitara is now known as Missenyi, a name invented by the Germans. I owe this information to Mr. Peter Schmidt, who is doing some work on Kiziba.
25. R. Oliver, "Discernible Developments in the Interior c.

1500–1840," in R. Oliver and G. Mathew, eds., *History of East Africa* (Oxford, 1963), Vol. I, pp. 187–88. This point is more subtly made in A. Kaggwa, *The Customs of the Baganda*, ed. M. M. Edel (Columbia U. P., 1934), pp. 162 ff.

26. For Luo tradition, *vide* J. P. Crazzolara, *The Lwoo* (Verona: Missioni Africane 1950–54); B. A. Ogot, *History of the Southern Luo*, East Africa Publishing House, 1967; and Canon Latigo, *Kitara Historical Texts* (henceforth, *K.H.T.*) (in my possession), No. 83.

27. John Tosh, "Techniques and Problems of Research in Lango," *Makerere Seminar Papers*.

28. The publication of Nyakatura's *Aspects of Bunyoro Custom and Traditions* will certainly mitigate this criticism.

29. J. H. Speke, *Journal of the Discovery of the Source of the Nile* (London, 1863).

30. J. A. Grant, *A Walk Across Africa*. (London, 1864).

31. S. W. Baker, *Albert Nyanza* (London, 1866); *Ismailia* (London, 1874).

32. H. M. Stanley, *Through the Dark Continent* (London, 1878); *In Darkest Africa* (London, 1890).

33. G. Schweinfurth, F. Ratzel, R. Felkin, and G. Hartlaub, eds., *Emin Pasha in Central Africa* (London, 1888).

34. G. Casati, *Ten Years in Equatoria* (London, 1898).

35. H. H. Johnston, *The Uganda Protectorate*. (London, 1902).

36. A. B. Fisher, *Twilight Tales of the Black Baganda* (London, 1911).

37. J. Gorju, *Entre le Victoria, l'Albert et l'Edouard* (Rennes, 1920).

38. J. Roscoe, *The Bakitara or Banyoro*. (C.U.P., 1923).

39. Bikunya, op. cit.

40. K.W., op. cit.

41. Karubanga, op. cit.

42. Sir G. K. Rukidi, *The Kings of Tooro*, translated by Joseph Muchope (Makerere History Department Archives).

43. J. H. M. Beattie, *Bunyoro: An African Kingdom* (New York and London, 1960); *The Nyoro State* (O.U.P.; 1971).

44. A. R., Dunbar, *A History of Bunyoro-Kitara* (O.U.P., 1965).

45. G. N. Uzoigwe, *U.J.*, 33, 2 (1969), pp. 221–24.

46. *Vide,* for example, G. N. Uzoigwe, *Revolution and Revolt in Bunyoro-Kitara* (Longmans, 1970), *Makerere History Paper* No. 5; and "Kabalega and the Making of a New Kitara" and "Inter-ethnic Co-operation in Northern Uganda" in *Tarikh,* 3, 2 (1970); "Pre-colonial Markets in Bunyoro-Kitara; *Comparative Studies in Society and History,* 14, 4 (1972), 422–55.
47. *Vide* Dunbar, op. cit., p. 15.
48. Ibid., p. 18.
49. K.W., op. cit.; J. Gray, "Kibuka," *U.J.,* 20 (1956), pp. 52–71; A. H. Cox, "The Growth and Expansion of Buganda," *U.J.,* 14 (1950), pp. 153–59; E. C. Lanning, "Ancient Earthworks in Western Uganda," *U.J.,* 17 (1953), pp. 51–62; Crazzolara, op. cit.; K. Ingham, "Some Aspects of the History of Western Uganda," *U.J.,* 21 (1957); E. E. Haddon, "Kibuka," *U.J.,* 21 (1957), 114–17.
50. *Vide* Dunbar, op. cit., p. 31.
51. K.W., op. cit.; *vide* also Dunbar, op. cit., p. 35.
52. Dunbar, op. cit., p. 37.
53. Ibid., p. 43.

PART I: PREHISTORY

Chapter 1: The Foundation of the Kingdom of Kitara

1. *Omukama* (king), singular of Abakama (kings).
2. Abahuma, a pastoralist people belonging to the same family as the Abahima of Nkore (Ankole) and the Tutsi of Rwanda.
3. This account is very similar to the one recorded by Nkore tradition. *Vide* Katate and Kamugungunu, *Abagabe b'Ankole;* H. F. Morris, *A History of Ankole* (Kampala, 1962); *Sam Karugire, A History of Nkore in Western Uganda* (Oxford, Clarendon, 1971).
4. For different lists of the kings of Kitara, *vide* Appendix to Introduction, *supra,* pp. xxx–xxxv.

Chapter 2: Abatembuzi

1. Kitara is a village in Kyaka County (now in Tooro). It was also the name of a place in Tanzania now known as Missenyi. It was probably from either of these two places that the kingdom took its name.

2. For the first time the name of the foreign king is disclosed in the text.

3. If Isaza swallowed the coffee seed he would then have entered into a blood brotherhood with Nyamiyonga. This would signify that the two monarchs would remain on friendly and brotherly terms.

4. Kinyoro tradition does not give the name of Nyamiyonga's kingdom but is content to describe it as the underworld. According to Nkore tradition (which is very similar to that of Bunyoro), the underworld turns out to be Nkore and Nyamiyonga assumes the name of Ruyonga. It is probable that the one tradition is a variation of the other although independent evolution may not be ruled out. For Nkore tradition *vide* Morris, op. cit., esp. Chap. 2.

5. A *Muiru* is the equivalent of the *Hutu* of Rwanda, i.e. agriculturist.

PART II: ABACHWEZI

Chapter 1: The Coming of the Abachwezi

1. Bukidi is the name given by Banyoro to the area now inhabited by the Langi. It means the land of the naked people.

2. It would appear that in Kitara custom to kill a child of that age was an abomination.

3. It would appear that Nyinamwiru was trying to create the impression that she believed her child to be still in Bukuku's palace.

Chapter 2: Abachwezi Rule

1. *Omuchwezi* is the singular of Abachwezi (plural).

2. The Kabale of the text is in modern Bunyoro and should not therefore be confused with Kabale, capital of Kigezi.

3. According to the textual account it would appear that the Abachwezi met with no opposition during their initial occupation of Kitara but that resistance against their rule developed afterwards. Non-Nyoro sources, however, tend to hold a contrary view. *Vide*, for example, Crazzolara, *The Lwoo*, Part I (1950); and

"The Hamites—Who were they?" in *U.J.* 33, 1 (1969), pp. 41–48.

4. The question as to how many Bachwezi came to Kitara has not been tackled by the author. The available evidence, however, would seem to suggest that they were not many. This raises two other fundamental issues. First, if the Bachwezi were numerically insignificant, then the theory of their forcible overthrow of the Batembuzi becomes very thin on that ground. And, second, given this numerical insignificance, one wonders how the indigenous population would have passively allowed them to impose their domination over them. The rather simple explanation of Kitara tradition is hardly convincing; nor can Luo tradition on this point stand up to critical examination.

5. It must be pointed out that when the author writes of Ganyi, Madi, and Bukidi, he does not necessarily mean the Luo groups or Semi-Luo groups who now inhabit the districts of Acholi, Madi, and Lango, respectively. The Luo did not migrate into Northern Uganda until about the fifteenth or sixteenth century. *Vide* Ogot, *History of the Southern Luo,* p. 55–57.

6. For a different version of the Nyangoma-Mulindwa incident, *vide* A. R. Dunbar, *A History of Bunyoro-Kitara* (O.U.P., 2d ed., 1969), pp. 18–19. Dunbar confuses Nyangoma with her sister Nyangoro. His account is based on (Mrs.) A. B. Fisher, *Twilight Tales of the Black Baganda* (London, 1911), pp. 99–102, 105–110. According to this version, it was Mugenyi rather than Kagoro who avenged the attempted murder of Mulindwa. Unlike Nyakatura this version also states that Nyangoro (Nyangoma) was not killed but that Mulindwa pronounced a curse on the Basingo clan as a result of which princes desisted from marrying into that clan.

7. The original name of Mubende was Kisozi.

8. This is why he is usually referred to as Wamara of Bwera (Buddu).

9. For a slightly different version of this story, *vide* E. C. Lanning, "Excavations at Mubende Hill," *U.J.* 30, 2 (1966), pp. 153–55. The last Nyakahuma was an old lady called Nyanjara. The author, Nyakatura, visited the site of these trees on 12 September 1929 to ex-

amine them himself. His companions included Michael Rusoke, the ex-Katikiro (Chief Minister) of Tooro, and Nicodemus Kakuroza, ex-Kasujju (official title of the saza chief of Bwamba) of Tooro. The biggest of these trees—known as Ndahura in Runyoro—is now generally known as the "Witch Tree."

10. The reader's attention must be drawn to what appears to be a confusion in the author's mind here. It will be remembered that he has earlier stated that Mubende was ruled by the Nyakahuma.

11. Since the position of the chief rainmaker has been abolished, it would then be assumed that Rwangirra had no official recognition and was probably not known to the authorities.

12. It is worth noting that all my informants regard Mubimba as the founder of their clan.

13. The author states that he has seen this iron post while it was in the possession of Inyaso (Ignatius) Lule, Saza Chief of Buyaga at the time. Lule had removed it from its original place in Mahugera.

14. For works on Burundi, *vide* M. D'Hertefelt, A. A. Trouwborst, et J. H. Scherer, *Les Anciens royaumes de la zone interlacustre meridionale. Ruanda, Rundi et HA* (Tervueren, 1962); Jan Vansina, "Notes sur l'Histoire du Burundi," *Aequatoria*, Vol. XXXIV, Part 1, Coquilhatville, 1961; and bibliography supplied there.

Chapter 3: The Disappearance of the Abachwezi from Kitara

1. *Abafumu*—There is no good English rendering of this word. But it is usually translated as witchcraft or divination. In this book, however, I have preferred to use divination.

2. *Kaijuire*—This was the most important military drum. It was sounded to inform the population of the imminence of war. It could be heard for many miles away from the capital and signified that the kingdom must always be preserved intact.

3. This expression, like most Nyoro expressions, is very difficult to render into English. It would appear that Wamara was accusing the people of Kitara of ingratitude. As far as he was concerned, they had become

his enemies. But how this can be connected with the spilling of the butter is not easy to comprehend.

4. It will be remembered that Mulindwa had been an invalid since the incident between him and Mugenyi's mother.

5. The present heir, Mr. Z. B. M. Kyanku, told me that not even during the era of Kabalega did the authority of the saza chief of Buyaga extend to the domain his ancestors had inherited. But now, although the situation has considerably altered, the Kyankus are still very much respected in Buyaga.

6. Or the lake which kills locusts.

7. Mugasa Ibebe Kirimani.

8. Nyamiyonga, King of the Underworld, was the father of Nyamata, wife of Mutembuzi Isaza.

9. It follows from this account that the Bachwezi preceded the Bahuma in Kitara.

PART III: ABABIITO

Chapter 1: The Coming of the Ababiito

1. From this account it does appear, as in the case of the Bachwezi, that not many people followed Rukidi to Kitara. And if this is so, the theory of Luo invasion so elegantly and heroically described by Crazzolara becomes rather thin on the ground. I am inclined to agree with Canon Latigo of Acholi's view that the Babiito occupation was essentially peaceful, but violent when necessary. *Vide K.H.T.* No. 83.

2. *Vide supra*, Part II, Chapter 3, Note 1.

3. Afterwards these men took on another clan, that of the Bakurubyo, because they had rowed [*kukurubya*] the Babiito across the lake; *kukurubya* is another word for rowing in Runyoro and so these men came to be called *Bakurubyo*—the rowers of the king. From now onwards the members of the Bakurubyo clan started to sacrifice a baby from time to time by throwing it into the lake. They were afraid of the bad luck which might be caused to befall them by the Mubiito baby who had been first sacrificed in this way. They were therefore atoning for its death.—Author.

4. This would seem to imply that the Sese clan was abolished and was replaced by the Bagweri clan.

5. It is interesting to note that cowrie shells were known in Kitara at this time. It was not, however, until the second half of the nineteenth century that these shells began to be used for monetary exchange. They are said to have been introduced by the Arabs in this period.

Chapter 2: Babiito Kings of Kitara

1. This does not seem to be a strong argument since it has been shown that there were more succession wars in Buganda than in Kitara unless it can be shown that Kitara succession wars normally lasted much longer than Ganda ones. And this is not easy to prove. *Vide* Kiwanuka, "Bunyoro and the British."

2. This would be a more valid argument if this principle is strictly observed. It must be pointed out, however, that Olimi IV Kasoma (1782–86) ruled for only four years. So did Olimi V Rwakabale (1848–52). A possible explanation may be that certain Kitara kings like Duhaga I Chwa Mujwiga (1731–82) and Kyebambe III Nyamutukura (1786–1835) ruled for far too long.

3. The sovereignty of Kooki must indeed have been a very limited one since Buganda exercised a lot of influence over it after it had seceded from Kitara in the eighteenth century.

4. This is rather an odd statement since Kaboyo and Nyaika were, by any standard, Babiito kings of Tooro. There is no evidence to suggest that Kitara exercised any tangible influence over Tooro between 1830 and 1876.

5. This would seem to suggest that the Bachwezi cult, which became very important later on, was a conscious policy of the Babiito dynasty. But then one wonders why a discredited ruling class should be turned into a cult by their successors!

6. Karokarungi was only a very small portion of modern Nkore.

7. New Moon celebrations—The moon was greatly revered by Banyoro. They attribute to it powers to cure illnesses, relieve hunger, and to bring good health, food and milk. The celebrations were therefore undertaken

at the appearance of each new moon to welcome the moon and pray it to bring prosperity.

8. Kaggwa and Nyakatura are in agreement as to the names of those who accompanied Kimera to Buganda. Curiously enough their names coincide with the names of those who, according to Kaggwa, had accompanied Kalemera to Kitara before Kimera was born!

9. For the original size of Buganda *vide supra*, p. xxv.

10. According to Karubanga: "In the old days Buganda was called Muwawa; in Runyoro it is the name of a tree which they call Omuhwahwa. It came to be called Buganda in the reign of Omukama Ndahura Omuchwezi." For the rest of this story, *vide* Karubanga, *Bukya Nibwira*, Chap. 2, p. 9.

11. According to Roscoe the name Bunyoro was given to the remnants of the Kitara Empire of late years by Baganda in derision. It was a nickname which arose out of the custom of Abakama of showing favor to the *bairu* (peasantry) by bestowing on them the title of *Abanyoro* (singular, *Omunyoro*) *b'Omukama* (free men and thus chiefs). Baganda learnt of this custom and were reported to have exclaimed: "You are only a nation of freed slaves; you are Banyoro, and your country is Bunyoro, the country of freed slaves." Unfortunately the name has ever since been in popular usage. Even today Banyoro males address one another as *Omunyoro* (equivalent of Mr.) as a matter of respect. *Vide* Roscoe, *The Bakitara or Banyoro*, pp. 2–3.

12. This is very revealing since it seems to suggest that the occupation of the first Babiito was hunting rather than pastoralism. It will be remembered that their successors were notorious for their love of cattle.

13. This would suggest that Bukidi country at this time was part of the Babiito Kitara Empire.

14. This, too, would suggest a loss of influence in Bukidi country.

15. It may seem curious that while Olimi was persuaded not to annex Buganda to Kitara, he was apparently allowed to annex Nkore. A possible explanation may be that Buganda was ruled by a Mubiito while Nkore was ruled by a Muhuma, the descendant of Ruhinda.

16. For discussions relating to this eclipse, *vide* J. Sykes, "The Eclipse at Biharwe," *U.J.*, 23 (1959), pp. 44–50; Sir

John Gray, "The Solar Eclipse in Ankole in 1492,"
U.J., 27 (1963), pp. 217–22; and "Eclipse Maps,"
J.A.H., 6 (1965), pp. 251–62; Kiwanuka, "Sir Apolo
Kaggwa and the Pre-Colonial History of Buganda,"
pp. 146–47.

17. From this account it would appear that, contrary to the
claim of Kinyoro tradition, Madi had not hitherto been
part of the Babiito Kitara Empire. Or perhaps it had
seceded from that empire and was being reduced once
more to obedience. It will be remembered that Madi
is said to have been annexed to Kitara during the reign
of Ndahura, *vide supra*, p. 25.

18. This is the first recorded succession war during the Babiito
dynasty.

19. For Rwanda tradition, *vide* A. Pages, *Un royaume hamite
. . . le Ruanda* (Brussels, 1933), in which this Kitara
invasion of Rwanda is admitted. *Vide* also Jan Vansina, *L'evolution du royaume rwanda des origines a
1900* (Brussels, 1962); and *Kingdoms of the Sa-
vanah* (Madison, 1966); A. Kagame, *Histoire du
Rwanda* (Leverville, 1958).

20. Chwa's (Chwamali in Nkore) occupation of Nkore [sic]
and Rwanda is confirmed by Nkore tradition. Morris
writes: "Cwamali occupied the country for several
years and then went on to conquer Ruanda. Here,
however, the Banyoro [sic] over-reached themselves.
Cwamali was defeated and killed and his army, retreating through Kaarokarungi, was set upon by Ntare
and slaughtered, Ntare thus earning the name of
Kiitabanyoro. Cwamali's mother when she heard the
news is said to have cried, 'Ebi shi! Ente za Kaaro
zankora omunda [the cows of Kaaro have broken my
heart].' Thus did Kaaro get the name of Nkore," Morris, *A History of Ankole*, pp. 10–11.

21. Another name for the Omukama's official sister is *Kalyota*.

22. The modern name of Ankole was coined by the British
in the 1890s.

23. Kyaka is now a county in Tooro bordering on the Buganda county of Buwekula.

24. This is surprising since Mashamba was not the Omukama
but a regent. When Wamara replaced Mulindwa, this
was not regarded as usurpation.

25. Some of the original texts may have given Gawa's clan

as Balisa. She is known, however, to have belonged to the Bakwonga clan.

26. This suggests that there was no convention permitting a reigning monarch to nominate his successor and that the general wish of the people does not legitimize a nominee.

27. It was the accepted practice in Kitara that an Omukama who had shed his blood or had become incapacitated was in honor bound to take his own life.

Chapter 3: Babiito Kings of Kitara (continued)

1. In Buganda, *Mukwenda* is the official title of the saza chief of Ssingo.

2. In such moments he was likened to an infuriated poisonous snake.

3. He was likened to a poisonous caterpillar which attacks anybody it comes into contact with.

4. *Enjeru, vide infra*, Part V, Chapter 2, Note 3. *Vide* also Karubanga, op. cit., p. 13. Kabalega was the only Omukama who was sufficiently wrongheaded to refuse to obey this custom.

5. *Bamuroga* was the head of the saza chiefs but he was not a Katikiro in the Buganda sense.

6. *Mugema* was the saza chief whose responsibilities included the guardianship of the royal tombs of Kitara.

7. No prediction could have been farther from the truth, for there was no peace in Bunyoro-Kitara for well over half a century afterwards.

8. *Vide* Grant, *A Walk across Africa*, pp. 286–87; Speke, *Journal of the Discovery of the Source of the Nile*, pp. 510–11.

9. This account is largely taken from Speke, op. cit. *Vide* also Dunbar, op. cit., 51–57; Grant, op. cit.

10. For fuller account *vide* Baker, *Albert Nyanza*.

PART IV: BABIITO KINGS OF KITARA (concluded): OMUKAMA CHWA II KABALEGA, (1870–99)

Chapter 1: The Succession War

1. Prince Kabagungu was killed in place of Prince Kabigumire, who had eluded Kabalega's capture and execution.

2. Ireeta later on became one of the great generals of Kabalega's Abarusura (national standing army). He commanded the *Ekirwana* division of this army and was the most consistent of Kabalega's supporters. It was Kabalega who gave him the name of Ireeta, his original name having been forgotten by informants. He was the father of Byakutaga and Samusoni (Samson) Ireeta. For further information *vide infra*, pp. 131–33.

Chapter 2: The Partition of Africa

1. It is probable that the author is here expressing the views of the White Fathers, who either wrote or supplied the information on which this chapter is based. There is no good study of the partition of Africa. But R. E. Robinson and J. Gallagher, *Africa and the Victorians* (London, 1961) is useful. So also is R. O. Collins, ed., *The Partition of Africa: Illusion or Necessity* (New York, 1969); and J. S. Keltie, *The Partition of Africa* (London, 1895).
2. By Nubians Banyoro mean people from Makraha and Latuka to the north of Gulu, Monbuttu and Lendu in the Congo, as well as Dinkas and Shilluks.
3. Adapted from Schweinfurth *et al*, *Emin Pasha in Central Africa*, op. cit.
4. For Baker's own account of his second visit to Kitara, *vide* Baker, *Ismailia*, Vol. 2.

Chapter 3: Internal Developments

1. *Vide* also *K.H.T.*, No. 82.
2. Kitagwenda is now in Tooro.
3. Later Omukama Kitahimbwa I.
4. For a contrary view, *vide* Morris, op. cit., p. 29.
5. For a contrary view, *vide* Morris, op. cit., Chap. 5.
6. Acholi and Langi tradition deny that their countries were ruled by Kabalega. For the nature of the relations between these countries and Kabalega, *vide*, Uzoigwe, "Inter-ethnic Co-operation in Northern Uganda," *Tarikh*, 3, 2 (1970), pp. 69–76.
7. Part of Buruli is still in Bunyoro but is now called Bujenje.
8. For a detailed analysis of the significance of Kabalega's creation of the Abarusura, *vide* Uzoigwe, *Revolution and Revolt*, Part I.

9. It is significant to note that the practice of having the lower teeth pulled is a Luo custom.
10. According to Stuhlmann, Ruyonga, Kabalega's great enemy and father of Komwiswa, had earlier died in 1882. *Vide* Sir J. Gray, "Acholi History, 1860–1901 Part I," *U.J.*, 15, 2 (1951), p. 142, citing Stuhlmann, *Die Tagerbücher*, 11, 353.

Chapter 4: Kabalega, Baganda, and Europeans, 1886–92

1. According to Stuhlmann, Mupina died in February 1887. *Vide* Gray, op. cit., p. 133, citing Stuhlmann, op. cit., pp. 315–16.
2. It would appear that Nyakamatura did not obey the king's order because Kabalega dissociated himself from the chief's action. *Vide* Sir J. Gray, "The Diaries of Emin Pasha—Extracts IX," *U.J.*, 29, 1 (1965), p. 82.
3. For accounts of developments in Kitara at this time *vide* Casati, *Ten Years in Equatoria;* Schweinfurth *et al,* op. cit.; various articles by Sir John Gray in *Uganda Journal,* including his serialization of extracts from "The Diaries of Emin Pasha"; Dunbar, op. cit., Part II, Chap. 10; and accounts by Ganda writers such as Kagwa and Zimbe.
4. Emin Pasha was not part of this return expedition, having refused to be relieved by Stanley.
5. *Vide* also H. M. Stanley, *In Darkest Africa,* for his own account of the return expedition from the relief of Emin Pasha.
6. For the account of the civil wars in Buganda and the role played by Kabalega *vide* also R. P. Ashe, *Chronicles of Uganda* (London, 1894); T. B. Fletcher, "Kabaka Mwanga and His Times," *U.J.*, 4 (1936), pp. 162–67; Sir J. Gray, "The Year of the Three Kings," *U.J.*, 14 (1950), pp. 15–52; M. S. M. Kiwanuka, "Kabaka Mwanga and His Political Parties," *U.J.*, 33 (1969), pp. 1–16; J. A. Rowe, *Lugard at Kampala, Makerere History Paper* No. 3; D. Kavulu, "The Islamic-Christian Civil Wars in Buganda, 1888–1890," U.S.S.C.C. Paper, Nairobi, December 1969.
7. For events in this period *vide* Dame Margery Perham, ed., *The Diaries of Lord Lugard,* Vols. I–III (London, 1959); *Lugard: The Years of Adventure, 1858–1898* (London, 1956), Part III.

8. It is interesting to note that the majority of those on the side of peace had already confronted Lugard and assessed his strength. Nyakatura, in this account, confuses Nyangi with Nyamutahingurwa. The latter in fact was Kabalega's mother and was also called Kanyanye.

9. Vide also Perham, *The Diaries of Lord Lugard;* and *Lugard;* A. B. Thruston, *African Incidents* (London, 1900); Colvile, *The Land of the Nile Springs.*

Chapter 5: Kabalega, Baganda, and Europeans, 1893–99

1. There is a lot of European literature on this theme. The importance of this chapter, however, lies in the fact that we are given the Banyoro account of the same story.

2. Vide also Sir Gerald Portal, *The British Mission to Uganda* (London, 1894).

3. For Colvile's own account *vide* Colvile, op. cit.: Chap. 6 et seqq.

4. Colvile admits having only seven hundred Baganda and Basoga soldiers with him, ibid, p. 71. But according to Thruston, "on Christmas Day between 15,000 and 20,000 men joined us at the frontier." Thruston, op. cit., p. 129.

5. Vide also Colvile, op. cit.; Thruston, op. cit.; M. Bovill, and G. R. Askwith, *Roddy Owen* (London, 1897).

6. Musaija Mukuru is the name of a hill near Hoima on the Fort Portal Road and means the hill of "old men."

7. For the European Version *vide* Thruston, op. cit.; and Colvile, op. cit.

8. Vide also Trevor Ternan, *Some Experiences of an old Bromsgrovian* (Birmingham, 1930).

9. Actually the Sudanese mutinied in October 1897. They were not ordered into Kenya but rather into the Sudan.

10. Those interested in the reasons behind this mutiny should see F.O.2/132–34, 144, 154–58, and esp. 161 (W.O. to F.O., 21 March 1898 (Secret.), incl. a provisional précis of events connected with the mutiny by Major H. Ramsey entitled: "The Mutiny in Uganda, 1897–98," 24 pp. print'; H. H. Austin, *With Macdonald in Uganda* (London, 1903), pp. 36–37, 90–114; F. Jackson, *Early Days in East Africa* (London, 1930), pp. 304–15; R. W. Beachey, "Macdonald's Expedition and

the Uganda Mutiny, 1897–1898," *Historical Journal*, Vol. 10 (1967), No. 2.

11. For a description of this event *vide* Thruston, op. cit., Introduction.

12. For the campaign against Kabalega in Bukidi, *vide* Bovill and Askwith, op. cit.; Fisher, *Twilight Tales*, pp. 176–77.

13. For the best account of the capture of Kabalega *vide* Princess Lucy Olive Katyanku and Semu Bulera, *Obwomezi Bw'Omukama Duhaga II* (Kampala, 1950), Chap. 4, pp. 26–37.

14. Kabalega was baptized John while in exile.

Chapter 6: Later Babiito

1. Kitahimbwa, a minor, was placed on the throne in an attempt to win people's sympathy away from Kabalega. His coronation was preceded by some curious rumors that Kabalega was dead. The country was then ruled by three regents headed by Byabachwezi. *Vide* Entebbe Secretariat Archives [E.S.A.] A5/4/1898, Wilson to Fowler, 5 March 1898; E.S.A. A34/4/1898, Entebbe to Salisbury, 16 March 1897, No. 27.

2. No territory of Kitara was alienated to Buganda by Evatt. The alienation was done by Colvile in 1894 and confirmed by Lord Salisbury in 1896. *Vide* E.S.A. A33/2/1896, F.O. to Berkeley, 8 August 1896, No. 115; E.S.A. A4/7/1897, Forster to Ternan, 30 December 1896; E.S.A. A5/2/1896, Note by Berkeley, 19 November 1896.

3. Kitahimbwa was deposed for alleged incompetence. But according to Banyoro he was removed because he protested against the ill-treatment of his kingdom by the imperial government. *Vide* Molson, *Report*, p. 5.

4. With the establishment of British administration by 1901, the name of Kitara ceases to be of practical significance and that of Bunyoro begins to be more meaningful. In the colonial period therefore the name of Bunyoro will be used in the text.

5. It will be remembered that Duhaga I was also a small man.

6. Perhaps so. But he was generally regarded as a weak king and was under the thumb of Jemusi Miti, the

      Ganda agent of British imperialism in Bunyoro. *Vide* Uzoigwe, *Revolution and Revolt,* Part II.

7. Ruyonga was the implacable enemy of Kamurasi and Kabalega; and Rujumba was the father of prince Kosia Labwoni, who still lives in the Bujenje County of Bunyoro.

8. *Obwesengeze* is a Luganda word. Banyoro however use it to denote a personal possession with all rights of disposal. This may involve the ownership of *official* land and also the possession of soldiers in an official capacity.

9. The author's account of the Nyangire revolt is incredibly poor and in many instances historically incorrect. It contrasts vividly with the series of magnificent interviews he has given to me on this topic. The account in this book may have been influenced by the fact that it was written when the author was a civil servant. For a detailed study of this episode in Kinyoro history, *vide* Uzoigwe, *Revolution and Revolt,* Part II.

10. Byabachwezi was the saza chief of Bugahya from 1893 to 1912.

11. It must be noted however that Bugahya had all along been a hereditary saza, at any rate, since the time of Nyakamatura Nyakatura.

12. Because it was too big and for internal political reasons, *vide* Secretariat Minute Paper, Entebbe [S.M.P.], 1251/09, Minute No. 124, 28 October 1912.

13. *Vide* also Katyanku and Bulera, op. cit.

14. According to Dunbar, it would appear that cotton and tobacco were introduced into Bunyoro by the Europeans much earlier than 1927. *Vide* Dunbar, op. cit., p. 127.

15. For more details *vide* H. B. Thomas and Rubie, *Enquiry into Land Tenure and the Kibanja System in Bunyoro 1931* (Entebbe, 1932).

16. For details, *vide The Bunyoro Agreement of 1933* (Makerere College Library); and Dunbar, op. cit., pp. 143–49.

17. *R.A.* means Rukirabasaija Agutamba [one who is above all men].

PART V: KITARA MONARCHY

Chapter 1: The Regalia of Kitara, the Government, and Miscellaneous

1. But it is also admitted that Kitara bark cloth was of inferior quality to that of Buganda and that, in fact, they imported a lot of their bark cloth from Buganda. It is also fair to point out that before the defection of the important bark cloth producing areas to Buganda, the reverse may have been the case.

Chapter 2: The King's Palace

1. For receiving people from Northern Uganda.
2. This is a special name given to the king's cows.
3. This is a kind of Jubilee celebration to mark an Omukama's succession to the throne. It is also a solemn declaration peace.

PART VI: KINGS OF BUGANDA, TOORO, NKORE, AND KOOKI

Chapter 1: The Kings of Buganda

1. I.e., Muteesa I.
2. The author cites H. H. Johnston, *The Uganda Protectorate*, Vol. II, p. 681; Speke, op. cit., p. 252; *Munno* of 1913, p. 21.
3. The author cites J. M. Gray, "Early History of Buganda," *U.J.*, 2, 4 (1935), p. 269, for the periodization of this king's reign.
4. The author cites *Uganda Journal*, loc. cit., for the periodization of this king's reign.
5. For a good biography of Muteesa I *vide* M. S. M. Kiwanuka, *Muteesa of Uganda* (East Africa Literature Bureau, 1967); *vide* also Sir John Gray, "Muteesa of Buganda," *U.J.*, 1, 1 (1934); "Sir John Kirk and Mutesa," *U.J.*, 15 (1951).
6. There is a lot of literature on Mwanga II. In addition to works cited *supra*, p. 257, Note 6, *vide* R. P. Ashe, *Two Kings of Uganda* (London, 1890); C. C. Wrigley, "The Christian Revolution in Buganda," *Com-*

parative Studies in Society and History, II (1959); J. A. Rowe, "The Purge of Christians at Mwanga's Court," *J.A.H.,* 5, 1 (1964); David Kavulu, *The Uganda Martyrs* (London, Longmans, 1969), *Makerere History Paper* No. 2; J. Taylor, *The Growth of the Church in Buganda.* (SCM Press: 1958.)

7. Mwanga died in *1903* and *not* in 1908.

8. The best account of Buganda history in the second half of the nineteenth century is J. A. Rowe, *Revolution in Buganda* (forthcoming). *Vide* also D. A. Low, *Buganda in Modern History* (London, 1971), Chap. 1; Semakula Kiwanuka, *A History of Buganda from the Foundation of the Kingdom to 1900* (Longmans, 1971), Chaps. 6–10.

9. For a good account of this period *vide* D. A. Low, and R. C. Pratt, *Buganda and British Overrule 1900–1955: Two Studies* (Oxford, 1960); and "Uganda: The Establishment of the Protectorate, 1894–1919" in *History of East Africa,* II, V. Harlow, E. M. Chilver, and A. Smith, eds. (Oxon, 1965); A. D. Roberts, "The Sub-Imperialism of the Baganda," *J.A.H.,* 3, 3 (1962); M. Twaddle, "The Bakungu Chiefs of Buganda under British Colonial Rule, 1900–1930," *J.A.H.,* 10 (1969).

10. For traditional history of Buganda *vide* Apolo Kaggwa, *Basekabaka;* and, *Empisa;* M. S. M. Kiwanuka, *The Traditional history of the Buganda Kingdom: With special reference to the historical writings of Apolo Kaggwa* (Unpublished London Ph.D. Thesis, 1965).

Chapter 2: The Kingdom of Tooro

1. For more particulars of Kaboyo's rebellion read the stories of Omukama Kyebambe III.—Author.

2. At this time Tooro had become a troubled kingdom mainly due to the activities of one Mubiitokati (princess), the sister of Nyaika, called Byanjeru. This lady put many people to death because she suspected them of having poisoned her brother. She caused a lot of disturbance in the country and this resulted in the division of the country into two because the central government lacked a strong leader.

3. For other works on Tooro *vide* B. K. Taylor, *The Western Lacustrine Bantu, Ethnographic Survey of Africa,* Daryll Forde, ed., East-Central Africa, Part III (Lon-

don, 1962); Rukidi, *The Kings of Tooro;* Mrs. A. B. Fisher, *On the Borders of Pigmy-Land* (London, 1905); O. W. Furley, "Kasagama of Tooro," *U.J.,* 25, 2 (1961); and "The reign of Kasagama in Tooro from a contemporary account," *U.J.,* 31, 2 (1967); M. R. Nyakazingo, "Kasagama of Tooro—A despotic and Missionary King," Makerere History Archives (1968).

4. Omukama George Kamurasi died on 21 December 1965 at twelve noon and was buried on 30 December at Karambi in Burahya county near his father's grave. He is the author of *The Kings of Tooro.*—Author.

Chapter 3: The Kings of Nkore (*The Bahinda Dynasty*)

1. *Abahinda* is the clan of the royal family of Nkore. It is equivalent to that of the Ababiito of Bunyoro-Kitara and Tooro. However, there are some common people who belong to the Bahinda clan. But there is a distinction between the "Bahinda of the Drum" and other Bahinda of the royal family.

2. For a full-length traditional history of Nkore *vide* S. Karugire, *A History of Nkore in Western Uganda to 1896* (Clarendon, 1971). *Vide* also Morris, op. cit.; Katate and Kamungungunu, op. cit.; J. Roscoe, *The Banyankolo* (C.U.P., 1923).

3. In Runyoro the word *Kati* when added at the end of another word always denotes a female, for example, *mubiito* (prince) and *mubiitokati* (princess).

4. According to this account this would seem to be the first succession war in Nkore history.

5. Later translated by the British as Nkore.

6. According to Morris, op. cit., this Omugabe is known as Ntare V (1870–95).

Chapter 4: The Kings of Kooki

1. I have been unable to trace this book. Apparently it never got off the ground. The only thing available in Kooki history would appear to be E. C. Lanning's "The Cairns of Koki, Buganda," *U.J.,* 21, 2 (1957), pp. 176–83. Dr. Phares Mutibwa is at present researching the history of Kooki.

Suggestions for Further Reading

Only the most important books and articles mentioned in the text will be repeated here.

BUNYORO-KITARA

Babiiha, J. K. "The Buyaga Clan of Western Uganda," *Uganda Journal,* 22, 2 (1958).

Baker, J. R. "Baker and Ruyonga," *Uganda Journal,* 25 (1961).

Baker, S. J. K. "Bunyoro: A Regional Appreciation," *Uganda Journal,* 18 (1954).

Beattie, J. H. M. *Bunyoro: An African Kingdom* (New York: Holt, Rinehart and Winston, 1960).

——. *Nyoro Kinship, Marriage and Affinity* (O.U.P., 1958).

——. *Bunyoro's Lost Counties* (Oxford, 1962).

Bikunya, Petero. *Ky'Abakama ba Bunyoro-Kitara* (London, 1927).

Blackledge "Bugerere," *Uganda Notes,* 111, No. 7, 1902.

Brewer, M. A. "Hoima during 1914–1915," *Uganda Notes,* 1915.

Dunbar, A. R. *A History of Bunyoro-Kitara* (O.U.P., 1965).

Gray, J. M. "The Riddle of Biggo," *Uganda Journal,* 2 (1935).

——. "Kabarega's Embassy to the Mahdists in 1897," *Uganda Journal,* 19 (1955).

——. "The Sieges of Bukumi, Mubende District, in 1898," *Uganda Journal,* 25 (1961).

Ingham, K. "The *Amagasani* of the Abakama of Bunyoro," *Uganda Journal,* 21, 2 (1953).

Karubanga, H. K. *Bukya Nibwira* (Kampala, 1949).

K.W. (i.e. Kabalega and Winyi) "Abakama ba Bunyoro-Kitara," *Uganda Journal,* Vols. 3–5 (1935, 1936, and 1937).

Kiwanuka, M. S. M. *The Empire of Bunyoro-Kitara: Myth or*

reality? *Makerere History Paper* No. 1 (London: Longmans, 1968).

Lanning, E. C. "Excavations at Mubende Hill," *Uganda Journal,* 30 (1966).

Nyakatura, J. W. *Aspects of Bunyoro Custom and Tradition,*
translated by Zebiya Rigby (East African Literature Bureau, 1971).

Roberts, A. D. "The Lost Counties of Bunyoro," *Uganda Journal,* 26 (1962).

Roscoe, Rev. J. *The Bakitara or Banyoro* (C.U.P., 1923).

Rukidi, Sir George. *The Kings of Tooro,* translated by Joseph
Muchope (Makerere History Department Archives).

Shinnie, P. L. "Excavations at Bigo, 1957," *Uganda Journal,*
24 (1960).

Uzoigwe, G. N. *Revolution and Revolt in Bunyoro-Kitara,*
Makerere History Paper No. 5. (London, Longmans,
1970).

——. "Kabalega and the Making of a New Kitara," *Tarikh,*
III, 2 (1970).

——. "Inter-ethnic Co-operation in Northern Uganda,"
Tarikh, III, 2 (1970).

——. "Precolonial Markets in Bunyoro-Kitara," *Comparative
Studies in Society and History,* 14, 4 (1972).

——. "Succession and Civil War in Bunyoro-Kitara," *International Journal of African Historical Studies* (Spring,
1973).

——. "Recording the oral history of Africa: Reflections from
field experiences from Bunyoro," *African Studies Review*
(Fall, 1973).

BUGANDA

Cox, A. H. "The Growth and Expansion of Buganda," *Uganda
Journal,* (1950).

Gray, J. M. "Early History of Buganda," *Uganda Journal,* 2,
4 (1935).

——. "Kibuka," *Uganda Journal,* 20 (1956).

Ingham, K. "Some Aspects of the History of Buganda," *Uganda
Journal,* 20 (1956).

Kabuga, C. S. *Ebyo Bwakabaka bwa Buganda, Obuzaalebwa
Ssekabaka Kintu ne Bassekabaka Abasooka* (Kampala,
1963).

Kaggwa, Sir Apolo. *Basekabaka be Buganda* (Kampala, 1953).

——. *Empisa za Baganda* (Kampala, 1952).

——. *Ebika Bya Baganda* (Kampala, 1949).

Kaizi, Mordecai. *Kabaka Daudi Chwa, Omulembe n'Ebiro-woozo Bye* (Kampala, 1947).

Kiwanuka, M. S. M. *History of Buganda from the Foundation of the Kingdom to 1900* (Longmans, London, 1971).

Low, D. A. *Religion and Society in Buganda, 1875–1900* (London, 1962).

Lwanga, P. M. K. *Obulamu Bw'Omutaka J. K. Miti Kabazzi* (Copy Makerere University Library, Kampala).

Mukasa, Hamu. *Simuda Nyuma: Ebiro bya Nutesa* (London, 1938).

——. *Simuda Nyuma: Ebya Mwanga* (London, 1942).

——. "The Rule of the Kings of Buganda," *Uganda Journal*, 5 (1946).

Oliver, R. "The Royal Tombs of Buganda," *Uganda Journal*, (1959).

Roberts, A. D. "The Sub-Imperialism of the Baganda," *Journal of African History*, III, 3 (1962).

Roscoe, J. *The Baganda* (London, 1911).

Rowe, J. A. *Revolution in Buganda: 1856–1900* (forthcoming).

Wild, J. V. *The Story of the Uganda Agreement* (Nairobi, 1950).

Wrigley, C. C. "Sir Apolo Kaggwa," *Tarikh*, I, 2 (1966).

——. "Kimera," *Uganda Journal*, 23 (1959).

Zimbe, Reverend B. M. *Buganda: ne Kabaka* (Mengo, 1939). (trans. MCL)

WESTERN UGANDA

Baker, S. J. K. "The Geographical Background of Western Uganda," *Uganda Journal*, 22 (1958).

Edel, M. M. *The Chiga of Western Uganda* (O.U.P., 1957).

Fisher, Mrs. A. B. "Western Uganda," *Geog. Journal* 24 (1904).

——. *On the Borders of Pigmy-Land* (London, 1905).

Geraud, F. R. "Ancient Kigezi" (Unpublished ms., 1968).

Gray, J. M. "Toro in 1897," *Uganda Journal*, 17 (1953).

Ingham, K. "Some Aspects of the History of Western Uganda," *Uganda Journal*, 21 (1957).

Karugire, S. *A History of Nkore in Western Uganda to 1896* (Clarendon, 1971).

———. "Relations between the Bairu and Bahima in 19th century Nkore," *Tarikh*, III, 2 (1970).

Katate, A. G., and Kamugungunu, L. *Abagabe b'Ankole* (Kampala, 1955).

Lanning, E. C. "Ancient Earthworks in Western Uganda," *Uganda Journal*, (1953).

Lukyn-Williams, F., "Nuwa Mbaguta, Nganzi of Ankole," *Uganda Journal*, 10 (1946).

Morris, H. F. *History of Ankole* (Kampala, 1962).

———. "The Making of Ankole," *Uganda Journal*, 21 (1957).

———. "Historic Sites in Ankole," *Uganda Journal*, (1956).

Ngologoza, P. *History of Kigezi* (East African Literature Bureau, 1969), edited by Donald Denoon and Benon T. Rugyema.

Oberg, K. "The Kingdom of Ankole in Uganda" in *African Political Systems*, Evans-Pritchard and Fortes, eds. (London, 1966).

Oliver, R. "Ancient Capital Sites of Ankole," *Uganda Journal*, 23, 1 (1959).

Roscoe, J. *The Banyankole* (C.U.P., 1923).

Taylor, B. K. *The Western Lacustrine Bantu* (London, 1962).

Thiel, P. H. Van. "Businza unter der Dynastie der Bahinda," *Anthropos*, 6 (1911), pp. 497–520.

EASTERN UGANDA

Fallers, L. A. *Bantu Bureaucracy* (C.U.P., 1956).

Fallers, Margaret C. *The Eastern Lacustrine Bantu* (London, 1960).

Fontaine, J. S. *The Gisu of Uganda* (London, 1959).

Gray, J. M. "The Basoga," *Uganda Journal*, 3, 4 (1936).

———. "Kakungulu in Bukedi," *Uganda Journal*, 27, 1 (1963).

Hobley, C. W. *Eastern Uganda, An Ethnographic Survey* (London, 1902).

Lawrance, J. D. *The Iteso* (Oxford, 1937).

———. "A History of Teso to 1937," *Uganda Journal*, 19 (1955).

Lubogo, Y. K. *A History of Busoga* (East African Literature Bureau, 1960).

Perze, E. M. "The Bagwe," *Uganda Journal*, 3, 4 (1936).

Robertson, D. W. *The Historical Considerations Contributing to the Soga System of Land Tenure* (Entebbe, 1940).

Roscoe, J. *The Bagisu* (O.U.P., 1924).

Skeens, S. R. "Reminiscences of Busoga and Its Chiefs," *Uganda Journal*, 2, 4 (1935).

Thomas, H. B. "Capax Imperii—The Story of Semei Kakungulu," *Uganda Journal*, 6 (1938–39).

Webster, J. B. "Teso Pioneers," *Tarikh*, III, 2 (1970).

——. "The Civil War in Usuku" (University of East Africa Social Science Conference Paper, Nairobi, December 1969).

—— and others. *The Iteso during the Asonya* (Uganda Publishing House, forthcoming).

NORTHERN UGANDA

Anywar, R. S. "The Life of Rwot Iburaim Awich" (originally written in Acholi—translated by J. V. Wild), *Uganda Journal*, 12 (1948).

Beaton, A. C. "A Chapter in Bari History," *Sudan Notes and Records* 17 (1934).

Bere, R. M. "Awich—a Biographical Note and a Chapter of Acholi History," *Uganda Journal*, 10, 2 (1946).

——. "An Outline of Acholi History," *Uganda Journal*, 11 (1947).

——. "Notes on the Origin of Payera and Acholi," *Uganda Journal*, 1 (1934).

Crazzolara, J. P. *The Lwoo*, Part I (1950), II (1951), and III (1954) (Verona, Italy: Missioni Africane).

——. "The Hamites—Who were they?" *Uganda Journal*, 33, 1 (1969).

——. "Notes on the Lango-Omiru," *Anthropos*, 55 (1960).

Driberg, J. M. *The Lango* (London, 1923).

Evans-Pritchard, E. E. "Luo Tribes and Clans," *Rhodes-Livingstone Journal*, VII (1949).

Girling, F. K. *The Acholi of Uganda* (London: H.M.S.O., 1960).

Gray, J. M. "Acholi History, 1860–1901," Part I, *Uganda Journal*, 15, 2 (1951).

——. "Rwot Ochama of Payera," *Uganda Journal*, 12, 2 (1948).

Gulliver, P. J. "The Karomojong Cluster," *Africa*, XXII (1952).

Lowth, N. L. C. "The Story of the Entry of the Alur into the West Nile," *Uganda Journal*, 2, 3 (1935).

Ogwal, Reuben. *History of Lango Clans*, translated by J. A. Otima (Makerere History Department Archives).

Southall, A. *Alur Society* (C.U.P., 1956).

———. "Alur Tradition and Its Historical Significance," *Uganda Journal*, 18, 2 (1954).

———. "The Alur Legend of Sir Samuel Baker and the Omukama Kabarega," *Uganda Journal*, 15, 2 (1951).

Tarantino, F. A. "The Origin of the Lango," *Uganda Journal*, 10, 1 (1946).

———. "Notes on the Lango," *Uganda Journal*, 13, 2 (1949).

Tosh, J. "The Langi of Northern Uganda in the 19th century," *Tarikh*, III, 2 (1970).

RWANDA, BURUNDI, AND THE CONGO

Cuvelier, J., and Jadin, L. *L'Ancien Congo 1518–1640* (Brussels, 1954).

Heusch, Luc de. *Le Rwanda et la civilisation inter-lacustre* (Brussels, 1966); and Cohen, D. W., review of same in *Journal of African History*, IX, 4 (1968), pp. 651–57.

Ihle, A. *Das alte Königreich Kongo* (Leipzig, 1929).

Kabqay, A. (ed.). *History and Chronology of Rwanda* (Rwanda, 1956).

Kagame, A. *Histoire du Rwanda* (Leverville, 1958).

———. *Le notion de génération appliquée à la généalogie dynastique et à l'histoire du Ruanda* (Brussels, 1958).

Louis, W. R. *Ruanda-Urundi, 1884–1919* (London, 1963).

Pages, A. *Un royaume hamite . . . le Ruanda* (Brussels, 1933).

Vansina, J. *L'Evolution du royaume rwanda des origines a 1900* (Brussels, 1962).

———. "Notes sur l'Histoire du Burundi," *Aequatoria*, Vol. XXXIV, Part I, Coquilhatville, 1961.

TANZANIA

Cory, H. *History of the Bukoba District* (Dar es Salaam, 1958).

Cosard, E. "Le Muhaya," *Anthropos*, 32 (1937).

Ford, J., and Hall, R. de Z. "The History of Karagwe," *Tanganyika Notes and Records*, 24 (1947).

Kimambo, I. N. and Temu, A. (eds.). *History of Tanzania* (EAPH, 1968).

Lawmgira, F. X. *The History of Kiziba and Its Kings* (2d ed. 1949) translated by E. R. Kamuhangire, Makerere History Department Archives.

Rehse, H. *Kiziba, Land und Leute* (Stuttgart, 1910).

Roberts, A. (ed.). *Tanzania Before 1900* (East Africa Publishing House, 1968).

KENYA

Barker, E. E. *A Short History of Nyanza* (Nairobi, 1958).

Hobley, C. W. "Kavirondo," *Journal of the Royal Geographical Society*, Vol. 12, No. 4, pp. 361–72.

Ogot, B. A. "The Concept of Jok," *African Studies*, XX, 2 (1961), pp. 123–30.

Osogo, J. *A History of the Baluyia* (O.U.P., 1966).

Stam, N. "Bantu Kavirondo of Mumias district," *Anthropos*, 14–15 (1919–1920), pp. 968–80.

Wagner, G. *The Bantu of North Kavirondo*, 2 vols. (London, 1949 and 1956).

——. "The Political Organisation of the Bantu Kavirondo," in *African Political Systems*, Evans-Pritchard and Fortes, eds., (London, 1966), pp. 197–236.

Were, G. S. *A History of the Abaluyia of Western Kenya c. 1500–1930* (East Africa Publishing House, 1967).

——. *Western Kenya Historical Texts* (Nairobi, 1967).

GENERAL

Bryant, A. T. *Bantu Origins* (Cape Town, 1963).

Butt, A. J. *The Nilotes of the Sudan and Uganda* (London, 1952).

Coles, S. *The Pre-History of East Africa* (London, 1959).

Fisher, A. B. *Diaries,* Book XI, Folder C, (1899) Makerere University Library, Kampala.

Gulliver, P. and P. H. *The Central Nilo-Hamites* (London, 1953).

Hamilton, R. A. (ed.). *History and Archaeology in Africa: report of a Conference held in July 1953 at the School of Oriental and African Studies,* London, 1955.

Herskovits, M. J. "Culture Areas of Africa," *Africa* 3 (1930), pp. 59–77.

Hobley, C. W. "British East Africa. Anthropological studies in Kavirondo and Nandi," *Journal of the Royal Anthropological Institute,* Vol. 33, pp. 325–49 (London, 1903).

Huntingford, G. W. B. *The Northern Nilo-Hamites* (London, 1953).

———. *The Southern Nilo-Hamites* (London, 1953).

Ingham, K. *The Making of Modern Uganda* (London, 1958).

———. *A History of East Africa* (London, 1962).

Mathew, G. "Recent Discoveries in East African Archaeology," *Antiquity,* 27 (1953).

Ogot, B. A. *A History of the Southern Luo Peoples 1500–1900,* Vol. I (Nairobi, 1967).

—— and Kieran (eds.). *Zamani: A Survey of East African History* (East Africa Publishing House, 1968).

Oliver, R., and Mathew, G. (eds.). *History of East Africa,* Vol. I, (Oxford, 1963).

Oliver, R. "The Traditional Histories of Buganda, Bunyoro, and Ankole," *Journal of the Royal Anthropological Society,* 85 (1955).

———. "A Question about the Bachwezi," *Uganda Journal,* 17 (1953).

Posnansky, M. "Kinship, Archaeology and Historical Myths," *Uganda Journal,* 30, 1 (1966).

———. "Towards a historical Geography of Uganda," *East Africa Geographical Review* 1 (1963).

———. (ed.). *Prelude to East African History* (O.U.P., 1966).

———. "Bantu Genesis," *Uganda Journal,* 25 (1961).

———. "Pottery Types from Archaeological Sites in East Africa," *Journal of African History,* 2 (1961).

Richards, A. I. (ed.). *East African Chiefs* (London, 1960).

Roscoe, J. *The Northern Bantu* (C.U.P., 1915).

Seligman, C. G. *Races of Africa,* 3d ed. (London, 1957).

Tew, M. *The Peoples of the Lake Nyasa Region* (London, 1950).

Trowell, M. "Clues to African Tribal History," *Uganda Journal*, 10 (1946).

Vansina, J., Raymond, M., and Thomas, L. V. (eds.). *The Historian in Tropical Africa* (O.U.P., 1964).

Were, G. S., and Wilson, D. A. *East Africa through a Thousand Years* (London, 1968).

Wilson, M. *The Peoples of the Nyasa-Tanganyika Corridor* (Cape Town, 1958).

Wrigley, C. C. "Some Thoughts on the Bachwezi," *Uganda Journal*, 22 (1958).

Index